*Communist Propaganda Techniques*

# *Communist Propaganda Techniques*

JOHN C. CLEWS

*Foreword by*
*G. F. Hudson*

FREDERICK A. PRAEGER, *Publisher*
NEW YORK

To the memory of
John F. Kennedy



BOOKS THAT MATTER

*Published in the United States of America in 1964*
*by Frederick A. Praeger, Inc., Publisher*
*64 University Place, New York 3, N.Y.*





*Library of Congress Catalog Card Number : 64-19955*
*Printed in Great Britain*

# Contents

# *Foreword*

By G. F. HUDSON

The propaganda campaign carried on by Communist states and Communist parties throughout the world to convince people everywhere that the United States was using bacterial weapons in the Korean war marked the climax of the immense effort of organized publicity deployed by the Marxist–Leninist faith in the Stalin era. Today the apparatus of publicity is still there, and is as formidable as ever when the engine is started. But since de-Stalinization and the Sino–Soviet split there cannot be any more the same perfect world-wide unanimity, the same unqualified assertion of infallibility, as in the days of the 'the Leader of Progressive Mankind'. Since it was officially admitted in Moscow that the Communist Party of the Soviet Union had been headed for twenty years by a tyrant and a fool, and since the Russian heirs of Lenin were denounced from China as traitors and cowards, the oracular voices have no longer spoken with the same confident and unhesitating certainty. But as long as large-scale political propaganda remains a major factor in international affairs, the study of its classic examples must be a highly rewarding enterprise, and there is probably no specimen which yields such valuable data for research as the germ warfare campaign in which Communist China, the Soviet Union and all the Communist parties combined in magnificent orchestration to persuade the world of the truth of a story that was fabricated from start to finish.

Mr. John Clews has made a special study of the germ warfare campaign in the context of the more permanent themes of Communist propaganda, and has shown the genesis of the idea in Stalinist secret police mythology before its specific application in charges against the American army during the Korean war. In the confessions extracted by Soviet police interrogation from Japanese prisoners of war in the trial at Khabarovsk support was given to charges of preparation to wage bacterial warfare against the Soviet Union by Japanese military authorities under orders from the Japanese emperor. This appears to have been part of a design for arraigning the emperor as a war criminal – a project deemed likely to help the cause of Communism in Japan – but it was never resolutely followed up, since no good tactical opportunity presented itself before the Korean war created an entirely new situation in the Far East. At an earlier date, even before the Second World War, accusations of intention to commit mass murder by means of bacterial infection had already been developed in the 'confessioneering' of Stalin's police. The Trotskyites, according to confessions elicited by Vishinsky as Public Prosecutor in the show trials of the Old Bolsheviks, had planned to infect troop trains of the Red Army with deadly bacteria in order to hasten the defeat of their own country in a war against the imperialist aggressors whose puppet Trotsky had become. The idea was in character with the monstrous villainy attributed to Trotsky without a single dissenting voice in the Moscow trial confessions and through all media of mass communications throughout the Soviet Union; it had a parallel in the story of the murder of Maxim Gorky and others 'by medical means', a theme which Stalin was preparing to repeat with new variations for the destruction of new victims in the 'Doctors' Plot' fabricated just before his death in 1953. No crime could be too outrageous for the Trotskyites to undertake, and it was just because they had no support among the masses of the Soviet people and no hope of overthrowing Stalin by open insurrection that they resorted, according to Stalinist propaganda, to the most treacherous and secret forms of murder. But once these devices had become part of the official mythology, once they had been identified as forms of struggle to be expected from the enemies of the working class, it was natural to extend their attribution from Trotsky to his imperialist masters; thus, after the war, the accusation was brought first against the Japanese – though without any serious attempt to prove actual belligerent use of bacterial weapons – and then, as a full-blown atrocity story, against the Americans, who had replaced the Japanese as imperialist aggressors in the Far East. The important change in the new variant on the Soviet theme which was produced by the Chinese communists was the evidence offered in support of the charge that bacterial warfare had been not merely plotted, but actually waged.

In seeking to persuade world opinion that the Americans had tried to spread epidemic diseases in North Korea the communists had one great advantage which they would not have had if for example accusation had been made that their enemies were using poison gas against them. To support charges of chemical warfare they would have had to produce casualties clearly due to toxic gases not encountered in ordinary life. If, on the other hand, a man is ill with cholera or plague, his symptoms are the same whether the epidemic is due to natural causes or to enemy action, and what has to be proved is not that there are epidemics, but that they have been artificially caused. It is still very difficult to obtain any definite knowledge about health conditions in North Korea during the period before the germ warfare allegations were launched by Communist China, but it seems quite likely that the devastation from bombing and invasion in North Korea created conditions favourable to epidemics, and that the Chinese People's Volunteers brought certain infections with them from the interior. If this was so, it may well have been that the charge of germ warfare against the Americans was originally put forward by the Chinese to absolve their own troops of any responsibility for bringing diseases into Korea, and was only inflated into a world-wide propaganda campaign when the possibilities of its political exploitation were fully perceived by the Chinese communist régime.

In this book Mr Clews surveys the evidence which was adduced as 'proof' of the accusation, and shows conclusively that it cannot, and never could, stand up to political analysis. He also shows, however, that the propaganda had a considerable effect throughout the world and not only convinced numerous left-wing intellectuals inclined to expect truth from Moscow or Peking rather than from Washington, but also created suspicions in the minds of many people who had no sympathy for Communism, but thought the

Pentagon might be 'up to something'. But there was one essential condition for such success as was achieved and it is one which should be duly noted, because it is today very relevant in the different context of disarmament inspection. The Communists had their accusations endorsed by hand-picked commissions of fellow-travellers, but they never permitted investigation of them by any genuinely neutral and impartial body. They would not allow either the International Red Cross or any agency not controlled by a communist front organisation to examine their evidence on the spot. They held fast to the principle that nobody who has not already shown himself a reliable friend of the communist cause can give a fair judgement on any issue, or, as Khruschov was later to express it, that, 'although there may be neutral nations, there are no neutral individuals'.

G. F. H.

## AUTHOR'S NOTE

This book is an attempt to synthesize a very large subject and much has had to be omitted or discussed only in passing. Extensive footnotes have been avoided deliberately, as most of the basic texts are available in many different editions and translations. My statistical tables are compiled from various Western sources, except where otherwise stated.

I am grateful to Mr G. F. Hudson and St Antony's College, Oxford, for their help and advice with my original research, I also express my thanks to the following organizations, among many others, through which I was able to obtain much of my basic material and commentaries: The Lenin Library, Moscow; the London School of Economics Library; the Library of Radio Free Europe, Munich; Collet's Russian Bookshop and Central Books Ltd., London; the Foreign Languages Publishing House, Moscow; the Foreign Languages Press, Peking; the U.S. Information Agency, Washington; the Central Office of Information, London; the Library of the Royal Institute of International Affairs, London.

J. C. C.

PART ONE

# *The World Apparatus of Communist Propaganda*

CHAPTER ONE

# *What is Propaganda?*

Propaganda is a vogue-word of the twentieth-century. The original meaning, perfectly respectable and quite neutral, through constant application in journalese has acquired a positive, and often derogatory, political sense.

Its first official association with some sort of organized campaign can be traced in Europe to the seventeenth century when in 1622, after the Reformation, Pope Gregory XV founded his Sacre Congregatio de Propaganda Fide to do missionary work abroad. By 1842 it had acquired the following dictionary definition: 'The spread of opinions and principles by secret associations, which are viewed by most governments with horror and aversion.'

Today the standard works, Webster or the Oxford dictionary, fighting a losing battle to maintain correct usage, define propaganda as representing organized groups which propagate particular ideas or practices, and which stand for those ideas themselves; Ozhegov, the standard Russian equivalent, is equally circumspect.

But as a contemporary vogue-word, the political connotations of propaganda have increased and quickly usurped the original meaning. In the opening weeks of the Second World War, Penguin Books of London published an ABC of international affairs, *The Penguin Political Dictionary*. The compiler of the day, Walter Theimer, considered propaganda of such little importance that he did not even list it. Two decades later (in 1957) Penguin published *A Dictionary of Politics*, in which the compilers – Florence Elliott and Michael Summerskill – described propaganda (using the word in the incorrect plural sense) as: 'Statements of policy or facts, usually of a political nature, the real purpose of which is different from their apparent purpose.' They go on to elaborate the term as: '. . . a statement by a government or political party which is believed to be insincere or untrue, and designed to impress the public at large rather than to reach the truth or to bring about a genuine understanding between opposing governments or parties.'

Leonard Doob in his standard work *Public Opinion and Propaganda*[1] offers the opinion that propaganda can be called: '. . . the attempt to affect the personalities and to control the behaviour of individuals towards ends considered unscientific or of doubtful value in a society at a particular time.' That is to say, if a person systematically puts forward a view which the other members of his group consider by their standards to be anti-social, then that person is creating propaganda.

But where British and American definitions still use fairly general terms, the standard Soviet Dictionary-encyclopedia is far more specific. 'Propaganda,' it defines, 'is the interpretation of ideas, teachings, political opinions and knowledge, component parts of the work of the communist and workers' parties in the ideological training of the party masses and the toilers.' In short, to communists propaganda is an essential feature of their system.

The exponents of dynamic propaganda – dynamic in the sense that it is a deliberately planned campaign aimed at influencing the minds, emotions and ultimately the actions of specific groups – can be found in history as far back as the spoken word can be traced. In its wider sense propaganda can even be seen in the lower vertebrates, such as the tropical fish which puff themselves up to double their real size in order to scare away potential enemies, visual stratagems which have been emulated by human beings throughout history.

The Crusades – and the myths which have been perpetuated about them centuries later – were an early example in European history of the sustained use of propaganda on a large scale. With the propaganda symbol of the Cross at the head of the armies, the fighting men and those they left behind were sustained and spurred on by all manner of atrocity stories about the Saracens, just as the Allies were in 1914–18 by stories of German atrocities in Belgium – and as the Germans were in 1939 by stories about British atrocities against the Boers in the South African War of 1899–1901.

If the Crusades of the Middle Ages represented planned

[1] Henry Holt & Co., New York, 1948.

propaganda on the part of the Christians, so did the techniques used by the Muslims of the day, and since, to gain adherents to their faith, where they felt persuasion would pay better than force. The Muslim techniques had much in common with those used by dictatorships in modern times – the choice between conversion and extinction; the constant participation in public ceremonies after conversion with the obligatory intonation of the formal language of the new faith. These and further refinements have repeated themselves over and over again during the late 40's and 50's in the countries where the commmunist system has come to power.

In Ancient Rome the Emperor Nero formed a corps of 5,000 young *augustales*, men deliberately trained to incite crowds at the circus, when fervour had to be stimulated for the execution of the Christians. Around the political arena of today the *augustales* can be found in the communist front organizations.

The hordes of Genghis Khan were a figment of propaganda, put out by Genghis himself as part of a deliberate plan to make his power seem greater than it was. After seven centuries a communist Chinese unit in Korea successfully bluffed the U.N. forces into over-estimating its size by the simple ruse of scattered camp fires at night.

In the fifth century it was St Augustine who wrote slogans on the sacristy walls and turned out polemical pamphlet after pamphlet, an example which repeated itself at an increasing rate after the introduction of the printing press and the ever-widening ability to read and write. No doubt he would have fully approved the indelible 'Ban The Bomb' slogans daubed on the pillars of Stonehenge some fifteen centuries later.

The introduction of printing brought with it the pamphleteering propagandist for all manner of causes. During the American War of Independence it was Gibbons's ghosting in French of the English version of the war which helped to keep the French out of it for a while.

Perhaps the outstanding propaganda work of the nineteenth century was Harriet Beecher Stowe's *Uncle Tom's Cabin*. This story of the privations of Negro slavery in the Southern States of America in the late 1850's had a direct effect on Northern opinion and the outbreak of the Civil War, which in its turn led to the liberation of the slaves.

The book was written in the full polemical style, planned to appeal to every sentiment of pity, horror and anger in the reader. The picture was painted in black and white, with no greys to tone down the impression left on the mind. In modern communist terms, *Uncle Tom's Cabin* was an outstanding example of agitational literature. Less known was its accompanying volume, *The Key to Uncle Tom's Cabin*, a documentary collection prepared by Mrs Stowe for the use of what communists today would call propagandist cadres. *The Key* supplemented with its cold detail the emotional word-pictures of *Uncle Tom* itself.

But it was not until the last few months of the 1914–18 War that official recognition was given to propaganda as a weapon in its own right. Both sides used propaganda sporadically during the war, but it was the formation of the special propaganda Directorate at Crewe House, Lord Northcliffe's London home, which formalized the matter in the minds of the Allies. H. G. Wells prepared a memorandum on propaganda to Germany which had a great influence on the immediate post-war international developments and the formation of the League of Nations, but the war was over before much else could be done.

In the years following the First World War there was a general tendency to count the Allied propaganda as successful, especially as various German generals attributed their defeat to the undermining influence of this psychological warfare rather than to the superiority of their enemies on the battlefield. It is only in more recent years and with a better understanding of the fundamentals of psychology that these earlier attempts at winning over the minds and behaviour of the enemy have been put into a proper perspective.

For most people in the West, propaganda started to take on meaning with the rise of Hitler, with his uniformed storm-troopers, his mass rallies, his invective and all the other totalitarian symbols associated with Nazism and its parallel, Fascism, in Italy. The Nazis succeeded in winning the effective support of the Germans, at the same time as they alienated thinking Europeans elsewhere. Nothing succeeds like success and Hitler's propaganda achieved its purpose so long as his cause was strong. It was only when defeat came that the propaganda lost its impact.

If the Nazis set the pace of psychological warfare before 1939, it was on the basis of the lessons they learned from earlier exponents. Napoleon, after all, was a firm believer in the mass use of the uniform to build up confidence and pride in his armies. The French Revolution provided many lessons on the manipulation of crowds for propaganda purposes. Nearly seventy years ago the French writer Gustave le Bon in his book *The Crowd* detailed for us some fundamental ideas on the propaganda use of crowds which gave Lenin inspiration in 1917, Hitler in 1932, and the communist leaderships in every country of the Sino-Soviet Bloc since 1945.

A man alone, said le Bon, may be a cultivated individual, but put him in a crowd and he is a barbarian, a creature acting by instinct. In crowds it is stupidity, not motherwit, which is accumulated, so crowds are incapable by their group character of doing anything demanding a high degree of intelligence. They do not want ideas other than those which are absolute, uncompromising and simple. Crowds think in extremes, accepting or rejecting beliefs as a whole, as we would expect when these beliefs are induced by suggestion instead of being developed by reasoning. Crowds like force and are little impressed by kindness, which they see as a form of weakness. The loftiest statues, he observed, are erected to the tyrants!

A number of analyses of Nazi propaganda techniques have been made since 1943[1] and their conclusions bear out much of what le Bon had observed at the end of the nineteenth century from the earlier experience in France.

Hitler's strategy was to get the support of the whole population, not just the voters. Accordingly his propaganda was adapted to different sections of the public, even to the extent of promises to German womanhood that, when the Nazis came into power, every woman would have a husband. To a generation which had lost its husbands and sweethearts in the Flanders trenches such a promise – however illogical in cold print – was powerful medicine at a mass rally.

[1] For example, Lindley Fraser, *Propaganda*, Oxford U.P., 1957.

Nazi propaganda was essentially simple in character. It had to appeal to emotion, not reason. It asserted, avoiding argument. It dwelt on clearly identifiable enemies, usually the Jews, with no vagueness of image. It made wide use of slogans, some permanent, others suited to specific campaigns. Repetition was highly important in the form of symbols, badges and slogans plastered in public places.

At meetings there were always plenty of 'stewards' to deal with interrupters. Vigorous advance publicity was always given locally and the crowds warmed up with rousing music, marching and counter-marching displays, and mass singing. Of course such features are not associated solely with Nazi propaganda, they can be recognized as part and parcel of all kinds of organizations. But it was the Nazis who brought into the open the full power of such conscious and deliberate manipulations of mass emotion.

Goebbels's theories of propaganda organization were precise. He considered it needed to be planned, laid down and executed by one authority; the propaganda consequences of any action should be considered before anything was done: propaganda need not necessarily be true, but it must be credible, while it needed some definite information as base, no matter how slight; if it were to have any effectiveness, it had to evoke interest in the audience. It was no secret that the Nazis took many of their propaganda methods straight out of the New York advertising textbooks, but once again Hitler and Goebbels took everything a significant step further in placing the whole system on a centralized national scale.

At the same time Hitler learned a great deal from the communists, both in Russia itself and in Germany, where in the early twenties Willi Muenzenberg – a founder of the German Communist Party and one of the most brilliant of the early communist propaganda experts – had organized a whole network of communist fronts and a group of highly successful communist papers and magazines.

The native communists, who had built up a formidable apparatus in Germany by the beginning of the 1930's, provided him with more profitable instruction. Then he showed the world a fresh lesson by wiping out the German Communist Party apparatus almost overnight when he came into power in 1933. As he wrote in *Mein Kampf*: 'A resolute bandit can always prevent an honest man from carrying on political propaganda.' This dictum was specifically concerned with breaking up the meetings of other organizations before the Nazis were in full power, but it was shown to be equally applicable to the bodies themselves when the dictator was sure of his position.

If Hitler learned from others, so we have learned much from Hitler. The Allied propaganda machine in the Second World War – psychological warfare or sykewar as its operations became known – grew to the size of a small army.[1] No holds were barred by either side and the major axiom of Crewe House in 1918 'that only truthful statements be made' was swept away by a series of planned campaigns of lies and rumours throughout occupied Europe, carefully conceived to alarm, confuse and damage the enemy.[2] Truth was used scrupulously in all 'white' propaganda (propaganda with a known and acknowledged origin), but with the increasing amounts of 'black' (origin hidden) and 'grey' (origin only partly revealed) propaganda the ends were considered important enough to justify the means of half-truths and complete fabrication.

Of course, these black and grey propaganda campaigns had limited objectives, with the main campaigns on a strictly white basis. As far as the Allies were concerned, there were many campaign successes and one notable failure – the 'total surrender' formula, which sounded dramatically fine in Allied ears, but which made no allowance for manœuvres and face-saving among professional soldiers on both sides when it was clear that Hitler had lost. Here was the case of a propaganda slogan being used without any consideration of its wider implications.

The war ended in 1945, but propaganda by régimes has continued at an ever-increasing rate. 'The political struggle never ceases,' it has been said, 'and propaganda must be unwearying.' Though to the thinking individual propaganda is not so much unwearying as wearisome, it is with us and it must be taken into account: it will not be removed by a mental shrugging of the shoulders.

[1] See Daniel Lerner, *Sykewar*, Stewart Inc., New York, 1959.
[2] See John Baker White, *The Big Lie*, Pan Books, London, 1958.

What fundamentally is propaganda expected to do to us? According to Serge Chakotin in his *Rape of the Masses*[1] the reactions of all living beings come from four basic instincts: that of struggle against death and danger; the instinct for food and drink; the sexual instinct, whether in a purely primitive form or in a more sophisticated sublimated form; the maternal instinct, expressed as pity or anger. Pavlov's experiments with conditioned reflexes were based on the first instinct of struggle in some cases, though his best-known trials were based on the second, alimentary instinct. These are the most common instincts activated by propaganda techniques, with more limited plays on the maternal urge and the different forms of the sexual instinct.

On this basis, Chakotin states, any good propaganda campaign must be planned. If it is to be rational then it must clearly define the different groups of people to be influenced, work out the psychological approach to each group, create the actual instruments to carry out the action decided as best suited to each group, and plan to carry out and supervise the campaigns both in time and in space. In other words, he applies the simple rules of good organization, which are equally effective whether used as the basis of a sales drive in industry, or in national and world politics. This clear definition of the groups is most important, for to be successful propaganda must activate emotions and it can only do this when they are already in existence or lying dormant. An anti-blood sports campaign at a hunt ball, or unilateralism at a football match, would be extreme cases in point.

Chakotin includes a further group concept, which has been a fundamental basis of communist propaganda for more than sixty years. He divides people into two groups – the ten per cent which make up the active minority and the ninety per cent which total the passive majority. Though he does not say so, this is the same grouping as that classified by the communists as cadres and masses. For the former propaganda is sophisticated, for the latter it is simple, categoric and direct, designed to influence the emotions, not the mind.

There is, however, one aspect of this classification which Chako-

[1] Routledge, 1940, and in a revised French edition, Gallimard, Paris, 1952.

tin neglected to take into account. He divided society up into two definite groups of people, the ten per cent active and the ninety per cent passive. In fact, every individual's personality is made up of active and passive aspects in varying degrees. We all have our weak spots, our uncritical self which accepts a line of thought without question. The factors behind such blind acceptance are usually complex but the fact remains that in certain circumstances all of us react in this way.

With the growing complexities of the modern world, it is becoming harder and harder to differentiate between truth and lies. For many the choice is simple – we tell the truth, they make propaganda! This is not an over-statement of popular reaction, irrespective of political opinion. The sheer inability of the ordinary person to find out the truth himself forces such a polarization on him. In such a situation, the skilled operator of deliberate lies has a receptive audience, for where an accidental half-lie becomes accepted as fact, things are made easy for the complete and deliberate fabrication. Occasionally, as they mount up, so the lies will react on those who make them.

In some Western circles it is held that lying propaganda defeats itself in the long run. This may be so under the conditions of open warfare, but there is reason to doubt this assumption today. The experience of communist campaigns in particular, point to a reversal of the righteous concept that to lie is wrong. It may be morally wrong, but this does not mean it is ineffective. Everything depends on the length of 'the long run'. In these days we may well ask ourselves whether obvious lies and mistakes in propaganda stories matter in the long run, providing the whole campaign is planned and centrally directed. In such circumstances the individual items are buried as forgotten details in a vaster picture as the experience of the 1950's show.

One thing is certain – effective propaganda is always on the offensive. It is an unsure proponent who constantly asserts that he is not as bad as he is painted by the other chap; this simply draws attention to the propaganda being fought. In propaganda any denial is dangerous, for it implies that there is something in the original accusation, and gives the other side the opportunity to raise the whole matter again and again. This is the dilemma of the scrupulous when dealing with the unscrupulous. This in fact is one of the fundamental problems facing the non-communist world. By its very nature communist propaganda operates without the scruples we would like to employ. Must we reply in the same way?

In the more sophisticated societies we have become accustomed to dismiss communist propaganda – or what we conceive to be communist propaganda – with a shrug and forget all about it. The very term is seized upon time after time to nullify unpopular or unwanted lines of thought in others, or as an excuse for not discussing a matter further – as indeed is the term propaganda in its wider sense. We prefer to ignore the lessons of history, which have shown repeatedly the vital strategic and tactical function of propaganda at decisive periods in the progress of civilization.

This was realized by the communist movement from Lenin's earliest days. In *What is to be Done?*, written sixty years ago, Lenin discusses the work of the propagandist in a revolutionary movement and gives interesting details of this work in Russia during the 1890's. Just before the outbreak of the First World War the Stalinist historians told us Stalin ran a propaganda apparatus in Baku, financed, together with other underground activities, by the proceeds of bank raids.

After the October Revolution a formal Department of Agitation and Propaganda was set up in Moscow by the All-Union Communist Party under its Central Committee.[1] *Agitprop*, as the department became known, soon came under the party secretariat and took over the control of literary groups in the Soviet Union; 1925 saw it running the League of the Godless for the party, an official atheist organization of the late twenties. In 1930 the agitational and propaganda aspects were divided into two sections, the Department of Agitation and Mass Campaigns, and the Department for Culture and Propaganda, *Kultprop*, to cope with the new party demands for greater control of mass activity. In 1934 they were remerged into *Agitprop* again and at the Eighteenth Party Congress in 1939 *Agitprop* was delegated to the status of directorate under A. A. Zhdanov, later to become known outside Party

[1] The structural development and changes of *Agitprop* in the U.S.S.R. are summarized in Leonard Shapiro, *The Communist Party of the Soviet Union*, Eyre & Spottiswoode, London 1960.

circles for his tight Zhdanov Line hold on Soviet cultural activities and creative freedom in the 1946–8 period when, having left *Agitprop*, he became the Central Committee member responsible for ideological control of the arts. In 1948 the party abandoned the directorate system and *Agitprop* became a department again, as it is today.

It is important at this stage to emphasize the dichotomy of the communist system, the split between the State and the Party. The formal apparatus of the State and its governing bodies is considered ideologically as a temporary necessity, so long as other non-communist states remain in existence and frontiers remain a reality. Only when communism becomes fully established will the State wither away. In more pragmatic terms the Soviet State with all its institutions, such as the Supreme Soviets and the ministries, is an absolute necessity for dealing with the governments and officials of other countries as well as for the day-to-day running of the Soviet Union's internal affairs; similarly with the other communist countries.

But it is the Party which really rules the country, as distinct from governing it. It has far greater powers than the State, the organs of which are dominated in all their aspects by the Party through its policies as stated by the leadership and as carried out by the cells which permeate all non-Party organizations.

This division between the Party and the State must be clearly understood when assessing Communist Party techniques. It might be said that the message put out by the State is information, while that put out by the Party is propaganda. But when – as is the case with Mr Khruschov – the Premier and the First Secretary of the Communist Party are the same person, it is difficult to reconcile apparently contradictory statements unless the State and Party relationship is borne in mind.[1]

From its early organizational days the communist movement has

[1] In 1920 for instance, the Soviet Government stated that propaganda activities were not its concern, but that of the newly-formed Comintern. When the United Kingdom officially recognized the Soviet State in 1924, the Soviet Government was able to sign an agreement of mutual abstention from conducting propaganda against each other's institutions and government, repeating a similar undertaking in 1933 when United States recognition was given the Soviet Union.

clearly differentiated its publics into a minority to whom a variety of ideas may be presented, and a majority, who will best respond to a single idea repeated many times. Propaganda in the narrow sense is intended for the first group and agitation is the system for the second. A propagandist, wrote Lenin in *What is to be Done?*, must present many ideas, so many indeed that they will be understood only by comparatively few people. On the other hand, an agitator dealing with the same subject must direct all his efforts to presenting a single idea to the masses, to arouse their feelings over the single idea, leaving a more complete explanation to the propagandist. For this purpose Lenin saw the propagandist using the printed word and the agitator the spoken word.

This principle was enunciated in 1902 and still holds true today. It can be found in many other circles as well as in the communist movement, but it is the communists who have formalized the whole matter and who have taken the concept beyond mere words.[1] They are linked with action and are both merged into organization. So communist propaganda cannot be assessed in isolation. It must be judged dynamically against the situation of the moment, the happenings of the past and the likely trends in the foreseeable future.

But in its narrower agitational aspect, propaganda is seen as: 'the main means of linking the Party with the masses, the well-tried method of persuading the workers, explaining to them the policies of the Party'.[2] The primary party organizations were described by Lenin as 'rifle pits', linking through their *Agitprop* and organizational work the masses and the Central Committee.

A picture of this internal agitational work in the Soviet Union is given by the Party Resolution on propaganda published in January 1960.[3] This is a good model for all the communist countries, with the possible exception of China. An important part of the Resolution of the Central Committee of the Communist

[1] 'There is propaganda in words and propaganda in deeds. Propaganda and agitation in deeds are more effective': M. I. Kalinin *On Communist Education*, Moscow, 1949, p. 354.

[2] From the article 'Agitational Work' in *Spravochnik sekretariya pyervichnoi partinnoi organizatsii* (Secretary's Handbook for Primary Party Organizations), Moscow, 1960.

[3] As given in the Soviet Press January 9, 1960 and reprinted in full in the *Spravochnik* above.

Party of the Soviet Union on the Tasks of the Party Propaganda under Present-day Conditions – to give it its full title – in many respects repeats much that has been basic since the communists came to power in Russia and as such is valuable in giving a clear picture of the propaganda task in a communist society. At the same time the Resolution brings the whole subject up to date, both in terms of content and presentation.

Being a Party resolution, its emphasis is on the Party machine and the Party member. But there is no doubt that it is intended to be applied to the whole of Soviet society.[1] Propaganda, it states, should be adapted to the needs of different groups – the intelligentsia, youth, women and the various minority nationalities. The use of textbooks, teaching aids, the Press, radio and television is detailed. The role of the social sciences and the work of propagandists in secondary and higher schools, ways of getting better results from meetings are laid down.

The content of propaganda for the 1960's – or the first half at least – is discussed, together with the ways individual propagandists can do their jobs better. Some of the directives refer to work inside the Party and Young Communist League organizations, others discuss how the work can be carried on not only in other organizations, but also with the individual member of Soviet society in his own home. As a general directive the Resolution is a thorough and, in terms of communist semantics, a clearly-phrased document.[2]

'Communist propaganda,' declares the Resolution, 'must take into account the peculiarities of profession, age, education and other factors inherent in the different strata of Soviet society'. Workers and collective farmers must be trained in a consciously comradely spirit of co-operation in working towards a communist society, while actively rejecting remnants of the past. Among the intelligentsia, this work must get them to link their activities with those of the masses and to play their full part in Soviet society.

[1] The listings given here are not necessarily in the order given them in the Resolution itself.

[2] The discussion of the Resolution which follows gives the main sense of the various sections without any extensive verbatim quotations. Only where passages or expressions are of special interest are they put in quotation marks.

Similarly young people must understand social happenings, must make firm personal convictions based on communist morality, be intolerant towards bourgeois ideology, apolitical ideas and 'philistinism' (anti-social self-interest). The rising generation must be cheerful, manly, brave and unshakeably convinced of the triumph of communism. So youth propaganda must be versatile and interesting, lively and picturesque. It must be based on the main points of Marxist-Leninist theory, the Party and national history, the examples set by the glories of the past, the heroic deeds of the present.

Propaganda among women must raise their ideological requirements and interests, getting them – particularly housewives – to take active parts in public and political life, fighting religious influences and the petty bourgeois ideas which still remain. Taking into account their work, they should be given more talks and lectures, while 'it is essential to wage a merciless struggle against manifestations of an attitude towards women that is feudal and reminiscent of Central Asian landowners'.

Propaganda work must take into account the national peculiarities at the various levels of the Soviet population, placing the main emphasis on co-operation between the nationalities for the 'all-round mutual enrichment of socialist nations'. Bourgeois nationalism must be crushed, together with tendencies to idealize the past and its contradictions. Similarly 'individual expressions of national self-sufficiency and exclusiveness' must be fought.

More textbooks and visual aids of a popular nature are called for dealing with philosophical aspects of Marxism-Leninism, atheism, industrial and agricultural economic questions, the history of international communism and of the national liberation struggle in Asia, Africa and Latin America, questions of communist upbringing and the philosophical problems of the natural sciences. Places of political education are to be equipped with the latest visual aid material, while the Ministry of Culture is to allow these places free access to its library and historical-revolutionary documentary films. At the same time the Ministry is instructed to make more such films and other material for political education. The whole lecture system has to be overhauled, made more lively and less superficial. The local organizations of the All-Union Society for the Dissemination of Political and Scientific Knowledge – the main apparatus for systematic agitation on current questions – are to be improved, while there is to be stronger Party control over the lecture groups of the Young Communist League, *Komsomol*. More leaders from the different professions and trades are to be put on lecture work.

The Press is to play a greater propaganda role, with greater attention to matters of the moment and their Marxist-Leninist theoretical background. There must be greater variety of material and presentation, more militancy and exposures of alien ideas. A wider range of writers is to be recruited, with new recruits to journalism from people 'who know life' and with experience in other organizations, as well as from workers' and rural correspondents.[1] 'It is necessary to rally around every newspaper and magazine gifted publicists and propagandists, skilful popularizers of revolutionary theory, able to respond in an operative manner to burning questions with vivid and striking writing in the Press.'

On the papers themselves the propaganda sections of the editorial offices are to be improved and trained propaganda workers 'who know their job' engaged. On the local papers the system of creating propaganda departments within the editorial offices made up of people from outside the paper – a system apparently at work – is to be approved formally, as well as other unstated ways of drawing the public into Press work.

While drawing on the experience of the best propagandists on newspapers and magazines, with discussions on the practice and methods of the written and the spoken word, more mass-political literature is to be published. It is to be bright and readable, compact and cheap, interpreting the questions of the moment for the millions.[2]

[1] Correspondents from factories and collective farms for national and local papers, whose reports are very often the basis of shortcoming exposures. This system of voluntary correspondents is both long-established and widely practiced, though there have been many examples of the unpopularity of such correspondents among their fellow-workers.

[2] Little wonder that in the autumn of 1960 an All-Union conference was called to discuss the woodpulp resources of the U.S.S.R. and means of increasing paper output!

Similarly, better use is to be made of radio and television for ideological purposes by Party organizations at all levels, with leading Party workers and other officials dealing with questions 'stirring the working people'.

The social sciences – here the term is used in a specialized Marxist sense – are allocated a more important role in propaganda activity than hitherto. Party propaganda can only be really profound and effective when it is constantly enriched by inquisitive and investigating thought, when the best scientific forces are taking a direct active part in it. In their turn the social sciences can only fulfil their task if they are organically linked with the practice of communist building and ideological work, with the topical requirements of Party propaganda. Social workers must study and generalize the experience of the Party and people's struggle for the victory of communism. They must break into life, evolve creatively radical theoretical problems of the present day, the basic conformities to natural laws in the development of socialism into communism.

During the 1960's Soviet social scientists have the following tasks set them in the Resolution: a detailed study of the history of the Communist Party of the Soviet Union and the historical significance of its experience for the world communist movement; a joint philosophical, economic and historical research programme on the topical problems of building communism in the U.S.S.R.: 'Scientific works on the paths to communist building, on the development of the world system of socialism in conformity with natural laws, on the world communist, workers' and democratic movement, on the present stage of a general crisis of capitalism, on the disintegration of the colonial system of imperialism and the development of the national-liberation struggle of the peoples of Asia, Africa and Latin America.' (Works attacking bourgeois, right-wing socialist and revisionist theories.) In general scientific workers and social science lecturers have to take a more active personal role in propaganda activities, both oral and printed.

Propaganda work in the high secondary schools must be improved. As throughout, improved standards of Marxist-Leninist teachings are the fundamental demand of the Resolution. With the importance of inculcating the ideas into the youngsters thoroughly, a popular course on the basics of political knowledge has to be introduced in the upper classes of the schools by 1962, with a special textbook for the course.

For these groups – which span the whole of Soviet society – the directives lay down the general line of propaganda for the foreseeable future: economic and production successes, the superiority of the Marxist-Leninist ideology over all others, the need to fight bourgeois ideology, the explanation of the peace-loving foreign policy of the Soviet Union and the general need for more theoretical studies. In short, the same approach is to be applied as before. The very first item of the Resolution, that the shortcomings of the propagandists noted in its preamble should be corrected, also adopts this approach. But though the general purpose and procedure are the same, the detailed directives are interesting for the insight they give into internal propaganda drives in the 1960's.

Two sections of the Resolution are devoted to the need to get propaganda out of the old, unintelligible rut of aphorisms, meaningless quotations from the Marx-Engels-Lenin textbooks and to make it a vital, dynamic force. The existing methods of highlighting work records and of educating the cadres – giving them facts and concrete knowledge – are to be reinforced by regular briefing conferences of agitators and propagandists together with members of the intelligentsia, called under the auspices of the more important local and regional Party Central Committees: these conferences would discuss export reports on internal and foreign affairs and on local matters of importance.

'Strictly observing the principle of voluntariness,' more non-Party activists, leading production workers and innovators are to be used for agitational work on the radio and television, in the Press, and for lecturing. At the same time as the ideological level of such mass propaganda is to rise, more effective use must be made of the arts. 'Bibliographical work and the propaganda of books and music should be raised.' Similarly houses of culture, clubs, libraries, reading-rooms, museums, parks and other cultural and educational establishments must become true centres of agitation and propaganda work. In all this, it is repeated, the mass and artistic organizations play a leading part.

Greater emphasis is to be put on political self-education within a seminar system, with 'only those who really lack the grounding necessary to do bookwork on their own' going to study circles or political schools. This system is advocated as 'the main method of mastering Marxism-Leninism,' and more help is to be given those who are studying for themselves the theory and history of the Soviet Communist Party. Within this framework the political school is for those embarking on the first stage of Marxism-Leninism, with study circles and theoretical seminars for the courses to follow: the history of the Communist Party, the fundamentals of Marxism-Leninism, economic questions and current political affairs, atheism, the international situation and world communism. At the highest level, the Marxist-Leninist Universities,[1] stress is laid on individual work as well as on seminars. In this connexion the importance of the *Komsomol* is brought out as an organization for moulding young people and therefore needing 'the best and most highly informed communists who like to work among young people'.[2]

In general, better propagandists are needed and better instruction for them when they are found: 'more care must be taken in extending their horizons, in raising their cultural standards and in perfecting their methodological skill'. Their courses are to be improved, more is to be written about their work and their status in the eyes of the public raised. In general the study centres are to be stirred up into greater activity.

As the Resolution puts it: 'The Communist Party of the Soviet Union Central Committee[3] demands that Party organizations should intensify the guidance of ideological work and first of all its decisive section – Party propaganda'. Much of the Resolution only restates what has been said many times before in Party directives, but in present-day terms. Although repetitious and tedious, it is an important document.

It is important because it clearly shows how the Soviet propa-

[1] Though strictly speaking these are Party institutions, they have university status.

[2] One of their jobs is 'to put an end to high turnover and to create stable propaganda cadres in the *Komsomol*'. A rather unflattering revelation of the current state of the organization.

[3] Abbreviated in future to C.P.S.U. and C.C., respectively.

ganda system makes its impact everywhere: no sector of Soviet society is without its presence. It shows in a concise form how closely the communist propagandist inter-relates domestic and foreign events in a spectrum stretching in each direction as far as the mind can reach. It also shows the weaknesses of its own making, weaknesses which will be dealt with towards the end of the book. Although we are primarily interested in communist propaganda to the outside world, we must know something of the internal communist propaganda work. This Resolution published in the opening days of the 1960's will be a basic document for a long time to come.

To understand the full importance of communist propaganda in the world today it is essential to bear in mind the world outlook of communism itself – it is a political movement of world-wide dimensions and with world-wide aspirations. Whether expressed in pure ideological terms or in the simpler expressions of expansionism, communism internationally lays down no bounds beyond which it will not spread – with the sputniks, the luniks and the manned rockets its territorial claims spread out beyond the moon to Venus. Compared with this perspective, the dictatorships of the past were relatively modest in their claims: even Hitler's vision did not extend as far.

For a long time after the Second World War it was generally believed that communism could only come to power behind the ranks of the Red Army: the examples of such countries as Czechoslovakia, Poland and Hungry are usually cited in support. That may have been so in the early years, but the theory is now coming under fire as one more likely to mislead than to explain. With a greater understanding of the power of propaganda and the systematic use made of it by the communists there is a feeling that Soviet conquests in Europe have been made in part, as the French writer Suzanne Labin puts it '. . . by the effects of the intoxication of the democratic spirit'.[1]

In a generalized sense it is accepted that communism places great stress on controlling the mind as a means of getting people individually and in the mass to work for its world-wide aims

[1] S. Labin, *Il est moins cinq*, 2nd Ed. 1960 Editions Berger-Levvrault, Paris.

and objectives. In the long-term view full control of the mind is most obviously desirable, but in more immediate terms – and this is most important – the major aim of the communist movement is not to gain recruits to its ranks, but merely to get support for, or neutralize opposition against, its policies of the moment.[1]

The wide-spread misunderstanding of this point is of great value to the communist movement. It always claims that it is not out to convert everyone to communism overnight, that it is as sweetly reasonable as the next political group. In fact, the general ignorance of the majority about communism and its policies is one of its greatest propaganda advantages. In British political circles, the main parties publish detailed annual handbooks about each other, for the use of their own propagandists when attacking the rival parties. Yet no such handbook[2] is published by any of them about their mutual enemy, the communist movement. While it is in the minority, the communist party claims to be the political equal of the other parties. It is only when it is in power – as we have seen in Eastern Europe – that it expunges from the record the claims of the past and suppresses the opposition groups.

Communist strategy uses its propaganda in the non-communist world to help foster the complacent 'it cannot happen here' attitude, to encourage rivalries between others on the 'divide and rule' principle, to create the image of new enemies to divert attention from itself and overall to stimulate a belief in the inevitability of communism as a world force.

Communists, whether acting as governments or as party political groups, have the tactical advantage of playing the game as they choose, ignoring or invoking rules and laws as it suits them; while the non-communists in general, and Western régimes in particular, are hampered by having to keep to the generally accepted rules.

The communist exploitation of the general desire for peace and

[1] With the 1963 claimed world communist membership of $42\frac{1}{2}$ million, it is about keeping pace with world population increases.

[2] One of the only substantial works of this kind is Hans Koch, *Theorie Taktik Technik des Weltkommunismus*, Ilmgauverlag, Pfaffenhofen/Ilm, 1959.

good international relations is an accepted fact, but even then it is not admitted by many how this exploitation succeeds even among those who profess to see through it. After all, no one cares to admit a truth that carries a sting in its tail! Communist propaganda is able to exploit to the full the guilt feelings in many circles that we might not have done all we could to understand and co-exist with the communists: past failures are dimissed as exactly reasons why we should try again, with the onus – by implication if not by direct accusation – placed on the non-communist, to find the new measure of agreement. If any faces are to be saved, it is those of the communists, who again will never accept any concession offered to them, if they can twist circumstances so that they gain it as a victory. Ideologically nothing is worth having unless it has been fought for; it must be wrung from the opposition, not freely given or taken.

Communist propaganda has the further advantage of being able to switch on and off at will. It can work hard at a single issue as long as it feels the issue is worth keeping alive. As soon as its usefulness is done, it can be dropped – usually for ever, though kept in hand in case it has to be brought to bear again. Such strategies and tactics as these will be discussed in the chapters which follow. At this stage it is enough for us to keep the general principles in mind.

In all these functions the propaganda should not be considered alone. It is a part – in many individual cases the most important part – of a general scheme, which may involve military action, insurrection, espionage, sabotage and the deliberate fomenting of unrest in non-communist countries.[1]

Communist propaganda is expensive. In 1960 a Ministry of Defence estimate published in Bonn gave an annual figure of $2,000 million, excluding the cost of the diplomatic service and the expenses of economic dumping, both of which play their part in the wider aspect of propaganda. An unofficial British estimate goes higher still, but even $2,000 million is a lot of money to

[1] Lenin's 1920 instructions under the title *Left-Wing Communism, an Infantile Disorder*, explain the inter-relationships of these factors Soviet readers of the Party Press were reminded of them as important Party instructions in 1960.

spend every year on convincing people that you are right and everyone else is not only wrong, but diabolically wrong.[1]

Suzanne Labin in *Il est moins cinq* reckons that communist propaganda and political activities in France cost $20 million a year, in Italy $30 million. In Indonesia and India – 'where men cost less' – the annual charge is $10 million each, in Finland and Iraq $5 million each. This makes a total of $80 million for these six, as well as an estimated 65,000 paid workers. A further twenty countries which communist parties of lesser importance cost a total of $220 million annually, employing 50,000 paid personnel. All told, Labin estimates, direct communist agitation outside the Soviet Bloc costs $500 million annually and employs 140,000 people. The apparatus of indirect propaganda – the various fronts to which reference will be made later – costs, she reckons, more than $1,500 million annually and finds work for 350,000 people. Labin's estimates thus equate with those published in Bonn. On these reckonings Moscow and Peking are spending two dollars a head on every person outside their own areas every year.

These are only estimates, for we do not know enough about these matters to make more than estimates or intelligent guesses. But this figure of two dollars a head seems reasonable and brings the 2,000 million figure into better perspective. For anyone attempting world rule – whether in ideological terms or in those of crude physical domination – systematic propaganda can be a cheap weapon, whether in terms of financial cost or the saving of manpower: an army of half a million propagandists is cheaper at any time than an army of soldiers, not to mention a navy and an air force. For expanding dictatorships the function of propaganda helps to economize on the cost of the expanding domination.

So it is that, as Labin points out, the communist party in any country will put out a hundred times more literature per member than the richest of the other parties. The locally produced material is backed by dozens of heavily subsidized publications published in all the vital languages by the Communist Bloc for readers in the

[1] Compare this $2,000 million with the Western Community's annual total of $7,000 million economic aid to under-developed countries during the years 1956–9, a figure twice that for 1950–5 (I.E.E.C. calculation given in *New York Times International Edition*, 14 March 1961).

Western Community and in the uncommitted countries.[1] According to United States Customs statistics, in 1959 some 6 million parcels of printed matter – totalling 10 million items – were sent from communist countries to the U.S.A. by the ordinary printed matter post: this excluded an unknown quantity sent by first-class mail.

Though communism's main plank is ideological, its actions are strictly pragmatic and opportunist. While paying lip service to ideological fundamentals, communist propaganda for the Western Community and the uncommitted nations is one that could be tagged on to any dictator's line, so long as it had no racial character to limit its universality. Communist propaganda makes good use of the theory of historical inevitability, especially if the facts of a situation can be made to fit the Party line. To this end, there is a general three-stage approach: (1) alarm, to raise the audience from its apathy and acceptance of the present; (2) prophecy of the future course downhill combined with reminders of past failures of the system; (3) finally the inducement of hope based on the communist solution offered, channelling the negative energies roused by the prophecy and recollection phases into positive action along the new lines put forward. Strikes, peace campaigns, 'anti-' demonstrations, friendship rallies – all such problems can be dealt with agitationally by the three-stage approach.

Where communist doctrine is invoked it has a certain plausibility – which may be most striking in particular situations – with its talk of monopolistic capitalism, warmongering and sabre-rattling, crises of unemployment and labour-capitalist antagonisms, imperialist domination and colonialist exploitation. Here again many of the catch-phrases invoked are not necessarily peculiar to communism – a phenomenon of great value to it in the developing and uncommitted countries.

Though it has been modified in recent years, communist propaganda has an essentially polarized set of values. The virtues of the

[1] To avoid awkward and repetitious language, the communist countries of Europe (excluding Yugoslavia) and Asia will be ıeferred to collectively as the Communist Bloc, Western Europe and North America as the Western Community and the other countries as the uncommitted countries.

Communist Bloc are complemented by the vices of the West. The communists are for peace, the West for war; communists can never be militarist, the West cannot be otherwise; communists are all for co-operation, the West relies on exploitation. These are the types of over-simplification used in communist agitational propaganda – though avoided in material intended for more sophisticated audiences.

But communist double-talk[1] – with its exploitation of words meaning one thing to communists and something quite different to others – must not be dismissed as mere semantics. If we are confused by what the communists mean with their words, they are perfectly clear in their own minds, as witness Mr Khruschov's lucid interpretation of peaceful coexistence the Communist Bloc way, which will be discussed later.

If we make mistakes by misunderstanding the communists' use of words, we equally misunderstand their impartial use of truth and lies, to the extent that we are left wondering which is fact and which is fiction. At the agitational level it does not really matter tactically how true or false a line of talk may be, so long as it sounds logical. Accusations and challenges on any particular point can always be answered by ignoring the content of the challenge and casting doubts on the motives or the probity of the challenger. All this is nothing peculiar to communist agitation, it is common to all the more extreme political movements, who recognize it as an effective short-term weapon.

Our mistakes so often are to ignore these realities and to dismiss communist propaganda simply because it contains obvious lies and offends our intellectual senses. But if it achieves its purpose – and there are many cases where this technique has – what reason is there for us to laugh, or to feel indignantly and morally superior?

Particularly in these days of greater flexibility of action, the communist propaganda is able to exploit all manner of sophisms which have become established in our minds. Eight of these major

[1] Harry Hodgkinson's *Doubletalk* (In the U.S.A. *The Language of Communism*), Pitman, London and New York, 1955, is still probably one of the best concise discussions of the subject though since Stalin's death some of his points no longer apply.

fallacies are listed by Labin: (1) the fight is between Russia and America, so everyone else should be neutral; (2) the Communist Bloc arms itself because it is afraid of Western aggression, remove Western aggressiveness by disarmament and all will be well; (3) the Communist Bloc is afraid because it misunderstands the West, so it is up to us to make approaches and show our goodwill; (4) the West shuts itself up in a negative attitude, so again it is up to us to be more forthcoming; (5) atomic energy is the gravest world problem today, so we should concentrate on it rather than on communist political advances; (6) we cannot ignore a thousand million communists, that is the inhabitants living in the East Bloc – what we must ignore is that only a tiny fraction of these are in fact true communists; (7) communist successes result from social injustices, with the implication that no other political parties bother about such problems and that communism in Eastern Europe was swept forward by a tide of popular support; (8) the last sophism is one that has been very firmly held in leading Western political circles, that the answer to the Soviet advance is economic aid to the under-developed countries: certainly such aid is necessary, but it does not provide the answer to communist propaganda in the uncommitted countries. Under some circumstances, it could even help the opposition by giving the local people the means to receive and be influenced by communist propaganda, whether oral *via* the radio or visual *via* books and films.

The American commentator Alistair Cooke, broadcasting over the BBC in January 1961 made this point when discussing the relations between the U.S.A. and Cuba. 'I think,' he said, 'the communists are less naïve about the roots of effective political action. They have shown – from Azerbaijan to Budapest and perhaps to Cuba – that the very quality to stimulate in poor and bitter peoples is the sense of being exploited, whether that sense is healthy or neurotic. But we of the West cling to the noble delusion that a man is a rational being and that he is at best a man with a just grievance, at worst a man with a grudge which can be cured with a treaty of mutual assistance and a Senate appropriation for foreign aid.'

Communist propaganda sweeps right across the semantic spectrum. It is spread throughout the world by an apparatus that is as complex as it is comprehensive. From the giant printing presses in Moscow to a jungle duplicating machine in tropical Africa the word goes out in all languages. As we have seen from the Party Resolution on Propaganda in the U.S.S.R., every possible medium is used, and at an increasing rate.

This is not the occasion to discuss in detail the major communist means of disseminating printed propaganda inside or outside the Bloc. *Tass* and news agencies patterned on it in the other communist countries[1] probably plays the most important day-to-day role, and in February 1961 this service was supplemented in Moscow by the formation of a special agency A.P.N. or *Novosti* (News), which was given the task of putting over to the world Soviet ideas on peaceful understanding, of taking up specific questions relating to the Soviet Union and of acting as a general background information agency on the U.S.S.R. Unlike *Tass*, which is a state organization and enjoys diplomatic immunity abroad, A.P.N. is a 'public' body, with no protection from the State except that its material is copyrighted.[2]

The dichotomy of the Soviet system has already been mentioned, with the existence side by side of the State apparatus and the Party machine, the Party being the controlling factor. In diplomatic terms the Soviet Government deals with other governments. At the same time the Communist Party goes over the head of the government by aiming its propaganda directly at the people, with the object of influencing action from below. The classical case of this in modern times was the 1948 communist *coup d'état* in Czechoslovakia, which was largely achieved by such action from below, as we have since been told by those who helped organize the coup.[3]

[1] These are A.D.N. (East Germany), Agerpres (Rumania), A.T.A. (Albania), B.T.A. (Bulgaria), C.T.K. (Czechoslovakia), K.C.N.A. (North Korea), MONTSAME (Mongolia), M.T.I. (Hungary), N.C.N.A. (China), P.A.P. (Poland), V.N.A. (North Vietnam). From the evidence of a Bloc conference of Press agencies held in Prague in June 1962 it appears that Prensa Latina (Cuba) should also be included.

[2] Whether this copyright is to be put on an international basis remains to be seen.

[3] As described, for instance, by John Boynton, 'From Prague to Westminster' in *Socialist Commentary*, June 1962.

In the wider sense the propaganda apparatus for influencing from below is the old-established system of communist fronts, ostensibly independent of the Party, often seemingly free from any political influence at all. Sometimes they may be quite large organizations in a country – as with the women's organization in France – but usually they are relatively small. They can, however, be very active and, if they have an efficient caucus, can bring considerable pressure on parliamentary institutions.

While some of the fronts – such as those for scientists, doctors and lawyers – are meant to appeal to the minority and can thus be called true propaganda bodies, the important fronts – peace, women, youth – have an agitational function among the masses.

Communist propaganda leans strongly on the thesis that an *élite*, the activists, leads and controls the crowd, the masses. Linked with this is the communist preference for collective rather than individual appeals. This again is not peculiar to communism, it can be found in any evangelizing group. Like the evangelists, the communists use a good song where they can to help induce a mass hypnosis: this is particularly noticeable with the World Federation of Democratic Youth and its rollicking 'Freedom Song'. This has a good, strong tune with words acceptable among young people anywhere. It is sung as the climax to rallies with everyone holding hands, a technique that draws in the most reluctant.[1]

This emotional agitation is particularly important for conversion campaigns – conversion to acceptance of the communist line, not necessarily to membership of the Party. To this end it is important that not too many Party members be present, the need is for converts and possible converts. It is in such indirect work that the fronts play an essential role. Some fronts may be long established, others only lasting a short while. In fact, the temporary fronts set up for specific purposes seem to be on the increase in recent years.

In its work of getting support from among the ranks of other organizations, the communist movement is not alone. But its system of fronts allows it to operate by remote control and thus remain out of sight. Its use of what are familiarly known as

[1] The writer states this from vivid personal experience on several occasions.

fellow-travellers can be as subtle as it is often blatant, as is its use of overt and covert Party members.

The original term fellow-traveller dates back to the early days of the Bolshevik Revolution, to describe those Russian writers who, while not subscribing to the tenets of communism, were prepared to go along with the communist authorities of the day. Today the term is synonymous with crypto-communism, though this is not necessarily the case with individuals. Labin suggests the word 'auxiliary' would be better. Certainly it is less subjective, for many fellow-travellers do their communist propaganda job sincerely believing that they are acting quite independently of any group.

In the 1950's the fellow-traveller was easy to recognize, for Stalin's line was uncompromising and clear. But the auxiliaries of the 1960's – with communist propaganda growing in size, scope and complexity – are harder to spot. In the chapters which follow, I intend to discuss the changes that have brought all this about and to see how far we can use our experience of the past decade or so to look forward.

CHAPTER TWO

# *The Basic Directives 1919–64*

Communism is a proselytizing movement which by its expansionist nature is world-wide in concept. Its existence depends on the constant and consistent use of propaganda in every way possible. Every major action of the communists internationally, as well as within the borders of the Bloc itself, is related by their Party spokesmen to a tenet of Lenin or Marx.

In the beginning there was The Communist Manifesto. This was not only the first statement of communist policy, it was also the first piece of communist propaganda, with its key agitational message perpetuated daily in every Party organ of the East Bloc: 'Working men of all countries, unite!'

The Manifesto was a product of that great year of nineteenth-century revolt, 1848. Its authors Marx and Engels declared that they had something in common with other revolutionary movements in that the immediate aim of the communists was the same as that of other proletarian parties: the formation of the proletariat into a class, the overthrow of bourgeois supremacy and a conquest of political power by the proletariat. But though these immediate aims were the same, the theoretical basis of the communist movement was quite different: 'The distinguishing feature of communism is not the abolition of property generally, but the abolition of bourgeois property. Modern bourgeois property is the final and most complete expression of the system of producing and appropriating products, which is based on class antagonism, on the exploitation of the many by the few. In this sense, the theory of the communists may be summed up in the single sentence – Abolition of private property.'

To attain these aims, the Manifesto laid down a policy of communist action briefly and succinctly: 'The communists everywhere support every revolutionary movement against the existing social and political order of things. In all these movements they bring to the front, as the leading question in each, the property question, no matter what its degree of development at the time. Finally they labour everywhere for the union and agreement of the democratic parties of all countries. The communists disdain to conceal their views and aims. They openly declare that their ends can only be attained by the forcible overthrow of all existing social conditions.'

This was in February 1848. Sixty-nine years later, these words of two members of the German bourgeoisie were put into action not in Germany itself, as Marx and Engels visualized, but in Tsarist Russia, a country outside their political calculations. There, in accordance with the Manifesto's instructions, Lenin's Bolsheviks supported the original revolution of February 1917 only to rise once again against their erstwhile allies in November, setting up by force the first communist state, the first epicentre of a world-wide political earthquake.

Within two years of the October Revolution and the establishment of Bolshevik power in Russia, the leaders in Moscow set about establishing a world revolutionary movement, the Communist International, or Comintern, which was founded in 1919 at a congress attended by fifty-three delegates from nineteen countries, of which eight now form part of the U.S.S.R. The Comintern developed until by the time of its last Congress, in 1935, it could count delegates from sixty-five communist parties around the world. It was wound up as an organization at the height of the Second World War in 1943, as a gesture of Soviet solidarity with the non-communist world fighting the Nazis.

Ostensibly the Comintern was not under the direct control of the Soviet communist apparatus, though the very manner of its winding up belied this. It followed the changes of the Moscow line in all their intricacies throughout the 20's and 30's and acted as the main line of communication from the Soviet capital outwards to the communist parties throughout the world, both the legal and the underground organizations. The major directives were given at the infrequent Comintern congresses and in more detail in the pages of its journal, *International Press Correspondence*, or *Inprecorr*.

The basic directives of the Comintern were most clearly laid down by its Sixth Congress in 1928 (the next and last was not to be until 1935) and they link the original Communist Manifesto of 1848 with the next basic directive, which was given by Andrei Zhdanov in 1947 at the formation in Warsaw of the next international communist body, the Communist Information Bureau, or Cominform.[1]

The programme for world communist action as laid down by the 1928 Congress was based on the simple thesis that 'the ultimate aim of the Communist International is to replace world capitalist economy by a world system of communism'. This world dictatorship of the proletariat would only come as the final result of the process of international proletarian revolution. This revolution in its turn would be made up of processes varying in time and character; there would be purely proletarian revolutions (of the Russian type, for instance), revolutions of a bourgeois-democratic type which would grow into proletarian revolutions, wars of national liberation and colonial revolutions.

Schematically the Comintern Congress saw the variety of conditions and ways of achieving the dictatorship of the proletariat in various countries divided into three main types. In the countries of highly developed capitalism, the U.S.A., Britain and Germany, for instance, the fundamental demand was for the direct transition of the proletariat to the dictatorship. This would mean demands for the expropriation of large-scale industry in its entirety, the organization of a large number of State Soviet farms with a relatively small part of the land transferred to the peasants, the regulation of the markets and the collectivization of peasant farming.

In countries with a medium development of capitalism (for example, Spain, Portugal, the Balkan countries) the stages of transition would depend on the extent of semi-feudal survivals in agriculture. Here the dictatorship of the proletariat would not come immediately, but as a development of the democratic dictatorship of the proletariat and peasantry. The emphasis would be on agricultural reform, with expropriated land handed over in the first place to the peasants, who would be organized along

[1] The more usual shortened form used in communist circles was Informbureau, but here we shall use the term Cominform as the one most familiar in non-communist circles.

co-operative lines and later combined still closer in production. The rate of this transition would be comparatively slow.

The colonial and semi-colonial countries (India, China), together with countries dependent on the capitalist states (Argentina, Brazil) would have a mixture of industry and feudalism, resulting in the principal economic and political sectors – industrial, commercial and banking enterprises, the large estates and plantations – being concentrated in the hands of foreign imperialist groups. In these countries the fight would take two forms. On the one hand the struggle against feudalism and the pro-capitalist forms of exploitation, on the other against foreign imperialism for national independence. Here again the transition would be by stages, representing the transformation of a bourgeois-democratic revolution into proletarian revolution. In the majority of such cases, a successful outcome would only be possible if direct help were obtained from countries where communism was already established.

In still more backward countries, such as parts of Africa, where there were few or no wage earners, where most people still lived in tribal conditions, where the national bourgeoisie was non-existent and where foreign imperialism showed itself in military occupation and the usurpation of land, the main task was to fight for national independence. Successful national uprisings could open the way for the direct introduction of the communist system, provided 'powerful help' was given by the established communist countries. This last point was re-emphasized in the 1928 directives, the necessity for the colonial revolutionaries to receive 'the assistance and support of the proletarian dictatorship and of the international proletarian movement generally'.

Taking a long view of world communist developments, the 1928 Comintern Congress laid down the inter-relationships between revolution in the industrial and under-developed countries in the following words:

> Colonial revolutions and movements for national liberation play an extremely important part in the struggle against imperialism and in the struggle for the conquest of power by the working class. Colonies and semi-colonies are also important in the transition period because they represent the world rural district in relation to the industrial

countries, which represent the world city. Consequently the problem of organizing the socialist world economy, of properly combining agriculture with industry is, to a large extent, the problem of the relation towards the former colonies of imperialism. The establishment of a fraternal, militant alliance with the masses of toilers in the colonies represents one of the principal tasks the world industrial proletariat must fulfil as leader in the struggle against imperialism.

Thus, in rousing the workers in the home countries for the struggle for the dictatorship of the proletariat, the progress of the world revolution also rouses hundreds of millions of colonial workers and peasants for the struggle against foreign imperialism. In view of the existence of centres of socialism represented by Soviet Republics of growing economic power, the colonies which break away from imperialism economically gravitate towards and gradually combine with the industrial centres of world socialism, are drawn into the channels of socialist construction, and by skipping the further stage of the development of capitalism as the predominant system, obtain opportunities for rapid economic and cultural progress. The Peasants' Soviets in the backward ex-colonies and the Workers' and Peasants' Soviets in the more developed ex-colonies group themselves politically around the centres of proletarian dictatorship, join the growing Federation of Soviet Republics and thus enter the general system of the world proletarian dictatorship. Socialism as the new method of production thus obtains world-wide scope of development.

In all this revolutionary work, the key factor was the Soviet Union:

Being the land of the dictatorship of the proletariat and of socialist construction, the land of great working-class achievements, of the union of the workers and the peasants and of a new culture marching under the banner of Marxism, the U.S.S.R. inevitably becomes the base of the world movement of all oppressed classes, the centre of international revolution, the greatest factor in world history. In the U.S.S.R. the world proletariat for the first time acquires a country that is really its own, and for the colonial movements the U.S.S.R. becomes a powerful centre of attraction.

Thus the U.S.S.R. is . . . the international driving force of proletarian revolution that impels the proletariat of all countries to seize power; she is the living example proving that the working class is not only capable of destroying capitalism, but of building up socialism as well; she is the prototype of the fraternity of nationalities in all lands united in the World Union of Socialist Republics and of the economic unity of the toilers of all countries in a single world socialist economic system that the world proletariat must establish when it has captured political power.

In return, the international proletariat had a duty towards the U.S.S.R., particularly in the event of any attack being made upon the Soviet motherland:

In view of the fact that the U.S.S.R. is the only motherland of the international proletariat, the principal bulwark of its achievements and the most important factor for its international emancipation, the international proletariat must on its part facilitate the success of the work of socialist construction in the U.S.S.R. and defend her against the attacks of the capitalist powers by all means in its power.[1]

These general rules for the international communist movement were laid down ten years after the Russian Revolution and became the operational guidance line without substantial modification for the next quarter-century. In 1938 Stalin underlined the central thesis in his so-called Letter to Comrade Ivanov, when he used the term 'Socialism in one country' to restate the international nature of the communist system. Comrade Ivanov's question was whether it was sufficient for the Soviet Union itself to have become a socialist state, or whether it must be on a world scale. In his reply Stalin rephased the question: 'Is it possible to regard the victory of socialism in our country as final, that is as secure from the danger of a military aggression and of attempts to re-establish capitalism, provided the victory of socialism has been achieved in one single country and the capitalist surroundings still continue to exist?'

The answer to this rhetoric was obviously in the negative. Stalin cited Lenin as teaching that: 'The final victory of socialism in the sense of complete security from the restoration of bourgeois conditions is possible only on an international scale.' This meant that: '. . . the serious help of the international proletariat is that

[1] In fact, the 1928 Comintern Congress saw such an attack on Soviet Russia by the West as inevitable and desirable, for as its programme declaration went on to declare: 'The development of the contradictions within the modern world economy, the development of the general capitalist critics and the imperialist military attack upon the Soviet Union inevitably lead to a mighty revolutionary outbreak which must overwhelm capitalism in a number of so-called civilized countries, unleash the victorious revolution in the colonies, broaden the base of the proletarian dictatorship to an enormous degree, and thus with tremendous strides bring nearer the final world victory of socialism.'

force without which the problem of the final victory of socialism in one country cannot be solved.' To back up his argument of 1938, Stalin reminded Comrade Ivanov and all other communists of what Lenin stated in 1919, in his report of the Central Committee at the Eighth Congress of the Russian Communist Party:

> We are living not only in a State, but in a system of States, and the existence of the Soviet Republic next to a number of imperialist States for a long time is unthinkable. In the end either one or the other will have the better of it. Until that end comes, a series of most terrible conflicts between the Soviet Republic and the bourgeois States is inevitable. This means that the ruling class, the proletariat, if it wants to and will rule, must prove this also by its military organization.

This declaration of 1919 was made against the background of the civil war in Russia and the military intervention of the Allied forces, but twenty years later, Stalin still considered it to remain in force as a basic tenet of communist international relations. As he said to Comrade Ivanov, he had declared in his textbook writings under the general title *Problems of Leninism* that:

> The final victory of socialism means complete security from any attempts at intervention and therefore at restoration, for no serious attempt at restoration can take place unless with serious help from outside, with the help of international capital. Therefore the support of our revolution on the part of the workers of all countries is an indispensable condition of the complete security of the first victorious country from attempts at intervention and restoration, an indispensable condition of the final victory of socialism.

A year later, in his Central Committee report to the Eighteenth Congress of the Communist Party in Moscow, Stalin re-emphasized his concept of the capitalist encirclement of the Soviet Union. Since 1917, he said, the Soviet State had passed through two main stages of development. The first stage ended with the elimination of the exploiting classes by the destruction of the capitalist system in Russia. With the elimination of capitalism in the towns and the countryside came the second stage, the establishment of the socialist system in its place, the adoption of a new Constitution (that of 1936) and the change of State function from one of suppression of exploiters to one of protection of the people's property. The army, punitive organs and the intelligence services no longer had their edge turned inside towards the country, but outside, against the external enemies.

Lastly, Stalin took up the question of the withering away of the Soviet State as the final stage of the transition towards full communism. Will the Soviet State, he asked rhetorically, remain in this period of communism? 'Yes, it will, unless the capitalist encirclement is liquidated and unless the danger of foreign military attack has disappeared. Naturally, of course, the forms of our State will again change in conformity with the change in the situation at home and abroad.' On the other hand, he concluded, the Soviet State would atrophy if the capitalist encirclement were liquidated and a socialist encirclement took its place.

In May 1943 the Comintern was formally dissolved by a resolution of the Presidium of the Executive Committee. Looking back over the years, the resolution acknowledged that the world situation had not developed in such a straightforward manner as had been predicted in the early Congresses of the International, of which the programme statements of 1928 were typical. Though the original organizational form of the Comintern for uniting workers suited the conditions of its times, under the conditions of the early 1940's it had become outmoded and 'even a drag on the further strengthening of the national working-class parties'.

Under the conditions of the anti-Hitler war, it was better for the national communist movements to work on their own. With the dissolution of the Comintern, all its member parties were formally freed from their obligations as laid down by the statutes and resolutions of the Eighth Congress of the Cominform that had been held between 1919 and 1935. The most important task for the communist parties to tackle for the immediate future was to: '. . . concentrate their energies on the whole-hearted support of and active participation in the war of liberation of the peoples and the States of the anti-Hitler coalition, and for the speediest defeat of the deadly enemy of the working class and the toilers, German Fascism and its associates and vassals.'

Two years later the war in Europe was over and that against Japan drawing to its close. The Soviet Union had already established its control of the countries of Eastern Europe, while its occupation forces were settled in Manchuria and North Korea, busily engaged – as they were equally in the Soviet Zones of Germany and Austria – in dismantling and removing to Russia the industrial frameworks of the economies as war booty and reparations.

In February 1946 Stalin made his first major policy speech of the post-war era, in the form of a pre-election address.[1] The war which had just finished, he said, was quite in the order of the crisis of capitalism. As the First World War was the result of the first crisis of the world capitalist system, so the Second World War resulted from a second crisis.

The First World War was one between capitalist countries. But the second was fundamentally different, in that from the very outset it assumed the character of an anti-fascist war,[2] a war of liberation, one aim of which was also the restoration of democratic liberties: 'The entrance of the Soviet Union into the war against the Axis states could only enhance, and indeed did enhance, the anti-fascist and liberation character of the Second World War'.

This was the preamble to a speech extolling communism as a system that had been forged in the fires of war. The event was also the occasion for the wholesale public adulation of Stalin which was to become an increasingly common feature over the next seven years of his life.

Though Stalin acknowledged that the Soviet Union had fought side by side with capitalist States such as the United States, Britain and France, ideologically he saw the war as one of national liberation from capitalism in general, not just from the fascist variety of State capitalism.

Six weeks after this speech of Stalin, the 'national liberation' concept was put into operation afresh with the Soviet-inspired attempt to set up a communist republic on the other side of the border with the U.S.S.R.'s southern neighbour, Iran. An abortive attempt, it nevertheless brought the realities of Soviet foreign

[1] This uncompromising speech from Stalin was made a month before Mr Churchill's speech at Fulton, Missouri, at which the former British premier warned against the Soviet menace, a warning generally greeted as dangerous talk at the time.

[2] It must be remembered that in the Soviet context, the Second World War only really dates from the German invasion of Russia in June 1941 prior to which the Nazi-Soviet Pact was in operation.

policy on to the international scene with the crisis it provoked in the United Nations Security Council.

On the Soviet home front, Stalin was also setting the record straight that *bourgeois* ideologies – permitted but not encouraged during the war – would no longer be tolerated. Called the Zhdanov Line – after A. A. Zhdanov, the Party Central Committee's spokesman on cultural matters at the time – a series of edicts dealing with literature, the stage, music and the cinema were issued between 1946 and 1948. These linked culture and politics in the following manner:[1]

> The position of socialism was strengthened as a result of World War II. The question of socialism has been entered into the agenda of many countries of Europe. This displeases the imperialists of all shades; they fear socialism, fear our socialist country which is an example of the whole of progressive mankind. The imperialists, their ideological henchmen, their writers and journalists, their politicians and diplomats, are trying to slander our country in every way they can, to represent it in a wrong light, to slander socialism. Under these conditions the task of Soviet literature is not only to return blow for blow against all this vile slander and these attacks upon our Soviet culture, upon socialism,[2] but also boldly to attack bourgeois culture, which is in a state of degeneration and decay.

The Zhdanov Line demanded a rejection of this 'degenerate and decayed' bourgeois culture as 'Soviet writers and all our ideological workers now stand on the forward fighting line, for the tasks of the ideological front and of literature in the first place are not removed but on the contrary grow more important under conditions of peaceful development'. As the novelist Konstantin Simonov put it in the *Literary Gazette* at this time: 'An ideological war on a world scale is now being waged with unexampled ferocity. And under such circumstances we suddenly hear people propagat-

[1] This quotation comes from a 'condensed and integrated' text of two speeches by Zhdanov in 1946, printed at the time in the *V.O.K.S. Bulletin*, Moscow.

[2] The term 'socialism' as used here and elsewhere in the book is in the Marxist sense and should be read as meaning 'communism' for all practical purposes. To avoid confusion, its more normal bourgeois meaning will be denoted where necessary by the terms 'Labour' for Britain and 'Social Democracy' for Europe and elsewhere.

ing the idea of a "respite" after the war, of the necessity of resting a bit, of sitting down and reading the tea-leaves to find out what will happen. On the contrary there can be no respite in the ideological war. Any position which we abandon today will not remain empty – tomorrow the enemy will occupy it. And at the present moment our ideological enemies are extremely aggressive. They are trying to gain ground and wherever we representatives of Soviet art permit it, they will not only try it, but will actually gain ground. We should and shall have to fight on the ideological front. That follows naturally from what we have been taught by the party of Lenin and Stalin. That follows naturally from our traditions, from our character, trained by the periods of the five-year plans, tempered during the days of the war.'

It was in this Zhdanov Line barrage that the idea of the Iron Curtain appears for the first time, introduced not by the West, but by Moscow, in the words of the *V.O.K.S. Bulletin* text: 'As hard as bourgeois politicians and writers may try to conceal the truth about the achievements of the Soviet order and Soviet culture, as hard as they may try to erect an iron curtain beyond which the truth about the Soviet Union may not penetrate abroad . . .'[1] By a typical communist sleight of meaning, such phrases as this were used to cover the reality of a policy of erecting a cultural iron curtain against the inward flow of bourgeois Western ideas and culture, which were inimical to communist interest as interpreted by Stalin and his henchmen.

In September 1947 on the eight-hundredth anniversary of the founding of Moscow, Stalin in an official message, hailed the Soviet capital: '. . . not only the inspirer of the building of the new Soviet social and economic ways of life, which have substituted the supremacy of labour for the supremacy of capital and rejected the exploitation of man by man. Moscow is at the same time the champion of the movement of toiling mankind for liberation from capitalist slavery.' Finally, Stalin summed up: 'Moscow's service consists in being the champion of the struggle for durable peace and friendship among nations, the champion of the struggle against

[1] The term itself dates from the latter half of the nineteenth century, when it was applied to the fire curtain used on the stages of the Vienna theatres to separate the auditorium from the stage during the intervals.

the incendiaries of a new war. For the imperialists' war is a most profitable enterprise . . . Moscow's service consists in tirelessly exposing the incendiaries of a new war and rallying the peace-loving peoples around the banner of peace. It is common knowledge that the peace-loving peoples look with hope to Moscow as the capital of a great peace-loving power and a mighty bulwark of peace.'

A few weeks after this Moscow speech, on October 5th 1947, the formation of the Cominform was announced. This was established by nine of the European communist parties, including that of the Soviet Union. Whereas four years earlier, the Comintern had been dissolved because it had become outmoded, the Warsaw conference of European communist leaders which formed the new Cominform did so because they found the absence of 'connexions' between them 'a serious shortcoming'.

As set up in 1947, the Communist Information Bureau represented the Parties of Yugoslavia, Bulgaria, Rumania, Poland, the Soviet Union, Czechoslovakia, France and Italy. The headquarters were established in Belgrade, but following the expulsion of Yugoslavia from the Cominform after the Tito-Stalin split of 1948, were moved to Bucharest. The task of the Bureau was laid down quite simply: '. . . to organize and exchange experience and, in case of necessity, co-ordinate the activity of communist parties on foundations of mutual agreement.' An official organ was started – first fortnightly and later weekly – under the English title *For a Lasting Peace, For a People's Democracy!* This unwieldy name was rarely used in full and in non-communist circles it was usually called *The Cominform Journal*, by which name it will be referred to here.

The Manifesto published by this Warsaw Conference expounded the 'two camps' thesis of Stalin which was to dominate communist international thinking and actions for the next eight years. The Manifesto stated:

Two opposite political lines have crystallized. At the one extreme the U.S.S.R. and the democratic countries aim at whittling down imperialism and strengthening democracy. On the other side the United States of America and England aim at the strengthening of imperialism and the choking of democracy. Because the U.S.S.R. and the democratic countries stand in the way of fulfilling imperialistic plans aiming at world domination and the crushing of democratic movements, a campaign against the Soviet Union and the countries of the new democracy was undertaken, a campaign fed also by a threat of a war on the part of the most sanguine imperialistic politicians of the United States and England.

In this way there arose two camps – the camp of imperialism and anti-democratic forces, whose chief aim is the establishment of a world-wide American imperialists' hegemony and the crushing of democracy; and an anti-Imperialist democratic camp whose chief aim is the elimination of imperialism, the strengthening of democracy and the liquidation of the remnants of fascism.

The battle of the two opposing camps – capitalist and anti-imperialist – is waged amid conditions of a further sharpening of the universal crisis of capitalism, a weakening of the forces of capitalism and a strengthening of the forces of socialism and democracy.

From this basic argument it went on to attack American policies in Europe and Asia, echoing what had already been said in Moscow. The Marshall Plan of Aid for Eruope was part of the general American plan for world expansion, 'complemented by plans for the economic and political subjugation of China, Indonesia and South America'. Similarly the 'capitalist tycoons' of Germany and Japan – aggressors of yesterday – were being prepared by the U.S.A. for a new role, as tools of American imperialistic policy in Europe and Asia. The Manifesto continued:

The arsenal of tactical weapons used by the imperialist camp is further very complex. It combined direct threats of force, blackmail and intimidation, all sorts of political tricks and economic pressure, bribery, the using for its own ends of conflicting interests and disagreements with the aim of strengthening its position, and all that is camouflaged by a mask of liberalism and pacifism in order to deceive and befuddle people not too dexterous in politics.

In these conditions the anti-imperialist democratic camp has to close its ranks and draw up and agree on a common platform to work out its tactics against the chief forces of the imperialist camp, against American imperialism, against its English and French allies, against the Right-wing Socialists above all in England and Wales.

Further equating American policy with that of Hitler, the Manifesto concluded with a warning and an instruction for immediate united front action:

. . . The communist parties should place themselves in the vanguard of the Opposition against the imperialist plans of expansion and aggression in all its manifestations, whether in the sphere of State administration, politics, economies or ideology and at the same time they should unite and co-ordinate their efforts on the basis of a common anti-imperialist and democratic platform as well as gather around themselves all democratic forces in their respective nations.

The major policy speech at this Warsaw Conference of the Bureau was given by A. A. Zhdanov as one of the two Soviet delegates (the other was Malenkov). He elaborated the original Stalin thesis of the special significance of the two World Wars in the overthrow of the capitalist system. Following the First World War, he said, Russia had dropped from the ranks of the capitalist powers. Following the Second World War, capitalism was still further weakened by the loss of the countries of Eastern and Southeastern Europe to communism, or more accurately to the communist-controlled peoples' republics.

While the war 'immensely enhanced' the international significance and prestige of the U.S.S.R., the capitalist world 'had also undergone a substantial change'. Of the six imperialist powers, three – Germany, Italy and Japan – had suffered military defeat, while France had also been weakened and had lost its significance as a world power. Only two great imperialist powers remained, the U.S.A. and Britain, of which Britain was also weaker than before. In particular Britain was becoming increasingly dependent on American economic help and the United States influence was spreading to areas previously British domain, the dominions and South America.

The Second World War also aggravated the crisis of the colonial system, as expressed in the rise of the national liberation movements in the colonies and dependent territories. Old methods of rule there no longer applied and the national liberation movements placed the rear of the capitalist system in jeopardy.

At the same time as the Second World War weakened most of the capitalist countries, it strengthneed the United States, which now was undertaking an expansionist course to establish the world supremacy of American imperialism: 'The new policy of the United States is designed to consolidate its monopoly position and to reduce its capitalist partners to a state of subordination and dependence on America.' But in the U.S.S.R., the U.S.A. met its obstacle to world supremacy. Which was why, like the Hitlerites before the war, the American imperialists were 'disposed to take upon themselves the mission of "saviours" of the capitalist system from communism'.

The next meeting of the Cominform in June 1948 was to expel the Yugoslav communists from its ranks on the grounds that the Tito-Rankovic clique had abandoned democracy and socialism for bourgeois nationalism. By November 1949, when the Cominform next met at an unstated place in Hungary, the condemnation of Tito was complete when the accusation was made that 'this clique have definitely passed from bourgeois nationalism to fascism and outright betrayal of the national interests of Yugoslavia'. It was at this time, it will be remembered, that leading communists such as Rajk in Hungary, Kostov in Bulgaria, and later Slansky in Czechoslovakia, were being tried and condemned to death as traitors, Titoists and agents of American imperialism.

But the importance of the 1949 meeting of the Cominform was the set of instructions it gave to the communist movement 'in the great and noble work of saving mankind from the threat of a new war'. An eight point programme was laid down.

In the autumn of 1948, a conference was called in Poland from which grew the Partisans of Peace movement. This had held its first major congress in June 1949, simultaneously in Paris and Prague. The first task laid down by the Cominform resolution in November 1949 was for communists to extend this movement: 'Particular attention must be given to bringing into the peace movement trade unions, women's, youth, co-operative, sport, cultural and educational, religious and other organizations, as well as scientists, writers, journalists, cultural workers, members of parliament and other political and public men and women who come forward in defence of peace and against war.' In this work, stated the second point, 'the ranks of the peace champions' should be based on firm working-class unity. Thirdly, this unity could only be won by struggling against the right-wing splitters, that is against the anti-communist Labour and Social Democrat leaders, who must be constantly exposed 'as bitter enemies of peace'.

At the same time, united action must be sought with the rank-and-file members of the Social Democratic and Labour parties. The fourth directive was to constantly attack Western military-political alliances and defensive agreements, and to see 'that not a single utterance of the propagandists of a new war be allowed to pass without rebuff from the honest supporters of peace'. The fifth point was the wide application of protests, demonstrations, leaflets, fund collections, boycotts and similar action which together would add up to the 'mass struggle for peace'. Turning away from the narrow issues, the sixth point linked the struggle for peace with that for national independence. This meant exposing bourgeois régimes which become dependent on 'servile subordination to the American monopolies'. In this respect the Communist Parties of France, Italy, Britain and Western Germany were picked out for special mention as having the duty 'to develop with still greater energy the struggle for peace, the struggle to foil the criminal designs of the Anglo-American warmongers'. The seventh point was addressed specifically to the Communist Parties inside the U.S.S.R. and Eastern Europe. In addition to exposing the imperialist warmongers, they also had to strengthen further the Communist Bloc 'for the protection of the peace and security of the nations'. The eighth and last point was the need for the continued exposure of the 'nationalist Tito clique, who act as spies in the service of the imperialists'.

In its closing paragraphs, the Resolution of the 1949 Cominform meeting set out clearly the new 'peace offensive' and the way in which it was being directed by the Soviet communist apparatus:

For the first time in the history of mankind an organized peace front has arisen, headed by the Soviet Union, the bulwark and standard bearer of world peace. The courageous call of the Communist Parties, declaring that the peoples will never fight the first socialist country in the world, the Soviet Union, is reverberating ever wider among the masses of the capitalist countries. In the days of the war against fascism the Communist Parties were in the vanguard of the popular resistance to the invaders: in the post-war period the Communist and Workers' Parties are the vanguard fighters on behalf of the vital interests of their peoples and against a new war. United under the leadership of the working class, the opponents of another war – the men of labour, science and culture – constitute a mighty front of peace, capable of thwarting the criminal designs of the imperialists.

The outcome of the titanic and mounting struggle for peace largely depends upon the energy and initiative of the Communist Parties. It depends above all on the communists as the vanguard fighters whether the possibility of frustrating the plans of the warmongers will be turned into a reality. The forces of democracy, the forces of peace, are far superior to the forces of reaction. The whole thing now is still further to sharpen the vigilance of the peoples with regard to the instigators of war, and to organize and unite the broad masses of the people for active defence of the cause of peace, in protection of the vital interests of the peoples, of their life and liberty.

It is with this resolution of the 1949 Cominform meeting that we enter the main period covered by this study of communist propaganda techniques. A somewhat extended account of the development of the communist line internationally from 1928 to 1949 has been given to show how little the fundamentals changed. The changes were in adaptations to changing world situations, without getting away from the basic tenet of fundamental hostility between the communist and non-communist systems. Over this period, indeed, we saw how incompatability by the communist analysis became still more pronounced, reaching its ultimate in the 'two camps' thesis evolved within months of the ending of the Second World War.

The Nineteenth Congress of the Communist Party of the Soviet Union[1] was held in October 1952, twelve years after the previous Congress. A break with the past was made in that Stalin, General Secretary of the Party, did not himself present the Central Committee report, which was made instead by Malenkov. Stalin's major contribution came immediately before the Congress, with a long article in the Party journal *Bolshevik* under the title 'Economic Problems of Socialism in the U.S.S.R.'. This was reprinted widely as a pamphlet in many languages and for the next six months was holy writ for communists everywhere. Within weeks of his death in March 1953 it became a forgotten document.

[1] Until the 19th Congress, the full title was the Communist Party of the Soviet Union (Bolshevik), a titular relic of the pre-revolutionary days. At the 19th Congress 'Bolshevik' was dropped from the title and the name of the Party journal was changed from *Bolshevik* to *Kommunist*.

Stalin's analysis of the world situation as given in his 'Economic Problems' showed a development of the 'two camps' thesis. The most important economic consequence of the Second World War, he wrote, was the breaking up of the single, world market of capitalism, which was now faced with a new parallel market, that of the communist countries and those linked with them economically. This was a direct result of the war, which had not only led to the defeat of Germany, Italy and Japan, but also to a 'break away from capitalism' by China and the countries of Eastern Europe.

The growth of the 'new, parallel world market' was helped, stated Stalin, by the Western economic blockade of the communist countries. In this he was referring to the Western embargoes on the sale of strategic commodities by traders in Western Europe to any country of the Soviet Bloc and Communist China. This embargo was put into operation before the outbreak of the Korean war, and was widened in its scope and effectiveness after China entered the war on the North Korean side.

But the economic blockade was not fundamental. What was important was the pace of industrial development of the communist countries: 'It will soon come to pass that these countries will not only be in no need of imports from capitalist countries, but will themselves feel the need to find an outside market for their surplus products.' By the same argument, he went on, the capitalist share of the world market would decline and their industries would operate more and more below capacity: '. . . that, in fact, is what is meant by the deepening of the general crisis of the world capitalist system in connexion with the disintegration of the world market.' The capitalists knew this and were trying to offset these difficulties with the Marshall Plan, the Korean war, rearmament and industrial militarization: '. . . but that is very much like a drowning man clutching a straw.'

In his 'Economic Problems' Stalin also developed the theme of the inevitability of war between the capitalist countries. He saw this conflict as between Britain and France on the one hand, and the U.S.A. on the other. A new set of conditions would arise between the countries that suffered major defeat, Western Germany and Japan, and the U.S.A.: 'To think that these countries will not try to get on their feet again, will not try to smash the U.S.

"régime" and force their way to independent development, is to believe in miracles.' (The 'régime' referred to was the American occupation of her Zone of Germany and of Japan, which was still in force at the time.)

This concept of the struggle of the capitalist countries between themselves for markets was considered by Stalin to be of more import than the struggle between the 'two camps' of capitalism and socialism. It followed from this that the argument of inevitable war between capitalist countries, still bore considerable force.

Turning to the peace movement, then in its fourth year, Stalin introduced a new tactical note: 'The object of the present-day peace movement is to rouse the masses of the people to fight for the preservation of peace and for the prevention of another World War. Consequently the aim of this movement is not to overthrow capitalism and establish socialism – it confines itself to the democratic aim of preserving peace.' This rule was not rigid, however, for he went on to stress: 'It is possible that in a definite conjuncture of circumstances the fight for peace will develop here or there into a fight for socialism. But then it will no longer be the present-day peace movement. It will be a movement for the overthrow of capitalism.'

Specifically upholding Lenin's thesis that imperialism by its nature generates war, Stalin saw the peace movement of the 1950's as possibly preserving a particular peace or preventing a particular war by forcing 'the resignation of a bellicose government and its supercession by another that is prepared temporarily to keep the peace. But that will not be enough, for imperialism will remain, continue in force and consequently the inevitability of wars will also continue in force. To eliminate the inevitability of war, it is necessary to abolish imperialism'.

It is against this uncompromising ideological background that Malenkov gave the Central Committee report to the Nineteenth Congress, summing up Soviet international policy as being 'based on the premise that the peaceful coexistence and co-operation of capitalism and communism are quite possible, provided there is a mutual desire to co-operate, readiness to carry out commitments, and adherence to the principle of equal rights and non-interference in the internal affairs of other states'.

On this basis, he went on: 'We are confident that, in peaceful competition with capitalism, the socialist system of competition will year after year more and more strikingly demonstrate its superiority over the capitalist system of economy. But we have not the least insistence on forcing our ideology or our economic system upon anybody.' Quoting Stalin, Malenkov declared: 'The export of revolution is nonsense. Every country will make its own revolution if it wants to and if it does not want to there will be no revolution.'

Malenkov ended with a four-point Party plan for Soviet foreign policy. The first requirement was 'to continue the struggle against the preparation and unleashing of another war' by continuing and stepping up the anti-Western propaganda in general and the peace movement in particular. That is to say: 'To rally the mighty anti-war democratic front for the purpose of strengthening peace; strengthen the ties of friendship and solidarity with peace supporters the world over; persistently to expose all preparations for a new war and all the designs and intrigues of the warmongers.'

The second was aimed at the Western strategic embargoes then imposed on trade with the communist countries. 'To continue the policy of international co-operation and development of business relations with all countries.' Stalin's thesis of the two world markets revealed this apparently positive point as one with a purely tactical purpose. The third was to tighten up relationships between the Soviet Union and the other communist countries by strengthening and developing their 'inviolable friendly relations', while lastly there was the order 'tirelessly to strengthen the defence power of the Soviet State and enhance our preparedness devastatingly to repel any aggressor'.

At the end of the Congress Stalin contributed a short speech specifically directed to the fraternal delegates from foreign communist parties. He reminded them first of all that the Soviet Communist Party expected them to support it fully: 'It would be a mistake to think that our Party, having become a powerful force, no longer needs support. This is not correct. Our Party and our country always have needed and always shall, the trust, sympathy and support of the fraternal peoples abroad.' In return the Soviet Party helps communists everywhere. Countries where the communists and their supporters had not come to power 'are deserving of particular attention' and to them the U.S.S.R. and the other communist countries were the 'shock-brigades' of the world revolutionary movement.

The world of 1952 was easier for the revolutionaries than was the world of 1917, Stalin reminded the foreign communists. Firstly, they could learn from the successes and mistakes of the past, secondly, the bourgeoisie itself; 'the main enemy of the liberation movement', had changed and had become weaker, dependent on dollars. Formerly the bourgeoisie was considered the leaders of the nation, the champion of its rights and freedoms. Now it was for the communists to take up this banner.

Within six months of the Nineteenth Congress Stalin died, on March 5th 1953. In the days which followed, communist leaders everywhere hastened to reaffirm their loyalty to Moscow. The then Hungarian premier and Party General Secretary, Rakosi, in *Pravda* of March 12th declared this loyalty by quoting from Stalin: 'An internationalist is he who, unreservedly, without hesitation, without conditions, is ready to defend the U.S.S.R. because the U.S.S.R. is the base of the world revolutionary movement, and to defend, to advance this revolutionary movement is impossible without defending the U.S.S.R. He who thinks to defend the world revolutionary movement apart from and against the U.S.S.R. is going against the revolution and is necessarily slipping down into the camp of the enemies of the revolution.'

In a foreign policy statement on March 9th, Foreign Minister Molotov re-emphasized that proletarian internationalism remained basic policy: 'Faithful to the principles of proletarian internationalism, the peoples of the U.S.S.R. are developing and unswervingly strengthening fraternal friendship and co-operation with the great Chinese people, with the working people of all the people's democracies, strengthening friendly ties with the working people of the capitalist and colonial countries, who are struggling in the cause of peace, democracy and socialism.'

Stalin was an absolute dictator, demanding absolute obedience. He saw the world in terms of black and white. His writ was infallible and those who were not with him were against him, whether at home or abroad. All other communist parties were subordinated to the Soviet Party and had to follow Soviet example. Those who disagreed and preferred their own roads to socialism were in the imperialist camp; such was the case with Yugoslavia after 1948.

His death left something more than a political vacuum. The whole communist system had evolved under his direction for close on thirty years. Abroad as well as in the Soviet Union it owed its major features to Stalin. A spot check of the November 17th 1950 issue of *Pravda* found Stalin's name 101 times: Josef Vissarionovich Stalin 35 times, Comrade Stalin 35 times, Great Leader 10 times, dear and well-beloved Stalin 7 times, Great Stalin 6 times. By the summer of 1953 his name was hardly ever mentioned though his works continued to be published extensively.

The interregnum period between the death of Stalin and the emergence in 1955 of Khruschov as his successor was the period of the so-called collective leadership. This period saw the purge of Beria and the weakening of his secret police apparatus as a factor of Soviet internal control, although the State security system was left intact as a major control weapon of the Party and State. During this period a greater flexibility in both internal and external affairs developed, first becoming noticeable in the dropping of the anti-Yugoslav campaign. This came to a climax with Khruschov heading a Soviet delegation to Yugoslavia in the summer of 1955, and the signing of the Belgrade Declaration of June 2nd, in which the Soviet leaders acknowledged that there could be more than one form of communism.

This concept of the 'varying roads to socialism' was reaffirmed at the Twentieth Congress of the Soviet Communist Party, held in Moscow in February, 1956. At the same time a second dogma from the Stalin period was thrown overboard, with the rejection by Khruschov of the theory of the inevitability of war under imperialism. This concept, said Khruschov, dated from the time when imperialism was an all-embracing world system and its opponents weak. But now things had radically changed: 'In the circumstances the Leninist precept that so long as imperialism exists the economic base giving rise to wars will also be preserved, remains in force.' But, 'war is not fatalistically inevitable.' In the same context, Mikoyan once again stressed the role of the peace movement as a weapon against those opposing communism. If anyone exploded a hydrogen or an atomic bomb, he said, 'the best of mankind will not let civilization perish, but will immediately unite.' This 'unity' would not be just to end war, but to end capitalism as well.

The Twentieth Congress emphasized four main factors. First that the wedge-driving tactics against the West were to be retained in accordance with the Lenin-Stalin dictum that the downfall of capitalism could be brought about by exacerbating the inherent contradictions of the system. As Khruschov said, quoting Stalin without actually referring to him by name: 'The problem of markets is also becoming all the more acute because the frontiers of the capitalist world market are increasingly contracting because of the formation of the new and growing socialist market.'

Secondly, economic warfare against the capitalist system was to be stepped up and translated from theory into practice in Asia, Africa and Latin America. Speaking of the newly-emergent countries, Khruschov said: 'These countries, although they do not belong to the socialist world system, can draw on its achievements to build up an independent national economy and to raise the living standards of their peoples. . . .'

Thirdly, the ideological war against the West was to continue. Khruschov made it clear that peaceful coexistence could not apply to the ideological field and his thesis was amplified by another major speaker, Suslov: 'In trying to achieve a further relaxation of international tension, we must not reduce our criticism of the bourgeois ideology, or of imperialism and colonialism. We must, on the contrary and for the very same purpose, increase it and expose by convincing examples and facts imperialism's aggressive policy and ideology.'

Lastly, the weapon of political disruption was endorsed. In the words of Molotov: 'We must put an end to underestimating the immense possibilities we have in the cause of defending peace and the security of the peoples, the basis of which is the creation and steady growth of the forces of the world socialist camp, the unprecedented upsurge of the liberation struggle of the colonial and dependent peoples, the fighting movement of workers in the capitalist countries, the international solidarity of the working class, the wide democratic movement of peace partisans, the activities of democratic organizations of women and youth and other forms of mass struggle in defence of peace and against war.'

This Twentieth Congress is more popularly associated with the dramatic attacks on Stalin's internal policies made by Khruschov in his secret speech, which was not made public (and then not by Moscow but by Washington) until 1956. This on top of the new idea of 'varying roads to socialism' and other relaxations of the hitherto tight Party controls – brought about waves of revolt in industrial and intellectual circles all over Eastern Europe. In Czechoslovakia students went on strike that summer and indulged in the rare luxury of political demonstrations against cultural repressions. In Poland there were strikes at Poznan coincidentally with the opening of the international trade fair there. In Hungary free debating groups were active, while in Moscow itself wall newspapers appeared at the university demanding greater freedoms. The culmination came in Hungary with the revolution of October 1956, which was only put down with the help of Soviet tanks. These shots by the Soviet tanks against the Hungarian people re-echoed throughout the world, bringing with them internal upheavals in every communist party outside the East Bloc, with wholesale resignations and the formation of splinter groups of the Right and the Left.

Faced with such doubts and dismay, Moscow hastened to restate the ideological facts of life. Even before the Hungarian revolution, there had been strong warnings that the permitted relaxations must not be abused. Immediately after the revolution had been crushed, an official reminder of the duties of international proletarians was given in an article in *Kommunist* No. 1 of January 1957:

Communists of all countries ascribe immense significance to the experience of the Soviet Union, the first to build socialism in the most difficult circumstances of capitalist encirclement and without any historical precedent whatsoever. This experience has shown that the existence of a powerful Communist Party, its guiding role within the dictatorship of the proletariat, the role of the socialist state in the planned development of a socialist economy, the policy of struggle against imperialist aggression and support of the national liberation movements . . . and the development of international solidarity among working people are all mandatory prerequisites for the building of socialism. As the Chinese paper *People's Daily* so correctly stated recently, the basic aspects of the Soviet experience 'reflect the universal law of revolution in a given phase of the general development of human society; this is not only the basic road of the proletariat of the U.S.S.R., but also the road on which all proletarians throughout the world must travel for the achievement of victory'.

In April 1956 the Cominform was dissolved and publication of its weekly *Cominform Journal* discontinued. This was another factor influencing the growing belief in communist circles in a new era of independence from Moscow. Between the spring of 1956 and the autumn of 1957 there was a hiatus in the communist world, only brought to an end by the celebrations in Moscow of the fortieth anniversary of the Bolshevik Revolution. During this period there had been many meetings between Soviet Party officials and delegations from other countries, mostly in Western Europe. But the next major post-Cominform policy declaration was made in November 1957, after the International Communist Congress which followed the anniversary celebrations and the successful launchings of the first two sputniks. This Congress was the first of its kind since the last Comintern Congress in 1935. From it came two policy documents, the first a Declaration signed by the twelve delegations from countries where communism was already in power and the second a Peace Manifesto signed by all the sixty-four parties present.

The fundamental dilemma facing this World Communist Congress was the contradiction between the unconditional Moscow line on international proletarianism and its explicit adherence to Moscow on the one hand, and the equally explicit declaration by Moscow of the new doctrine of 'varying roads to socialism'. The very nature of this dictum gave the national communist parties the ideological right to pursue their own 'road to socialism', as happened so catastrophically in Hungary. This could obviously not be allowed in such a world-embracing and expansionist system as communism and the Declaration of the Moscow conference condemned such tendencies as revisionism, at the same time stressing that the socialist States were led by the Soviet Union. In short, the main purpose behind the Declaration was to strengthen the internal unity of the world communist movement. It was signed in the names of the twelve ruling communist parties, but its appeal was to communists everywhere.

Yugoslavia was present at these Moscow talks, but did not take part in this first meeting of the inner caucus and did not sign the Declaration. Instead she signed the vaguer Peace Manifesto intended for wider consumption. This blamed the ruling circles of the capitalist countries for past wars and present aggressive intentions. It praised the communist efforts for peace and appealed to everyone to demand the end of the arms race, the banning of nuclear weapons and the liquidation of military bases. The dangers of German militarism were particularly stressed.

In short, while the Declaration attempted to lay down a policy for the Communist Bloc, the Manifesto was used as a propaganda platform for communist parties abroad and as a rallying call for the peace movement.

In June 1957, it will be remembered, there was a further step taken on the road away from collective leadership with the expulsion from the Central Committee of the Soviet Party of the so-called anti-Party group of Molotov, Kaganovich, Malenkov and Shepilov. More than a year later, in the autumn of 1958, the campaign against the group was renewed by Khruschov, who added yet another name to the list of the schismatics, Bulganin. At this time meetings were going on all over the Soviet Union in preparation for the special Twenty-first Congress of the Party, called for January 1959 to ratify the new seven-year plan 1959–65. Time and again at these meetings the 'despicable anti-Party group' was censured with unvarying severity of tone and phrase.

The main purpose of the Twenty-first Congress was to map the industrial and economic future of the U.S.S.R., but it was made clear that this could not be separated from communist world policy. 'At present we are exerting our main influence on the international revolution with our economic policy,' stated Lenin in the early days of the Revolution. The struggle on a world-wide scale had been transferred to this field of activity. If they solved this task, the communists would have won a certain and final victory on an international scale. Therefore economic development was exceptionally important. Some thirty-five years later Khruschov introduced to the Twenty-first Congress a new economic doctrine stemming directly from this directive of Lenin. The main points were to continue giving priority to heavy industry, as in Stalin's time; to co-ordinate the main sectors of the East European economics under Soviet leadership so as to compete with other industrial countries; gradually and persistently to penetrate the developing countries, squeezing out the Western countries by the strategic investment of Soviet capital, the use of barter, dumping, low-interest loans, economic missions and experts and, the training of specialists from these countries in Moscow.

This policy of world domination by economic means did not exclude the more traditional communist techniques – proletarian revolution organized from within or without and the Stalinist technique of actual communist military action. In Lenin's time the Soviet economy was only a passive element in the communist world plan. Under Khruschov by 1959 it had taken on an active role. Looking into the future Khruschov saw the Soviet economy becoming the dominant factor in this new stage of communism expansion. Taking Stalin's thesis of the contracting world market for capitalism a stage further, he saw his new policy drawing the emergent nations completely into the socialist camp. Once under communist control economically, the political control would follow closely behind.

This was the situation as the decade of the 1950's came to a close. It had opened with Stalin in complete control, seen him die and the fight for the succession from which Khruschov emerged victorious. Whereas Stalin's own victories of the 1930's had been achieved with considerable bloodshed, Khruschov's rise to power only witnessed the physical elimination of one close contendent, Beria. But – as will be discussed in more detail in Chapter 10 – a new rival to the Soviet Union for world leadership of communism was rapidly coming to the fore in Mao Tse-tung and the Communist Party of China. The unity which still showed itself on the surface at the 1957 Moscow meeting of world communists was far from apparent the next time they met there, three years later.

At the end of November 1960 – following the normal October Revolution celebrations – a secret conference of representatives of eighty-one communist parties was held for three weeks. During this time, there was much speculation by outside commentators, but nothing was said until early in December 1960, when a Declaration was published. This Declaration was a World Plan for communists, the first since the last Comintern Congress in 1935. The 1960 Declaration was the call to action for the new decade, a call declared binding on every communist party subscribing to it. It was a general directive to action, worded to give local communists ample scope to adapt the instructions contained in it to fit their local needs and conditions.

In one important respect it differed from the past. For the first time, the emphasis on the leading role of the Soviet Union was dropped. The Declaration stressed that all communist parties were equal and independent, with the Soviet Party as 'the generally acknowledged vanguard of the world communist movement', representing by its example 'the application in practice of the revolutionary principle of proletarian internationalism'. The Party which had once been the leader was now the vanguard. Whereas the 1957 Declaration described the Soviet Union as the leader of the Communist Bloc, the 1960 Declaration did not give it this title. Moscow certainly had its place at the top spiritually and historically for world communism, but from the 1960 conference onwards, it found itself sharing the leadership with Peking for all practical purposes.

The New World Plan for the 1960's as laid down by the Moscow conference was essentially the same as before. In practical terms it is in the present and in the future tense in the way it lays down the seizure of power wherever and whenever the chance occurs. But now the strong-arm tactics of the 40's and 50's are discarded and their place taken by subtler weapons.

The 1960 Moscow Statement still saw the world in two camps: 'Our epoch,' it declared, 'is the epoch of struggle of the two opposing social systems, the epoch of the downfall of imperialism, the epoch of the transition to the road of socialism for new peoples, of the triumph of socialism and communism on a world scale.'[1]

[1] In this connotation, the terms socialism and communism have essentially the same meaning.

Having been carefully avoided by Party propagandists for some years, the term 'world revolution' has crept back: '. . . the course of social development confirms Lenin's prediction that the countries of victorious socialism exert their main influence on the development of the world revolution by their economic construction.' This restatement of Khruschov's thesis to the Twenty-first Congress directly equates the Bloc's own economic growth with the spread of communist revolution to the rest of the world.

This more localized activity outside the Communist Bloc is to be intensified and better co-ordinated, ordered the Declaration, listing typical situations for exploitation in the immediate future. Every trouble centre that can be exploited for anti-Western purposes is construed as 'the striking proof that the waves of the anti-imperialist, national liberation, anti-war and class struggle are rising ever higher'.

The Stalin analysis, it will be remembered, argued that the rise of the communists to power in Eastern Europe and China came about through the historical inevitability of the Second World War; a Third World War would result in the complete victory of communism. With the advent of the nuclear deterrent this has changed. Instead the Declaration presents the 1960's as the period of competition between the communist and capitalist systems – as Khruschov had already declared – with the added factor that 'all revolutionary forces are united against imperialist oppression and exploitation'. These revolutionary forces comprise 'the peoples building socialism and communism, the revolutionary movement of the working class in capitalist countries, the national liberation struggle of the oppressed peoples, the common democratic movement'. All these are seen as a combined weapon 'undermining and destroying the world imperialist system', that is the world outside the communist countries.

Though war is no longer considered a major factor, it is still to be reckoned with locally: 'Communists have always recognized the progressive, revolutionary importance of national-liberation wars and are the most active champions of national independence.' Elaborating further on this, the Declaration claims that the world communist movement has helped decisively in 'the struggle of the peoples of colonies and dependent countries for liberation from the yoke of imperialism' while communism itself 'has become a reliable shield of the independent national development of the liberated peoples'.

Turning to peaceful coexistence, the Declaration is once again firm as to the limitations of the concept: 'Peaceful coexistence of States with different social systems does not mean a reconciliation between the socialist and *bourgeois* ideologies. On the contrary, it implies an intensification of the struggle of the working class and of all the communist parties for the triumph of socialist ideas.' But this does not mean that political quarrels between States must be settled by war. On the contrary, the settlement is to be by internal uprisings under communist control:

> The line of peaceful coexistence is a line of mobilization of the masses, of the development of intensified action against the enemies of peace.
>
> Peaceful coexistence is far from being a rejection of the class war: it is one of the forms taken by the class struggle and its use helps to intensify the class struggle within the capitalist countries and the national liberation struggle in the colonies, while they in their turn help to strengthen the communist peaceful coexistence campaign by helping towards world communism without the need for war.
>
> While ensuring that the communists retain the leadership at all times, greater use is to be made of the peace movements, the youth, student and trade union rumps and women's groups to exploit all possible sources of discontent, joining forces where possible with social democratic and labour groups for tactical ends.

Such were the instructions sent out to the eighty-seven communist parties in the world from Moscow at the end of 1960. A year later, Khruschov elaborated on it in his Central Committee report to the Twenty-second Congress of the Soviet Communist Party, held in Moscow in October 1961. In this report he dealt extensively with the world situation as well as with internal Soviet affairs.

He began his section on relations with the non-communist world with an apparent contradiction: 'We are convinced,' he said, 'that the socialist system in the final reckoning will be victorious everywhere. But this does not mean at all that we shall try to win this victory by interfering in the internal affairs of other countries.' What is happening, he said, is that communist ideas are spreading satisfactorily through the entire world, though not because they are imposed by the Soviet Union.

He continued to put this 'export of revolution' concept in the context of the sixties: 'Naturally, warring classes have always sought the support of kindred forces from outside. For a long time the bourgeoisie had an advantage in this respect. The world bourgeoisie acting in concert stamped out revolutionary centres elsewhere and by every means, including armed intervention. Of course, even the international proletariat was not indifferent to the struggles of its class brothers, but more often than not it could express its solidarity with them only through moral support.'[1] At this point the inflection altered to a sharper tone: 'The situation has changed since then. The people of a country who rise in struggle will not find themselves engaged in single combat with world imperialism. They will enjoy the support of powerful international forces possessing everything necessary for effective moral and material support.'

Khruschov reaffirmed that 'the communists are against the export of revolution', in order to continue with a new thesis: 'We do not recognize anyone's right to export counter-revolution, to perform the functions of an international gendarme.' By this he meant any attempt by non-communist authorities to suppress revolutions which had the support of the communist movement: 'Imperialist attempts to interfere in the affairs of insurgent peoples would be acts of aggression, endangering world peace. We must state outright that in the event of imperialist export of counter-revolution, the communists will call on the peoples of all countries to rally, to mobilize their forces and, supported by the might of the world socialist system, firmly repel the enemies of freedom and peace.'

[1] Though it is not stated on such occasions as Party Congresses, the world communist movement has been able to show its solidarity in more tangible forms than moral support, as was shown by the communist riots in India and the communist revolt in Burma in 1948, followed by the outbreak of the communist war in Malaya. The other side of this coin of armed intervention has been seen on more than one occasion since 1917, with communist suppressions of 'revolutionary hotbeds' in their own areas, from the early nationalist uprisings in the Caucasus in 1919 to Hungary in 1956 and the Berlin Wall in 1961.

In such circumstances, of course, all attempts by non-communists in general and the West in particular to protect their national and international interests will be interpreted by Moscow as counter-revolution, whenever it suits its purpose. In such a situation it reserves the right to do as it pleases, however much this might fly in the face of world opinion.

Turning to peaceful coexistence, Khruschov took up the well-known argument that with a little give and take on both sides world frictions would disappear. 'Certain pacifist-minded people in the West,' he said, 'are ingenuous enough to believe that if the Soviet Union made more concessions to the Western Powers, there would be no aggravation of international tension. They forget that the policy of the imperialist powers, including their foreign policy, is determined by the class interests of monopoly capital, in which aggression and war are inherent.'

So peaceful coexistence in 1961 was put into a context fundamentally little different from that described by Stalin in 1927, with relations with capitalist countries necessary to give a breathing-space until revolution broke out or the capitalist countries started to fight among themselves.

The Twenty-second Congress was notable for the wholesale repudiation of Stalin and his dogma. But his emphasis on the need for peaceful coexistence was only changed in direction by Khruschov: 'The peaceful coexistence of States with different social systems can be maintained and secured only by the selfless struggles of all the people against the imperialists' aggressive strivings. The greater the strength of the socialist camp and the more vigorously the struggle for peace is waged within the capitalist countries, the more difficult it is for the imperialists to carry out their aggressive plans.'

'Peace and peaceful coexistence are not quite the same thing,' he clarified. 'Peaceful coexistence does not merely imply the absence of war. It is not a temporary, unstable armistice between two wars, but the coexistence of two opposed social systems based on the mutual renunciation of war as a means of settling disputes between States. The experience of history shows that an aggressor cannot be placated by concessions. Concessions to the imperialists on matters of vital importance do not make up a policy of peaceful coexistence, but a policy of surrender to the forces of aggression. To that we will never agree.'

In this way the Soviet leader reiterated in yet another form the old-established communist policy of using internal strife in the non-communist world to undermine the political, economic and social bases of the non-communist countries and render their defences useless. To this end he told how he intended to reactivate the peace partisans movement. He said to the 1961 Congress: 'The peace supporters in many countries who have associated in various unions and movements, have made an important contribution to the struggle against the forces of aggression and war. Everyone will remember how, in the early 50's, hundreds of millions of people called for a ban on atomic weapons and how indignantly the peoples of Europe protested against the establishment of the notorious European Defence Community and Western Germany's participation in it. The pressure which the people exerted on parliaments and governments produced a powerful effect.'

Such work is particularly important now, said Khruschov: 'The peoples must tighten the vigilance with regard to the intrigues of the imperialist warmongers. Vigorous anti-war action by the peoples must not be put off until the war starts. Such action must be launched immediately, not when nuclear and thermonuclear bombs begin to fall. The strength of the Peace Movement lies in its mass scope, its organization and resolute actions. All peoples and all sections of society, except for a handful of monopolists, want peace. And all the peoples must insist that a peace policy be pursued and must use all forms of struggle to achieve that end. The peoples can and must render harmless those who are obsessed with the insane ideas of militarism and war. The peoples are the decisive form in the struggle for peace.'

With such directives as these, world communist policy continues to be based on the theory of the inherent hostility between the communist and capitalist systems. In everyday terms the only changes have been of a strategic and tactical nature to match the changing times. In this respect there is a significant difference between the doctrine of the early 1960's and the early 1950's. In Stalin's time and immediately afterwards every word of the

Marxist classics was golden, particularly the writings of Lenin and Stalin himself. But a decade later communist spokesmen were more and more putting the earlier tactical writings into historical perspective, only keeping those up to date which suited their current line.[1]

The spring of 1962, for instance, saw renewed Soviet insistence on the theme of peaceful coexistence and universal disarmament, with repeated accusations of lack of good faith on these issues against the Western Powers and their supporters. As part of this campaign a fresh Soviet drive was made to have what it called 'war propaganda' banned. A typical presentation of its case was given by Moscow Radio in a broadcast to Europe early in April 1962, when the argument ran thus:

> If the effective measures against war propaganda are not taken in the West, it may in the end become such an offensive that it pushes the world into the abyss of a nuclear conflict. As is well-known this odious propaganda works primarily on those employed at the numerous U.S. military bases in Western Europe and other regions. Who can guarantee that these people, their minds poisoned by the cannibal ideology of war, may not suddenly take leave of their senses and press the button for launching nuclear rockets? No one can give any such guarantees if the propagation of war and hostility towards other peoples does not cease immediately.

At the same time – the end of March and the beginning of April – a series of talks was being broadcast by Moscow in its service to Communist China, which discussed between them the inter-relationships of peaceful coexistence, war and peace and national liberation.

The first of these talks stated exactly why the Soviet Union did not want war: 'In accordance with the law of historical development, the inevitable victory of socialism does not want war between countries. This victory can be achieved on a basis of peaceful coexistence and the struggle for complete disarmament. The subjugated peoples can and should cast off the imperialist yoke. The superiority of the socialist system in various fields has

[1] In London the communist bookshop's catalogue of basic Marxist literature published in April 1961 continued to list seven of Stalin's works.

created a strategic situation in which the forces of imperialism are forced to admit that imperialism will destroy itself should it wage a war.' In other words, communism is inevitable and it is therefore not necessary to waste resources on war when it can be attained by other means. Again, war in this sense means a global, thermonuclear war. As we have already seen, local wars are quite a different matter. This is demonstrated more clearly than usual in these particular broadcasts to China, because their main purpose was to demonstrate to the Chinese communists that the Soviet Union was not being 'soft' in its relationships with the Western powers. 'Peaceful coexistence,' declared the broadcast dealing with national liberation, 'requires the forsaking of all aggression and this accords with the interests of the colonial peoples as it gives them security from without. The doctrine of peaceful coexistence demands non-interference in the internal affairs of other countries and upholds the right of self-determination. The national liberation struggle therefore does not run counter to the doctrine of coexistence and it can in fact be pursued to the utmost only in conditions of peaceful coexistence.'

Enlarging on this point in another of the talks, Moscow radio told its Chinese listeners: 'Under conditions of peaceful coexistence, people engaged in the national liberation struggle are safe from being invaded by the former colonialists. This is of special significance during the first stage of national liberation struggle.' In brief, the successful application of the communist doctrine of peaceful coexistence will effectively disarm the West and prevent attempts to deal with uprisings which have the support of the communists.

This new concept for the 60's is put into even sharper focus by an article which appeared in the Slovak political weekly *Predvoj* in March 1962. As a key passage stated: 'Peaceful coexistence and economic competition and the carrying out of general disarmament established conditions favourable for a broad development of all forms of the anti-imperialist movement – for the struggle of the working class and the peasantry for democracy and socialism as well as for the struggle for national independence and free development of the progress of the underdeveloped countries.' In speaking of 'general disarmament' the emphasis is on the West. Jozef Drozd, the writer of the *Predvoj* article, is quite definite on this: 'It must be emphasized again that the struggle for general and complete disarmament does not and cannot mean a weakening of our defensive strength. On the contrary. The events of last year have confirmed again that an increased defence potential of the socialist world system offers increased hopes for general and complete disarmament to become a reality, thwarts the aggressive plans of the most reactionary imperialist circles and compels them to negotiate.'

In the event, the early 60's were marked ideologically by a split between Moscow and Peking on the tactics of world revolution and the attainment of full communist power. The two lines were expressed in formal terms in the respective policy documents published as open letters in June and July 1963.

The first was that of the Chinese, entitled *A Proposal Concerning the General Line of the International Communist Movement*, published on June 16th. A long and complex document, it underlined once again many of the militant points that had been doctrine since the first years of the original Comintern. It stressed that all forms of struggle – 'including armed struggle' – must be used to attain power: 'Communists would always prefer to bring about the transition to socialism by peaceful means. But can peaceful transition be made into a new world-wide strategic principle for the international communist movement? Absolutely not. Marxism-Leninism consistently holds that the fundamental question in all revolutions is that of State power. The 1957 Declaration and the 1960 Statement both clearly point out: "Leninism teaches, and experience confirms that the ruling classes never relinquish power voluntarily." The old government never topples even in a period of crisis, unless it is pushed. This is a universal law of class struggle.'

Dealing with peace, the Peking open letter declared: 'According to the Leninist viewpoint, world peace can be won only by the struggle of the peoples in all countries and not by begging the imperialists for it. World peace can only be defended effectively by relying on the development of the forces of the socialist camp, on the revolutionary struggles of the proletariat and working people of all countries, on the liberation struggles of the oppressed nations and on the struggles of all peace-loving people and countries. Such is the Leninist policy. Any policy to the contrary definitely will not lead to world peace but will only encourage the ambitions of the imperialists and increase the danger of world war.'

'Peaceful coexistence,' stated the Peking letter, 'cannot replace the revolutionary struggles of the people. The transition from capitalism to socialism in any country can only be brought about through the proletarian revolution and the dictatorship of the proletariat in that country.' Peaceful coexistence was not a fundamental policy and should not form the general line of communist foreign policy.

On July 16th, Moscow replied with an open letter from the Central Committee of the C.P.S.U. This rejected the Chinese line as adding 'grist to the mill of the imperialist policy of "brinkmanship"'. 'The struggle for peace and peaceful coexistence,' stated the Moscow letter, 'weakens the front of imperialism, isolates its more aggressive circles from the mass of the people and helps the working class in its revolutionary struggle and the peoples in their struggle for national liberation. The struggle for peace and for peaceful coexistence is organically bound up with the revolutionary struggle against imperialism.' The letter went on to restate that the Moscow line on peace not only averted nuclear war, but was also 'the best way to help the international revolutionary working-class movement to achieve its principal class aims'.

In short, 'the struggle for peace and the peaceful coexistence of States with different social systems, far from hindering, far from delaying, makes it possible to develop in full measure the struggle for the attainment of the ultimate aims of the international working-class movement . . . The primary task of the communist parties is to rally together all the peace-loving forces in defence of peace and to save mankind from a nuclear catastrophe. The socialist revolution takes place as a result of the internal development of the class struggle in every country, and its forms and ways are determined by the concrete conditions of each given nation.'[1]

[1] At the beginning of 1964 the Soviet military paper *Red Star* published a series on the methods of Soviet military science. On February 4th it reiterated the basic thesis of just and unjust wars, just being those carried out or approved by the Soviet Union, unjust being those it opposed: 'whatever wars have been started in the modern epoch, their basic origin has been imperialism, its aggressive policy as a concentrated expression of its economy'.

In this way Moscow once again laid down the new line that world communism would be best brought about by non-violent methods, though it was necessary at the same time 'to be ready for the armed suppression of the resistance of the *bourgeoisie*'.

In his role as Soviet premier, Mr Khruschov greeted 1964 with two messages. In one to the American people he predicted that '1964 can become a year of decisive change for the better in the entire international situation'. At the same time he sent a message to the governments of all countries calling for an agreement to renounce the use of force for settling territorial and frontier disputes. Before January 1964 was out, Soviet forces in Eastern Germany had shot down an unarmed American plane which had strayed over the border from Western Germany, killing all three occupants. In mid-February the Soviet delegation to the disarmament talks in Geneva had walked out and effectively ended the talks because of the failure of the Americans to return to them a Russian official who had sought political asylum in the West. These are the apparent contradictions still basic to communist activities. This is why now more than ever we need to understand the workings of the world communist propaganda system.

CHAPTER THREE

# *The Instruments of Control*

To understand the communist system it is essential to remember the interlocking role of Party and State in the countries where the Party is in power, in the Communist Bloc itself. This has already been mentioned briefly in Chapter 1, and it cannot be overemphasized. Outside the communist world, we are so used to thinking of the State as something quite divorced from any individual political party that it is difficult for us to adjust our minds, to a different concept.

But we must rethink our traditional inter-relationships of Party and State if we are to understand Communist Bloc policies and to make proper sense of communist propaganda. As we have noted, when the Soviet premier Mr Khruschov writes to the other world political leaders, the pen is also held by the hand of the First Secretary of the Communist Party of the Soviet Union, Comrade Khruschov. To be more precise, the pen is *always* held by the First Secretary of the Communist Party, who issues the policy directives which govern the running of the Soviet State, both on the domestic front and in its relations with other peoples and countries.

This dual conception of Party and State is an important aspect of all communist political, social and economic policy, whether at home or abroad. The Party gives the people its *rukovodstvo*, its guiding hand, while the State gives the country its *upravlenie*, its administration. The *rukovodstvo* is *never* wrong. If mistakes are made, the blame is attached to the *upravlenie*. This applies when things go wrong in Soviet industry, and equally when mistakes are made by those who did not understand or those who intended to sabotage the Party policy of the moment, either because they were Left or because they were Right deviationists at that particular time.

So for our purpose the voice of the Party and of the State are taken as one, except when statements are made in different ways for the benefit of different audiences. This essential simplification does not run into any danger of over-simplification, as we shall see. It applies to propaganda from Moscow itself, the communist countries of Eastern Europe, Peking and the Asian communist countries of North Korea and North Vietnam. It is only when the propaganda is of an intra-Bloc nature that the divergences become apparent.

In this chapter I work on the assumption that Moscow is the major epicentre, as indeed it was until the latter half of the 50's. The system in Peking runs along much the same lines. There is the Communist Party of China (C.P.C.) corresponding to the Communist Party of the Soviet Union (C.P.S.U.). There is the National People's Congress, corresponding to the All-Union Supreme Soviet: both of these elect their respective premiers and governments. In Communist China there is another body which has no Soviet equivalent, the Chinese People's Political Consultative Committee. This is not an organ of State power, but a consultative body of the Democratic Front, which represents the various political and mass organizations on the mainland. In its external relations, Communist China relies less than the Soviet Union on its governmental organizations – for the most part because it still has relatively little diplomatic relationship with the non-communist world. In China the C.P.C. has far greater direct administrative control over the key government ministries than has the C.P.S.U. in the U.S.S.R.

I described the rise of the *Agitprop* apparatus in the Soviet Union towards the end of Chapter 1. Agitation and propaganda today come directly under the control of the Presidium, together with cultural affairs, science and foreign relations. All four are, in fact, closely inter-related. It is important to remember that in itself *Agitprop* performs a staff, not an operational, function. It is not a production department. Its concern is the planning, direction and overseeing of all the media of communist propaganda at home and abroad.

Here I am concerned with communist international propaganda and not that directed to the home audience. But the two are closely linked, the one being in essence the projection beyond the Soviet borders of the other. There is one major difference. The home audience is largely captive. All means of communication in the Soviet Union are controlled by the communist apparatus. It can relay its messages at any strength and in any direction it wishes. Press, radio, television, films and the theatre are all available for *Agitprop* and all are used extensively. Meetings, lectures, discussion groups and personal encounters are all fully utilized to put over current policies on general issues (propaganda) or to stir up emotions and generate action on specific matters (agitation). *Agitprop* both within the Soviet Union and within the other countries of the East Bloc has been dealt with extensively in other writings. Our concern is with the natural extension of this process outwards from the epicentre to the non-communist world.

The lines of command outwards from *Agitprop* separate into two main groups. The first we discuss in this chapter, the direct Party lines of control through the national communist parties locally and the governmental agencies of the Communist Bloc in their relationships with the rest of the world. The second group is made up of the communist fronts and the friendship societies, which Muenzenberg called 'the innocents' clubs'. These are dealt with in Chapter 4.

The national communist parties are organizationally the most important lines of command. It is so often forgotten that the international communist movement *is* world-wide in its operations, to an extent that has never before been seen in a political creed which by its very nature cannot but be dictatorial and totalitarian. Its very existence depends on the imposition of an anti-popular creed which can only benefit an *élite*, an *élite* which can only remain in power by using the weapon described by them as dictatorship of the proletariat. It is an over-simplification to attribute the world-wide nature of the communist movement to the vested interests of the *élite* in its perpetuation and extension. But communism is as essentially conspiratorial as it is messianic and this dual characteristic is a cohesive factor great enough to span seas, mountains, and the barriers of political states.

We have already seen how over the years Moscow had demanded the allegiance and support of all the communist parties for the

Soviet Union as the heartland of the world movement. This demand lasted into the early 60's and only ceased to be dominant when Peking became more active as an alternative source of Party inspiration. But the first forty years after the Bolshevik Revolution saw some kind of organization in being at most times to link together the national communist parties, large and small, overt and underground.

For most of the period this body, of course, was the Comintern. As I outlined in Chapter 2, this lasted from 1919 to 1943, when it was dissolved for tactical reasons at the height of the war. Then in 1947 the Cominform was founded. Unlike the Comintern, which was made up of all the communist parties of the day, the Cominform comprised twelve European communist parties only. Of these Yugoslavia was to be expelled within less than a year for deviation, the refusal to acknowledge the leading rule of the Soviet Union. While the Comintern was a brainchild of Lenin, the Cominform was born of Stalin. After Stalin's time it had only a limited existence left and it was dissolved in April 1956, two months after the Twentieth Congress of the C.P.S.U. and the 'secret speech' denunciation of Stalin and Stalinist practices by Khruschov.

No fresh organization was brought into being to replace the Cominform, though the next year saw a number of oblique demands for some co-ordinating body made by various European communist leaders. Finally, in September 1958, publication started in Prague of a monthly journal, *Problems of Peace and Socialism*, with the English edition entitled *World Marxist Review*. This has continued into the 60's as the leading international organ of the world communist movement, following in the footsteps of the Comintern's pre-war *Inprecorr* and its unreadable post-war successor *The Cominform Journal*. In the period directly under review here the major publication was *The Cominform Journal*, which came out fortnightly in Belgrade, moving to Bucharest after the expulsion of Yugoslavia. By this time it had become a weekly broadsheet which showed all the appearance in typography and layout of a multi-language edition of *Pravda*. It was published locally in the Communist Bloc languages and in Swedish, while the major West European language editions were published in Bucharest.

It is important to remember that *The Cominform Journal* was a completely overt publication and every means was made to widen its circulation.[1] In terms of reading matter it was dull, but to the reader with any sense of interpretation it gave a clear indication of communist, that is to say Moscow, policy for the week ahead, and maybe longer. For instance, a relatively small critical item on the internal situation of the Japanese Communist Party in 1950 was quickly followed by a wholesale reorganization of the Party and a new militant line. The *Journal* gave a great deal of information on communist propaganda activities throughout the world, together with articles clarifying and expanding the current Party lines. Its distribution was efficient and it was airmailed from Bucharest with a thoughtfulness for non-communist readers in that it was sealed in a plain envelope and mailed at air letter rate, all for a subscription of less than a pound a year!

Publication of *The Cominform Journal* was the major activity of the Cominform as an organization, with real control of international communism in those closing years of the 40's and the early years of the 50's being held by Stalin in Moscow. It ceased publication on the closing down of the Cominform in April 1956. Six months later Khruschov was telling a visiting journalist that a new journal was to be published in the next few months. Its purpose was to be a forum of discussion between fraternal parties, so that they could air their views and share common experiences. Khruschov was anxious in launching this new organ to avoid any suggestion that it represented a new Cominform.

As it happened, the next few months saw the unrest in Poland and the uprising in Hungary. In such circumstances the new journal was shelved. It was put aside, in fact, for nearly two years. It was announced in the summer of 1958 with one of the Soviet *Agitprop* and ideological chief, A. M. Rumyantsev, former editor of the Soviet Party ideological monthly *Kommunist*, as the editor-in-chief. In this way the continuity of editorship demonstrated by *The Cominform Journal*, with its Russian chief editors Yudin and Mitin toeing the Stalinist line in Bucharest, was ensured by the

[1] I took out a six-month subscription to the *Journal* in 1949 and from then onwards received it regularly, even after the subscription expired. My changes of address were conscientiously acted upon!

establishment of a Khruschov henchman in the new editorial chair in Prague.

The importance of the *World Marxist Review* in the 1960's is less than that of *The Cominform Journal* a decade earlier. Over this period there has been a permanent change in the pattern of inter-Party communication. In Stalin's day there was only one major international communist party gathering – the Nineteenth Congress of the Soviet Party in 1952. This was the first formal occasion since the Eighteenth Congress in 1939 for representatives of foreign parties to gather *en masse* in Moscow. The three Cominform meetings of 1947, 1948 and 1949 only comprised the eleven parties making up the Cominform, of which only the Italian and French Parties were outside the Communist Bloc.

The Twentieth Soviet Party Congress in 1956 was held according to schedule, itself a break with the Stalinist past. From this date onwards there have been several formal and informal gatherings of international communist leaders in Moscow, those highlighted being the international gathering after the 40th anniversary celebrations in 1957 (which followed a smaller meeting that summer in Bucharest) and the international conference in Moscow in November-December 1960. Party Congresses and anniversaries of revolutions will undoubtedly be used more often from now on as platforms of propaganda to the world communist movement.

If the international communist periodicals have changed in their importance, that of the anniversary slogans has not. They are an accurate reflection of the Party line of the moment. Taken individually, each slogan is an agitational call to action. Collectively they represent propaganda for Party adherent and auxiliary alike. The May Day slogans published by the Central Committee of the Soviet Party differ only in detail from those published by the Party for the October Revolution anniversary in the November. With but few exceptions, the hundred-odd slogans put out at the half-yearly intervals which separate these two events are almost identical in phrasing and content. The significance at any one time lies in the exceptions to the rule, as indications of changed emphasis. The slogans do not anticipate changes, they merely give them a relative importance.

Although the exceptions to the rule show a change in direction, the actual wording and presentation of the slogans is more important in the long run because it makes clear the scope and interlocking nature of communist policy. This is shown, for instance, by the comparative listing of the Central Committee slogans published in Moscow for May Day 1962 and the October Revolution Anniversary of November, 1961. Both lists begin with world-wide issues, continue with individual countries and areas and end with domestic exhortations. The Anniversary slogan references to the Twenty-second Party Congress which had only just been completed are omitted, of course, from the May Day list: this, on the other hand, includes: 'Long live peace and friendship among peoples!' which is replaced on the Anniversary list by the more militant: 'Long live the unbreakable unity and cohesion of the great army of communists of the whole world!'

The November reference to 'general and complete disarmament' is a new theme, while the May Day reference to Algeria takes account of the independence agreement, though it is not regarded as by any means final, being described as merely 'an outstanding victory along the path of a free, independent Algerian State'. Cuba is upgraded from thirty-seventh to twenty-sixth place in the listing. The most notable divergences in text come in the sections devoted to domestic issues, which are governed by various conferences and directives in the six months between November 1961 and May 1962, particularly those calling for changes in agricultural policies.

In November, workers in literature and art were enjoined to 'depict vividly in your works the grandeur and beauty of the heroic feats of Soviet man!' By May this had been changed in emphasis, telling them to do their job 'more vividly'! At the same time Press, radio and TV workers in November were told 'be tireless propagandaists and bears to the masses of the all-conquering ideas of communism, of leading experience, of the achievements of science and technology and of the spiritual riches amassed by mankind!' By May Day the slogan is blunter: 'Be active fighters for the great cause of the Party, for putting communist ideals and the gains of science and leading experience into practice!'

These slogan lists – and they are repeated with local variations in all the communist countries – have two important features. In the more general sense they represent a series of chapter headings in the half-yearly volume of world communist activity, and, as I have already remarked, they are phrased as commands from the Central Committee of the Party. The November slogans are directed more particularly to Party militants, while the May Day slogans are intended for a wider audience. But the differences are largely of emphasis. At all Party levels and for all communist parties and groups they are both directives to action and aids to an understanding of policy trends and changes.

The slogans are directives written in clear, simple form. They are complemented by more detailed directives written in the curious kind of communist code which has been called the indicative-imperative. The use of the indicative-imperative dates back to the Cominform days, when it was used extensively in the *Journal.* The technique is simple. By using the Party jargon with its words having specialized meanings, instructions could be given not in the imperative form, but in the indicative. Instead of saying 'communists *must* do this', they say 'communists are doing this'.

This use of the indicative-imperative has two advantages. Its superficial doubletalk is meaningless to the casual reader. As such it is dismissed as jargon and forgotten by the potential targets of communist propaganda. At the same time its real meaning is quite clear to the communist activist for whom it is intended. This gives it the first advantage of open distribution, which is always of greater administrative efficiency than clandestine work.

Secondly, the verbal avoidance of the imperative form with its obvious instruction and command reduces the risk of public alarm and official attention in the non-communist countries. This is particularly important where the Rule of Law operates, for under such rules, the indicative-imperative has no legal meaning.

As one of the many examples of this we can read the leading article in *The Cominform Journal* of January 9th, 1953 entitled 'Growing Upsurge of National-Liberation Movement in Colonial and Dependent Countries'. Though the text dates from the early 50's, the message – as we have seen from the ideological directives cited in Chapter 2 – applies equally in the 60's.

The very title of the leader with its indicative 'growing upsurge' is a directive, the imperative 'communists must intensify disruptive activities in Asia and Africa'.

A typical paragraph from the leader declares in the indicative:

The national-liberation struggle in the colonial and dependent countries is assuming a more active and resolute nature. The spontaneous and divided centres of the movement for independence are becoming more and more organized in separate countries; the struggle is assuming a nation-wide character. The imperialists are no longer able to rule in the old way in the dependent and colonial countries and the colonial peoples no longer want to live in the old way. Nor can any efforts on the part of the imperialists avert the progressive disintegration of the colonial system, hold back the liberation of the peoples from the colonial yoke.

Translated into the imperative, this would direct Party members as follows:

Communists are to intensify their activities in the colonial and newly-independent countries. Spontaneous nationalist movements are to be penetrated and brought under communist control. The present stage in the evolution of the colonies towards independence is ripe for exploitation in the communist interest, which is represented by the Soviet interest. Existing relationships between Western and Asian nations and non-self-governing territories in other parts of the world are changing. It is up to the communists to take advantage of this and to ensure that the change does not come about through co-operation and agreement but through violent clashes. If the present relationships can be made to collapse the colonial peoples can then be more easily 'liberated' into communism and dependence on the Soviet Union.

Later passages became more specific, thus the *Journal* put it:

The anti-imperialist and anti-feudal movement in the colonial and dependent countries is closely linked with the struggle for peace, for security and for friendship of the peoples. Broad masses of the oppressed and the exploited are becoming more and more convinced that a third world war, should the warmongers succeed in unleashing it, will bring the colonial and dependent countries additional and countless sufferings and sacrifices. Consequently they demand the expulsion of all foreign troops from their countries, the liquidation of foreign military bases and resolutely oppose the so-called 'unified military commands' and the involving of the colonial and dependent countries in the various aggressive U.S.-British military blocs. The peace movement is growing and developing.

Which, translated, means:

The communist agitation programme is to be carried out by means of the 'peace' campaign and 'peace' is to be used as the principal theme to justify whatever local communist interests demand. In particular all attempts to build up any organization to resist the possible use of force by the Soviet Union must be prevented. A particular agitation is to be conducted against defence arrangements made in co-operation with the Western Powers.

At the same time, declares the *Journal*:

The national-liberation struggle of the colonial peoples enjoys the profound sympathy and moral support of the communist and workers' parties[1] in all countries, of all the democratic and peace-loving forces of the world. The national-liberation struggle in the colonies – true ally of the fighters for peace, democracy and socialism – is the common cause of all advanced and progressive mankind. This just struggle has the support of all people of labour, honour and progress in the metropolitan countries, because a nation which oppresses other nations cannot be free. The nation which oppresses another nation forges chains for itself.

The imperative of this directs:

All communist agencies, particularly in the mother countries, are to support communist agitation in the colonies, which is made to appear as part of the 'struggle for peace, democracy and socialism'. Thereby liberal-minded people of all parties – generally ignorant of the communist meanings of so many vital political terms are to be persuaded by the communist agencies to lend their support as well.

In such ways the channels of communication carry the communist messages and commmands outwards to the national com-

[1] The joint term 'communist and workers parties' is often used in official communist statements to cover those communist parties which continue to use other names, as for instance the Polish United Workers' Party in Poland and the Irish Workers' League in the Irish Republic. In some countries where the communists are already in power these oblique names are usually historical reminders of past united front tactics prior to the communist coming to full power. In others they are adopted to hide the true identity of the organizations, especially in those countries where a communist party as such would be illegal or out of favour with the populace.

munist parties the world over. Meetings with Party leaders at the capital of the heartland, international Party journals – and in this connexion we must not forget the main Soviet journals such as *Kommunist*, which are systematically read by the hierarchies abroad for their instructions and explanations of current lines – and the many thousands of regional and local publications, anniversary slogans and all means of transmitting the indicative-imperative messages, such are the openly publicized means by which the international communist apparatus is kept in touch.[1]

The early 1960's saw over ninety communist parties in the world, communist parties in the sense that they were acknowledged openly as such by Moscow and Peking. The communist party is usually of a clandestine nature in any society where it is not the dominant factor. In 1963 communist parties were illegal in thirty-seven countries, including Spain, Portugal, South Africa, most of South and Central America except Cuba and Mexico, Thailand, Malaya, the Philippines, the Sudan Republic, the United Arab Republic and Algeria.

Forty-nine of these communist parties were from Asia, Africa and Latin America, the latest being that formed in the British Southern African protectorate of Basutoland early in 1962. In all, thirteen new communist parties were founded in the world in the years following the Twentieth Congress in 1956. A number of them were reconstituted groups originally set up by metropolitan parties in the former African colonial territories. With the membership of the United Nations past the hundredth country mark, it could be said that almost every sovereign state in the 60's has its communist party, either in the open or underground. The largest in the non-communist world is that of Indonesia, with 2 million members, the smallest that in the Irish Republic, with an estimated 150 members.

Considering the world nature of the communist movement, we are told almost nothing of its make-up and the state of the individual parties, except when they are exceptionally strong, as has been the case with the Indonesian party. After over forty years

[1] In this book I am not concerned with clandestine activities, though in specific situations these may be more important. My concern is the understanding of communist propaganda techniques and their impact.

of communist rule in the world, we still have to build up our overall picture from fragments and estimates. The only definite information we are given by Moscow is the world membership, which is claimed to have grown by one-third between the mid-50's and the early 60's, as the following table shows:

| | |
|---|---|
| 1956 (April) | 30 million |
| 1956 (November) | 32 ,, |
| 1957 (2nd half) | 33 ,, |
| 1960 | 36 ,, |
| 1961 | 40 ,, |
| 1962 | 42.5 ,, |

Of these the following fragments give an idea of the figures for the non-communist world during part of that period:

| | |
|---|---|
| 1957 | 4.6 million |
| 1960 | 5.2 million |
| 1961 | 5.3 ,, |
| 1962 | 6 ,, |

A significant feature of both sets of figures is that little apparent difference was made to total recruitment by the communist suppression of the Hungarian revolution in 1956, nor by the revelations of Khruschov earlier that year about the excesses of the Stalin régime. As the difference between the total and the non-communist world figures show, the bulk of party membership continues to come from parties in the Communist Bloc itself.

Breakdowns such as these suggest that the few figures given by Moscow are inflated in two ways. First of all, they include the lesser category of candidate membership of the Bloc parties, which could add up to six-figure totals and more, particularly in the Chinese Party. Secondly, Moscow's own estimates of its non-communist world support may well be over-optimistic. So many of the parties are small and relatively unorganized as to be unreliable statistical sources. As far as the world outside the Communist Bloc is concerned, the rate of growth matches that of world population, about two per cent per annum. Taken as a whole, therefore, this suggests little of the dynamic which one would expect from a movement with an expanding world outlook, particularly in the countries outside the Bloc itself where membership of the Communist Party brings with it none of the privileges it carries inside the Bloc.

But in communist terms, the parties throughout the world have a special *élite* function, in that they are the direct heirs of the Revolution and that their activities in their own areas closely correlate with the rumbling from the epicentre. Throughout the whole period of communist activity since 1917, it has always been a fetish at the local level to assert that the Communist Party acts independently of Moscow. This is part of the essential ritual, an incantation which can be heard simultaneously all over the world every time there is a major policy switch. The Party is there to act on instructions and the communist propaganda apparatus is there to help it do its job.

The actual Party situation throughout the world has been discussed in some detail at this stage as relatively little will be said about it in succeeding chapters. In this book I am not so much concerned with the workings of the individual communist parties in themselves as with the use of communist propaganda techniques directed at the overwhelming majority outside the Party machine's direct area of operations. To this extent the next chapter is more important. I have given it the cynical name which Willi Muenzenberg chose for the communist fronts, 'The Innocent's Clubs.' On this basis my main thesis might be described somewhat melodramatically as the Rape of the Innocents. In political terms this description is as apt as any, for that is exactly the function of such 'clubs' today, just as it was three decades ago. But before turning to the communist fronts we will look briefly at the other major media of communist propaganda which, like the communist parties themselves, come under the direct control of the central Party leadership. On the one hand, the Party in Moscow has a direct line to the party machines elsewhere in the world. On the other hand, it has an indirect but no less strong line of control by way of the East Bloc government agencies dealing with communications abroad.

Widest spread of course is the network of the East Bloc diplomatic services and trade delegations, with the Soviet Ministry of Foreign Affairs, the State Committee for Foreign Economic

Relations and the Ministry of Foreign Trade being the most important.

The Foreign Ministry is charged solely with the responsibility of Soviet foreign relations: negotiations with foreign diplomats in the U.S.S.R., the maintenance of diplomatic relations with governments abroad and the supervision of the representatives of other Soviet agencies abroad. In 1960 the Soviet Union had fifty-three embassies, four legations and a permanent mission to the United Nations: fourteen countries had been added to its diplomatic list in the preceding six years, mostly in Africa and South-east Asia.

The State Committee for Foreign Economic Relations comes under the U.S.S.R. Council for Ministers and has ministerial rank. In some ways it complements the Ministry of Foreign Trade. It develops economic contacts with foreign countries and supervises technical and economic aid, scientific collaboration, the construction of enterprises abroad and credit grants.

The Ministry of Foreign Trade starts its work after the Committee for Foreign Economic Relations has finished its task of establishing the economic basis for Soviet economic relations with another country. It is concerned with the overall control of foreign trade, but not with actual day-to-day operations.

These are carried out by some two dozen export-import associations which each have representatives at home and abroad. These are legal monopolies, each with an exclusive trading responsibility for certain commodities, though some have responsibility not by commodity but by trading area. All are legally independent economic organizations, liable for their own actions.

This is where the system of communist foreign trade has its own special dichotomy. It is a State monopoly subject to overall control by the Party through the Soviet State apparatus. This is certainly the case when negotiating trade agreements, particularly those involving long-term contracts. But the actual commodity negotiations are carried out through the import-export associations, which are independent bodies in Soviet law. In this circumstance, the Government of the U.S.S.R. cannot be held liable for debts and acts of the association either at home or abroad. Nor can the associations be held liable for the acts of the Soviet Government.

This obviously puts any foreign trader at a disadvantage when concluding a deal with a Soviet association, under a general trade agreement negotiated at inter-governmental level. He can be sued by a Soviet plaintiff for any breach of contract on his part according to the generally accepted rules of bourgeois law. If he suffers from breaches on the Soviet side he can take the matter to a special Soviet tribunal set up for dealing with foreign trade cases only, under conditions which put the foreigner at a complete disadvantage with little hope of redress, especially if considerable sums are involved. The purpose of the Soviet judiciary, as of all other organs of the Soviet State, is to protect the interests of the Soviet system first and foremost, even when it conflicts with the rights of an individual.

This particular aspect of the operations of Soviet foreign trade has an important propaganda function. The communists can – and do – make full use of their trading agreements to develop the theme of expanding economic relations: this is their *rukovodstvo*. Whatever goes wrong is no concern of the Party and State's *rukovodstvo*, but is the fault of the trading association involved, the *upravlenie*. If this dichotomy of Soviet foreign trading operations is appreciated, many apparent inconsistencies are cleared up.

Diplomacy and foreign trade are not overtly propaganda functions, of course, though they play their roles. The actual propaganda media of the Press, radio and television – whether for home or foreign audiences – also come under Party control either directly or through the State organizations.

The Soviet Press and publishing activities generally are all controlled by the Party through one fundamental weapon, the publishing licence. Every periodical, pamphlet and book must be submitted for licensing both at the proof and the printing stages. Except for those intended for foreign consumption, these publications must carry the licence details, including the number permitted and the technical specifications (details which many Western librarians would welcome for non-ideological reasons!) Little is known of the workings of this licensing system, but with it the Party, acting through the State, has a tight administrative grip on what is being published, from the local evening paper right up to the Great Soviet Encyclopedia.

Periodicals for abroad are published by a number of specialist organizations, usually as part of wider activities. Such is the case of the monthly *Soviet Woman*, the organ of the Soviet women's organization which appears in several languages. The colour magazine *Soviet Union* is published by the *Pravda* publishing house in various languages, while the weekly *Moscow News* is published in English and French and more recently in Portuguese for Latin America.

The Foreign Languages Publishing House is responsible for all non-periodical publishing in non-Soviet languages, including material for other communist countries. In 1960 it published over a thousand titles in two dozen languages totalling forty million copies. These excluded pamphlets of less than fifty pages.

The export of all Soviet publications – periodicals, pamphlets and books, as well as gramophone records – is carried out entirely through the export-import association *Mezhdunarodnaya Kniga*, which also imports books and papers from abroad for distribution in the Soviet Union. Only titles carried on the association's export list may be dispatched abroad. This embargo dates from the Stalinist days, when very little was allowed out. Since then the export list has grown tremendously. The trouble nowadays in obtaining particular books is attributed more often than not to their going out of stock as soon as they are on the market. The M.K. export list of Soviet periodicals for 1962 listed more than 2,000 titles compared with 500 in 1955 and even less in 1950.

*Mezhdunarodnaya Kniga* is concerned primarily with the sale of Soviet periodicals abroad. It does not control the exchange of Soviet and foreign periodicals between research institutes, though these come under the normal Soviet postal censorship regulations governing mails entering or leaving the country. By and large, the only publications not allowed to be sent abroad are the local papers from the remoter regions and certain highly-specialized scientific journals.

Together with the Press, the news agency *Tass* (Telegraph Agency of the Soviet Union) is a vital two-way organ of propaganda. It is the main source of Soviet news for abroad and in its turn is the main channel of news from abroad for internal Soviet consumption. It is a governmental agency, coming directly under the Council of Ministers. The heads of its offices throughout the world have diplomatic rank, which carries with it a corresponding diplomatic immunity from the normal processes of the laws of a country such as is not enjoyed by any other journalists: this applies particularly to actions for libel, and to charges of espionage.

The radio services – like television – come under the general supervision of another governmental body, the All-Union Radio and Television Committee, which is in its turn closely supervised by the Party *Agitprop* department.

Soviet broadcasts for abroad started in 1933, with long-wave programmes in German from Moscow. Short-wave transmitters were added later and by 1942 ten short-wave transmitters at Moscow and Kuibyshev were broadcasting 400 hours a week in seventeen foreign languages. This fell off immediately after the war, but by 1950 the Soviet Union was broadcasting more than 500 hours a week and by 1962 broadcasts abroad from the whole of the East Bloc totalled more than 3,800 hours a week in some sixty languages. These figures exclude programmes for home audiences.

Television is still largely for home audiences. But with a Helsinki-Leningrad landline operating from 1961, Soviet and East European TV can now be transmitted directly to any European transmitter that agrees to a link-up. At the same time, of course, West European programmes can be transmitted directly to Soviet and East European viewers, if the communist TV stations wish. In practice little use was made either way in 1963, the only programmes of any significance being sporting events. Exceptional at the time was Moscow's use of Telstar satellite facilities to give live coverage for Russian television viewers of the funeral of President Kennedy in November 1963. Outside Europe, there is no direct use made of television for communist propaganda abroad, though films are extensively offered for showing on local TV programmes.

Last of the major State organizations directly concerned with foreign relations is that covering cultural affairs.[1] Originally this was V.O.K.S. (the Russian initials for the All-Union Society for Cultural Relations with Foreign Countries). Early in 1958

[1] The Academy of Sciences also plays a propaganda role in its relations with foreign organizations, together with its scientific work. For our purpose the former is considered with the cultural propaganda.

V.O.K.S. was dissolved and its place was taken by the Union of Soviet Societies for Friendship and Cultural Relations with Foreign Countries, with the former chairman of V.O.K.S., Nina Popova, as its president.

In its day V.O.K.S. came under the State Committee for Cultural Relations with Foreign Countries. On the one hand the State Committee dealt with other governmental bodies in arranging official cultural exchanges. The job of V.O.K.S. was to deal with the various national Soviet friendship societies which operated outside the U.S.S.R. under communist direction. In the U.S.S.R. itself V.O.K.S. formed a number of corresponding friendship societies in the mid-fifties for other Bloc countries and for India, Finland and Italy, which maintained contacts with their opposite numbers abroad. These brought complaints from the non-communist Governments concerned that the Soviet authorities were negotiating with unofficial and unrepresentative bodies.

So the new Union of Soviet Friendship Societies was set up to meet these criticisms. It took over the V.O.K.S. premises in Moscow and its magazine *Culture and Life*, as well as some of its officers from the chairman downwards.

In February 1962 Mrs Popova reported that fifty organizations within the Soviet Union were affiliated to the Union of Friendship Societies, which 'had contacts with the public' in 118 countries, including forty-four countries with which the U.S.S.R. did not yet have diplomatic relations. The Soviet friendship societies had contacts with over 2,000 organizations abroad and with 'scores of thousands' of public figures.

Such are the main Soviet Party and State organizations concerned with propaganda for abroad. Their equivalants are to be found in all the other communist countries. Outside the Bloc their most important opposite numbers are the communist fronts.

As far as relations with organizations and individuals abroad are concerned, the Union of Friendship Societies acts in many ways as a co-ordinating body with what are officially known as 'public organizations', a third group comprising what in the non-communist world would be regarded by the Party as 'transmission belts'. As is discussed more fully in the next chapter, these transmission belts are organizations not openly connected with the

Communist Party, but which it uses as an indirect way of promoting its policies and actions.

In the Communist Bloc itself such 'public organizations' are the trade union movement, the women's organization, the Young Communist League and the other ancillary youth and student bodies and mass movements. Nominally independent, these come under Party control in the same way as other sectors of economic and social life in the communist countries, with communists holding the key positions and the Party Central Committee laying down the general policies within which they work.

In the Soviet Union, a new 'public organization' was set up in 1961 which has a specifically international responsibility. This is the news agency A.P.N. or *Novosti*. A.P.N. is quite distinct from *Tass*, which is a State organization with full State privileges abroad and the responsibility of putting forward the official viewpoint.

A.P.N. is run jointly by the major public organizations as an unofficial body, without any special privileges. It is a brain-child of Khruschov's son-in-law, Adzhubei, editor-in-chief of *Izvestia*. It has the wider brief of presenting not so much news as feature material about Soviet affairs to the outside world, at the same time as it prepares features on world affairs for Soviet readers. In both cases, the material is clearly marked as coming from the agency either as A.P.N. or as *Novosti*. Thus from 1962 onwards the already extensive booklet service of the Soviet Embassy in London was supplemented by essays on Soviet social, economic and political affairs by Russian specialists writing under A.P.N. auspices. Earlier still, features prepared under the *Novosti* symbol began appearing regularly in *Izvestia* and other Soviet publications.[1]

The A.P.N. *Novosti* organization is a valuable supplement to *Tass*, for it can always deny the official standing of any controversial statement it makes, if such a statement became embarrassing to Moscow. Its material – unlike that of *Tass* – is copyrighted abroad, so that it can invoke this protection if it wishes to prevent any embarrassing use made of its publications in direct quotation.

[1] In 1962, besides providing thousands of articles for the Soviet press, A.P.N. sent 50,000 items of copy to over 90 countries. It issued 387,000 photos.

CHAPTER FOUR

# *The Innocents' Clubs*

In the previous chapter we considered propaganda in relation to the Communist Party and State system in the East Bloc and the party system in the rest of the world. Right from the beginning the communist leaders realized that they could not foment world revolution by working within their own closed movement. By their own tenets they could not trust anyone else, but if they were to achieve their aims they had to get the co-operation of others, by whatever means available.[1]

So in the early days of Bolshevik power Lenin was quite clear in his own mind that: 'Only those who have no self-reliance can fear to enter into temporary alliances even with unreliable people; not a single political party could exist without entering such alliances.' But he was equally clear that in making such alliances with bourgeois democrats the communists should be given complete freedom 'to reveal to the working class that its interests were diametrically opposed to the interests of the bourgeoisie'. This conception of opportunism as a tactical weapon is a major theme of his pamphlet *What is to be Done?* published at the very beginning of the twentieth century, re-issued many times since and still underlined today by Party spokesmen, sixty years after its initial publication.

Lenin always stressed the need for temporary compromise, if that were likely to help attain a Party objective. He put it most succinctly in what remains the key directive at all Party levels: 'The strictest loyalty to the ideas of communism must be combined with the ability to make all the necessary compromises, to "tack", to

[1] It is not my purpose here to discuss the issues of ideological purity and the extent to which non-communist aid should be rejected. In terms of practical politics the thesis of Lenin, not Trotsky, are those operative.

make agreements, zigzags, retreats and so on, in order to accelerate the rise to power of the communists.'

In 1920, this compromise thesis was developed by Lenin in *Left-Wing Communism, an Infantile Disorder*, another of his works that has been kept continually up to date, with special attention on its fortieth anniversary in 1960. This was a criticism of the left-wing communists in other countries who clung to principles, instead of compromising to gain advantages for themselves.

'It is possible,' he wrote then, 'to conquer the more powerful enemy only by exerting the utmost effort and by necessarily, thoroughly, carefully, attentively and skilfully taking advantage of every, even the smallest, "fissure" among the enemies, of every antagonism of interest among the bourgeoisie of the various countries, among the various groups or types of bourgeoisie in the various countries; by taking advantage of every, even the smallest, opportunity of gaining a mass ally, even though this ally be temporary, vacillating, unstable, unreliable and conditional. Those who do not understand this fail to understand even a grain of Marxism and of scientific, modern socialism in general.'

These statements were no empty words, they were calls for action, calls which have been consistently answered in the years following the Revolution. Initially they were specifically related to the period before 1917 and immediately afterwards, but their general line did not have to be modified to deal with more recent situations.

The first of the communist fronts on an international scale was formed in the 1920's, as the International Workers' Aid. Originally this was a genuine relief organization which collected funds in Europe and America to send emergency food to Russia, at that time in the midst of a wide-spread famine.

The potentialities of the I.W.A. for wider, political activity was realized by Willi Muenzenberg, who had been elected chairman of the Communist Youth International in 1920 and who founded the I.W.A. a year later.[1] He soon changed its emphasis to solidarity

[1] Curiously enough, little has been published on Muenzenberg, even by his close associates, such as Ruth Fischer, who worked with him in Berlin and Moscow in the 1920's. When I wrote to Miss Fischer in 1961, some months before she died in Paris, she replied that she could tell me

(*Continued on next page*)

first and charity afterwards. In this way it could get sympathizers at all levels for Soviet policies and carry out considerable Party propaganda without the Party label being attached.

By the mid-20's, the I.W.A. had finished with Russian famine appeals and had turned its attention to inflation-ridden Germany, then to industrially-troubled Japan and then to Britain with its General Strike of 1926. In Germany, Muenzenberg developed the I.W.A. publications work into what has been called a publishing empire. Other organizations were added, including two dailies for the German capital, various specialist and hobbies journals, a book club, a film distribution company with branches in Europe and America and a complete newspaper chain in Japan. All were controlled by the communist machine through Muenzenberg.

After the Nazis came into power in Germany, Muenzenberg escaped to France and in Paris in the 30's he founded still more groups, such as the League Against War and Fascism and the World Committee for the Relief of Victims of Fascism. Groups of this kind personified the anti-fascist feelings exploited by the communists during the united front period in the European left-wing political movements of the mid-30's. Muenzenberg was killed (in circumstances which suggested that the Soviet secret police rather than Gestapo agents were responsible) during his flight from the Germans in France in 1940, by which time his utility to Moscow had come to an end. This break was in large part due to his own independence of action and his insistence on working alone, without directives from the Comintern or the local Parties.

The Party had direct control of a number of other fronts, which were considerably less refined than the Muenzenberg empire of what he called his Innocents' Clubs. The Young Communist International and the Red International of Labour Unions (more commonly the Profintern) were the major bodies to come under direct control. The Y.C.I. dated back as far as 1907 as an organiza-

---

nothing of value about his activities and that she was no longer interested in the subject. The only substantial narrative of Muenzenberg's work was that written by the late R.N. Carew Hunt in 1960 as part of a symposium *International Communism* in the series St Anthony's Papers No. 9 (ed. David Footman) published by Chatto & Windus, London.

tion, but came under Moscow's wing after the Revolution and the foundation of the Young Communist League immediately afterwards. Like the Comintern, it was dissolved in 1943. Since then no attempt has been made to start a fresh world communist youth organization, and references to the subject at the Fourteenth Young Communist League Congress in Moscow in April 1962 suggest that the existing machinery of the World Federation of Democratic Youth will continue to be used. The Profintern was founded in 1921, but it never achieved much, being too uncompromising towards other bodies, and it was dissolved in silence in 1937.

The Second World War and the immediate post-war years saw the emergence of the network of communist fronts we know today. In this chapter it is my intention to discuss them in fairly general terms, leaving a discussion of their activities and their changing functions to Chapters 9 and 10. The subject is at the same time simple and complex. It is simple in that the purpose of the fronts is clear: to act as a transmission belt for the communist machine. It is complex in that so many organizations are involved when we look at the world-wide situation.[1] Indeed, the communist fronts demand a book to themselves.

It will simplify matters for us if we divide the fronts up into major categories. One important group is outside the scope of this book, because it goes beyond the specific job of carrying out propaganda activities. This comprises what may be called the espionage fronts, which may take the form of political organizations, professional and scientific bodies, business firms, publishing houses, schools, clubs and so on, and which conceal straight spying and intelligence-collecting activities.

We are also concerned only in passing with Party operational fronts, such as sports clubs which give quasi-military training to young communist adherents or trading, commercial and publishing concerns whose profits help Party funds. Both these types of

[1] Thus in the U.S.A. alone by January 1962 there were 663 organizations and 122 publications which had been cited as communist or communist front by various Federal Agencies and 155 organizations and 25 publications cited as such by State or territorial investigating committees. These totals included many ephemeral bodies and papers, set up for immediate and temporary political purposes.

front activity can be carried on, of course, as part of the work of the more general political fronts.

These divide into three types. The one with which we are least concerned is the type which acts as a substitute for a communist party, usually in a country where the communist movement as such is too small to be effective or where it is banned. We are similarly little concerned here with the political fronts designed for the communist domination of other left-wing groups, so that they are communist-controlled, putting forward communist policies at the same time as they disclaim their communist character.

We are mainly concerned with what have been called the specific-issue fronts. These organize people along definite lines which may be of sex, occupation, profession or of feelings on specific issues. It is in this category that the major international and national communist fronts fit. Their job was laid down by Muenzenberg in a six-point Comintern programme in 1928 and the programme is as fresh today as it was then:

1. To arouse the interest of 'those millions of apathetic and indifferent workers' who are not interested in communist propaganda. They have to be attracted in new ways.
2. To act as 'bridges' for those who sympathize with the communists, but who have not taken the final step and joined the Party.
3. By means of mass organizations to extend the communist sphere of influence in itself.
4. To provide an organizational link with those sympathizing with the Soviet Union and with the communists.
5. To counteract the work of non-communist organizations.
6. By means of such sympathetic and mass organizations to provide training for 'cadres of militants and officials of the Communist Party possessing organizational skill'.

It is on the basis of these six points that the communist fronts have developed over more than thirty-five years. From these activities at all levels we are able to derive organizational factors common to them all, which are a good guide in identifying a communist front for what it is. There are something like a dozen of them. Individually, these characteristics may prove nothing – or they may be misleading. Taken together, a majority of them would constitute reasonable proof of communist front activity: in objective political terms, if not in a court of law.

The following are the major criteria that should be established in summing up a communist front, whether on an international, national, or local level. Many of the answers to the questions they raise cannot be given easily. It has been said that the organizational principles underlying the system of fronts are symbolized by the iceberg with one-eighth visible and seven-eighths submerged. Many of the questions we need to have answered are contained in the concealed seven-eighths.

Going from the top of the iceberg downwards, we can ask the following questions:

(1) To what extent does the organization co-operate with the campaigns, activities and publications of the communist party or other front organizations. This we can see by a general study of its own activities and those of the other bodies. We can also check on the extent to which its own officials and supporters are connected with the other bodies.

(2) Does it share the same address as other fronts? In checking this, it may be necessary to go back in time, because as one body leaves for bigger (or smaller!) premises, so it hands over to another front as successor. The property owner may well be a sympathizer.

(3) Does it co-operate with communist-controlled unions, perhaps to the exclusion of others? This may be important at a local level, where a non-communist union nationally has communist-controlled branches locally.

(4) Does it use entertainers for its fund-raising activities who are regularly associated professionally or privately with communist or front bodies? This phenomonon is quite common in the bigger cities.

(5) Does it receive favourable publicity in the communist Press? In itself, this criterion could be mis-interpreted, as the objectively independent actions of a body could be subjectively interpreted as favouring the communist cause.

(6) Do its publications reflect the Communist Party line, does it publish articles by communists or sympathisers, advertise communist or other front activities? Occasional references of this nature may mean nothing, of course. Systematic publication of such material can be very significant.

(7) Is the organization's printing done by a communist printing house? In countries where the publisher's and printer's imprint are legally required, this is immediately obvious, though in itself it may mean nothing other than the economy of cost offered by the printer in question!

(8) Does the organization itself follow the communist party line? This is not always so easy to distinguish as the criterion under item (6), as the organization itself may be better judged by its actions than by its words.

(9) Is it uniformly loyal to the Soviet Union or Communist China? At a national level we might get an answer to such a question, but locally it would be more difficult, especially where the activities are diffuse.

(10) Are the organization's funds transferred directly or indirectly to the communist party or to other fronts? Most of these organizations rarely, if ever, publish their accounts and it would be most difficult to answer this question from overt sources.

(11) Does the organization have communists or their trusted associates in positions of power? Are its meetings regularly addressed by such people? This can be the easiest question to answer – at the international or national level. But locally, it could pair with the previous question as the most difficult to answer with certainty. Prominent Party or front personalities are simple to identify, but not so the lesser luminaries whose reticence about their communist affiliations is so often masked by the prominence accorded their names in other, more acceptable circles.

In general these criteria, in total or in part, are essential aids to the recognition of a communist front. What about the individuals who support it? For their part, they can be divided into four distinct categories. First, there are the open members of the Communist Party. Second are those communists, not avowed, who can be shown to be Party members on the basis of documentary or other proof. Third, there is the bigger group who accept Party discipline, either because they are secret members of the Party or because for reasons best known to themselves they are content to accept such discipline. Last and most numerous of all are those for whose benefit the front is so often set up: the Innocents. These are usually attracted by the highlighted aims of the organization, the prominence of its sponsors or just because they think the front is a good way of getting together with people, especially if those people should come from the Communist Bloc, or, as the Innocents would put it, behind the Iron Curtain.

In such fronts, the Innocents are presented as prominently as possible, with frequent platform appearances for the public as well as for their own benefit. Very often they share their ranks with the sponsors whose names lend academic, political and other public respectability to the fronts. Such sponsors who are the first to deny vehemently that they are being used for political ends by the members of the first, second or indeed the third categories, who normally prefer to play their vital organizational roles in the background, appear publicly as infrequently as is possible.

The communist fronts which have evolved since the war fall into two main categories. The first is found entirely at the national and local level, the second is international in concept with a network of national affiliates.

The first and smaller group is that of the Communist Bloc friendship movement, made up of friendship societies and leagues in the major non-communist countries, formed with the object of generating support for the policies and interests of individual communist countries under the general blanket aims of promoting friendship and understanding. The most important in all countries where such societies exist are the Soviet friendship groups, such as the British-Soviet Friendship Society, the Scottish-U.S.S.R. Society, the *Association France-U.R.S.S.*, the National Council of American-Soviet Friendship. Many such bodies existed before the war, perhaps in other forms, and were able to develop during the war, capitalizing on the surge of pro-Russian feeling among the Allies at that time, a warmth of heart which was exploited to the full by the native communist parties in all the Allied countries. After the war these Soviet friendship groups had varying phases of development as the fellow-feeling abated with the chill of the Cold War. But though in individual countries – in Britain, for instance – popular support ebbed, the Soviet friendship movement in the world as a whole expanded, both in the Bloc itself and more particularly in the developing countries.

As the communists took over power in Eastern Europe and then in Korea, China and Vietnam, so their supporters elsewhere set up appropriate friendship groups. In Britain there is a typical complex of such organizations: the Britain-China Friendship Association, the British-Polish Friendship Society, the Society for Friendship with Bulgaria, the British-Hungarian Friendship Society, the British-Czechoslovak Friendship League and the British-Rumanian Friendship Association. All these are on the Labour Party's proscribed list as being communist organizations, membership of which is inimical to membership of the Labour Party.[1]

During the 50's there were no equivalent friendship groups in the Communist Bloc itself. In fact, this was still largely the case in 1962, with the exception of the Soviet Union, where a limited number of friendship societies with foreign countries was formed from 1959 onwards, to establish links not so much with the countries of the Western Democracies as with those of the developing areas of Asia and Africa. There are few such groups in China or in Eastern Europe. As was noted in the last chapter, the Soviet groups have been formed into the Union of Soviet Societies for Friendship and Cultural Relations.

Outside the Bloc these friendship groups are mainly concerned with the obvious activities of organizing delegation exchanges and exhibitions to show how well communism works in the respective countries. These visits and exhibitions, lectures and meetings organized nationally and locally all play an important propaganda role, often backed up by the publication of magazines and newsletters about the society's work and the country concerned. Side by side with these political activities are those of a cultural or quasi-cultural nature: art exhibitions, literature readings, musical programmes, visits of notables, scientific and cultural lectures. In the more sophisticated places, these activities are usually kept carefully apart. But this does not always follow and propaganda and culture may be as intermingled at such friendship meetings abroad as at home in the Bloc itself.

In the Communist Bloc the friendship groups again present

[1] In Britain the Society for Cultural Relations with the U.S.S.R. (S.C.R.) is not a proscribed organization, though it has always been a follower of the Party line.

political and cultural programmes, particularly where they are concerned with the countries of Asia and Africa. In these cases the political message is that of national liberation, the cultural message that of native art developing in spite of colonial oppression.

Far more important than the friendship societies are the international fronts and their national affiliates. None of them existed before the war, though one or two have considered themselves as carrying on where pre-war bodies have left off. Three of these were set up immediately after the war: the World Federation of Trade Unions (W.F.T.U.), the World Federation of Democratic Youth (W.F.D.Y.), and the Women's International Democratic Federation (W.I.D.F.). In the following year five more were added: the World Federation of Scientific Workers (W.F.S.W.), the World Federation of Teachers' Unions (known by the initials of its French name, F.I.S.E., it has since become absorbed into the W.F.T.U.), the International Association of Democratic Lawyers (I.A.D.L.), the International Organization of Journalists (I.O.J.), the International Union of Students (I.U.S.), and the International Broadcasting Union (again known by its French initials, O.I.R.).

In 1949 the Partisans of Peace movement – later the World Peace Council – was founded. Various offshoots of the W.P.C. were subsequently formed. In 1951 there was the Committee for the Promotion of International Trade, which was disbanded in 1956, though some national committees continued. In 1954 the World Congress of Doctors was formed as an offshoot of the W.P.C., but later became independent under the name of the International Medical Association. Then in 1957 was formed the International Institute for Peace as a front for the W.P.C. itself! In 1951 the International Federation of Resistance Fighters (F.I.R.) was formed by its predecessor, the International Federation of Former Political Prisoners of Fascism, which had itself been formed in 1947. In 1955 a World Congress of Mothers was organized under W.I.D.F. auspices, which set up a Permanent International Committee of Mothers (P.I.C.M.) under the W.I.D.F., with which it shares offices in East Berlin.

The history and development of such international fronts follow a similar pattern. Initially the organizations were apparently non-political and non-partisan. In this way they attracted groups that otherwise would never have responded to communist advances or which would have rejected Soviet policies.

In virtually every example, however, the non-communist members of the international gatherings organized by these bodies soon saw the communist controls being exerted. As a result there was a wave of disaffiliation during the 40's and early 50's, with the disgruntled members forming their own international bodies. Thus in 1949 the International Confederation of Free Trade Unions was formed by those West European and American unions which had worked out of the W.F.T.U., impotent to do anything inside the Union against its Soviet-directed policy opposing such programmes as the Marshall Plan. The World Assembly of Youth was formed in 1952 by those youth organizations which quit the W.F.D.Y., while the International Student Conference was started in 1950 by those Western national student unions which had lost all confidence in the I.U.S. In these two cases the withdrawals were precipitated by the expulsions of the Yugoslav youth and student bodies from the W.F.D.Y. and the I.U.S. following the Cominform break with Tito. The International Commission of Jurists was formed in 1955 by a group of lawyers recognizing the I.A.D.L. as a communist front.

The major international fronts are noteworthy for their 'interlocking directorates', with officials of one being represented on others. In every case leading positions in the fronts are held by Soviet and other Communist Bloc functionaries, though as such they do not necessarily take a large public role: this is left to prominent individuals whose job it is to give the organization popular acceptance. The membership claims for the international fronts are usually large, but presented in such a way as to defy detailed verification. When organizations are members – as distinct from individuals – their own membership figures are put together to make up the communist front head-count. In any case, every one of the fronts listed here relies on its East Bloc affiliates for its main support, whether in numbers, leadership or finance. That from the Western Community or from the uncommitted nations is of little consequence, except for its propaganda value.

These fronts between them cater for all social groups. Trade and professional organizations are covered by the World Federation of Trade Unions, the World Federation of Scientific Workers, the International Organization of Journalists, the International Medical Association and the International Association of Democratic Lawyers. Women are catered for by the Women's International Democratic Federation and its subsidiary, the Permanent International Committee of Mothers. Young people come under the wing of the World Federation of Democratic Youth and the International Union of Students. In the more generalized sense, international affairs are covered by the World Peace Council with a specialized aspect of peace coming under the International Federation of Resistance Fighters. Not only do they have interlocking membership at the top, but their policies on wider issues are co-ordinated whenever the occasion demands. This is particularly noticeable in the way that policy statements of the individual fronts follow the Soviet line of the moment.

All these international fronts have their affiliates and supporters at the national levels. This support is universal from the East Bloc, but it varies in quality and degree outside the Bloc. For such organizations as the W.F.T.U., the W.F.D.Y., the I.A.D.L., the I.O.J. and the I.U.S., which are faced with rival organizations, they have to seek their support in the Western Community from communist and other minority groups. Often, indeed, they can get no organizational support whatever but must rely on individual cadres working within non-communist organizations to agitate on their behalf.[1]

An occasional function of the international fronts is for them to agitate for a particular line of action which is favoured by the communists and opposed by others. This agitation is stimulated by the communist faction running the front. At the right time a Soviet spokesman replies to the demands made in the name of the front supporters and agrees to their 'proposals', which are rejected or ignored by Western spokesmen. In this way a semblance of democracy is given to the process by making it appear that the

[1] Typical was the situation in the 1962 Annual Delegate Meeting of the British National Union of Journalists, where an attempt was made to get the Union involved in preliminary talks with the I.O.J., although it is a firm supporter of the opposing International Federation of Journalists.

communist leadership is bowing to popular demands. This technique, however, is rarely used internationally, though it is frequently encountered in more domestic situations in the Bloc.

In this chapter we have discussed very generally the types of communist front and the means of identifying them. I have refrained from any extensive listing, being content to present a sample from Britain. I have done this deliberately since a complete list would be long and tedious. It would be invidious to include fronts from one part of the world and omit them from another. And again, the communist fronts are far from being static organizations. They come and they go almost overnight. A list prepared now would be out of date in part within months. Every time an issue of East-West politics arises, it brings with it a plethora of fronts rigged up by the communists. When the issue blows over, the front is allowed to collapse.

As we have already seen, the communist fronts are best judged other than by their names or their avowed aims and objects. They show themselves in their real colours by what they do and by the nature of those who run and support them. In such a situation they must be viewed critically both for what they are doing at any one time and what they were doing before then. As we have already said, a communist front is an iceberg, there is far more to it than what can be seen on the surface.

This is best demonstrated by an actual case history, the so-called germ warfare propaganda campaign which took place throughout the world at the time of the Korean fighting in the early 50's. This campaign involved many hundreds of individuals. If all the propagandists and agitators are counted, then the total goes up to thousands. More important, however, is the way in which it was carried out as a joint manœuvre by the world communist movement, the international fronts, their national affiliates and many communist and non-communist personalities. The purpose was to give credence to communist accusations that the Americans were carrying out bacterial warfare in Korea. The campaign lasted two and a half years and then was dropped and hardly referred to again.

This campaign is discussed in detail at the end of the book, so that we can get a real appreciation of the workings of the propaganda machine which was responsible for the campaign. By understanding the workings of this single, gigantic operation of hate we can better evaluate the wider aspects of communist propaganda techniques and the ways in which they have been developed over the 1950's and into the 60's.

# PART TWO

# *Propaganda in its Changing Aspects*

CHAPTER FIVE

# *The Stalinist Trim*

The history of international communism since the end of the Second World War divides itself roughly into three main stages. There was the tough, uncompromising period which marked the last years of Stalin's rule, ending with his death in March 1953. This period saw the Soviet Union continuing as unopposed leader of world communism – Mao Tse-tung's régime in China, established in power only after 1949, was still too busily engaged with internal affairs to take a very active part internationally, apart from the Korean war.

Following the death of Stalin came an interregnum period, that of the so-called collective leadership in Moscow. This lasted until 1957 when Khruschov emerged as the successor to Stalin, as acknowledged head of the Soviet Communist Party and State, with the former members of the old collegium in disgrace. This period was marked by the 1956 revelations of the Twentieth Party Congress in Moscow and the abandonment of the Stalin myth, with the resultant uprising in Hungary and associated troubles right across the Communist Bloc from China to Poland. The repercussions were felt not only within the Bloc, but also within the communist parties of Europe, Asia and Latin America. It was at this period that Communist China began to take a more active international role.

The last period overlaps that of the interregnum, beginning about 1955. From this time onwards communist propaganda began to lose its old Stalinist, unyielding character and took on more sophisticated forms. These in their turn were welcomed by many as signs of a thaw in the Cold War between the Communist Bloc and the rest of the world. With the launching of the sputniks in 1957, and the key to ultimate nuclear warfare in the hands of the Soviet, communist propaganda abandoned earlier defensive themes of capitalist encirclement which so restricted relations with the rest of the world in Stalin's day. Flexibility developed and greater subtleties were employed in propaganda for non-communist consumption, particularly in Asia and Latin America. Africa became a vital new field for operations.

But the monolith was shattered by Stalin's death, and Moscow no longer ruled supreme. There was no longer just one epicentre of world revolution in a curve of the river Moskva, another was breaking the surface south of the Great Wall, in the shadow of the Western Hills. The rise of Communist China as a world power brought with it not only a new propaganda force aimed at the rest of the world but also a new factor within the Communist Bloc itself. The resultant Sino-Soviet relationships and their impacts on communist propaganda are discussed in Chapter 10.

Outwardly, the years immediately following the end of the Second World War suggested the continued relaxation of Soviet relations with the West which had begun after the invasion of Russia by the Nazis in 1941. Looking back we now know that this whole period was one of delusion for the West. In Eastern Europe the consolidation of Moscow-directed communist power proceeded rapidly between 1944 in Rumania and 1948 in Czechoslovakia. From 1949 onwards Moscow was in control right up to a boundary stretching from the Baltic nearly to the Adriatic. Only the expulsion of Yugoslavia from the Cominform kept that line short of the southern sea. Following the expulsion of Tito from the fold there was a wholesale purge of Party leaders throughout the remainder of Eastern Europe, with only Eastern Germany remaining unscathed: Moscow's purge trials of 1936–8 were recreated in Budapest, Prague, Sofia and elsewhere between 1949 and 1952.

In Moscow Stalin reigned supreme, hailed as the genius[1] directly responsible for all the triumphs of Soviet science, art, literature,

[1] The use of the Russian phrase *genialnyi Stalin* ('the brilliant Stalin' or 'Stalin the genius'), showed an interesting example of the side-effects of propaganda intended for translation. It was very often mis-translated into English as 'the genial Stalin' and repeated as such by English communist propagandists!

industry, economics and political direction and the driving-force without whom the Soviet people could not have beaten the fascists during the war, and without whom they could not build communism in the future. These themes not only resounded throughout the Soviet Union itself but to an even greater extent at times in Eastern Europe and in larger communist parties of the non-communist world.

In the first couple of years after the war there was still some sort of contact between Eastern and Western Europe, carried out by relatively unrestricted student exchanges and trade relations. But this period lasted only into 1947 and by 1948 it was virtually finished; the communist coup in Prague ended the official exchange programmes. Even before then, Stalin's opposition to East European participation in the Marshall Plan for the economic rebuilding of Europe had clamped down on any likelihood of East-West economic relationships returning to the old, pre-war levels.

In these early post-war years there were signs of Moscow participating in the various international bodies which had resulted from the wartime co-operation of the Allies. The Soviet Union took part in the formation of the United Nations at the San Francisco Conference in 1945.[1] Soviet delegations were accredited to the specialized agencies of the U.N., while considerable amounts of international relief were accepted through U.N.R.R.A. (the United Nations Relief and Rehabilitation Administration) for the devastated areas of the Ukraine and for Eastern Europe, notably Poland.

But the later years – around 1950 – saw the Soviet Union and almost all the East European members of the specialized agencies resign on the grounds that these agencies were nothing more than tools of Western imperialism. By the time of Stalin's death, communist countries were represented only in the United Nations itself – the General Assembly, the Security Council and the Economic and Social Council – and in these only to use them as sounding-boards for current propaganda lines.

[1] It is worth remembering in this context that in November 1939 the Soviet Union invaded Finland, for which she was expelled from the League of Nations a fortnight later, December 14th, 1939.

In 1952, indeed, Stalin raised the issue as to whether the United Nations was as representative as it claimed. He complained that the system of voting in the General Assembly of one vote per delegation gave the small countries as much power as the Great Powers. This point was never pursued further than the pages of *New Times*, and any possible development was put to an end by his death some months later.

This rejection of the United Nations was symptomatic of Stalin's distrust of the whole of the non-communist world. He saw issues as quite clearly cut. Those not for Soviet policy were against it. There was no neutrality. The Soviet Union was surrounded by its enemies. This capitalist encirclement would mean war unless the world communist movement and its supporters rallied round Moscow and gave Stalin their full allegiance. Those who did not give it were traitors, renegades and deserters to the imperialist camp. Peace could only be equated with socialism, and capitalism meant war.

From the mid-40's onwards the theme of peace and socialism has been pre-eminent in communist propaganda, from the Cold War period which came into the open in 1947 with the formation of the Cominform right into the 1960's. It is around this general line that the propaganda has woven its twisting course.

Thus we see that in Stalin's time a major theme was developed, calling for the abolition of war propaganda. This was codified in 1950–1 by all the countries of Eastern Europe and by the Soviet Union in laws against disseminating war propaganda. The penalties were heavy and the phrasings such that virtually any statement not in official favour could be construed as such, in the sense that being considered anti-Soviet, it therefore favoured capitalist warmongering. In the event, little use was made of this device after the propaganda process had been completed. But it was referred to in Soviet publications ten years later and early in 1962 Soviet spokesmen at the Disarmament Conference in Geneva again raised the whole question of banning war propaganda, demanding that it be incorporated into future international agreements. In May 1962 a joint Soviet-American declaration against war propaganda was agreed affirming that war could no longer serve to settle international disputes. This was already the official Moscow line, as we have seen. The importance lay in the possible different interpretations of the 'war propaganda' concept.

All the time that this campaign was going on, the world communist movement was itself embroiled in a number of wars. Looking at this period we can see two expansionist lines develop. During the early period we see the process of what has been called 'contiguous revolution': the attainment of power by Stalin's henchmen in the countries of Eastern Europe and in North Korea. With a Soviet-held hinterland, Mao Tse-tung swept to power in China in a campaign which began in the north in 1947 and ended in 1949. Within five years of Mao entering Peking in triumph, civil war in the former French Indo-China came to an end with a communist régime in the north of Vietnam, a régime which had enjoyed the military and diplomatic help of her near neighbour, Communist China, as well as of Russia. To this list could be added the final conquest of Tibet by Chinese forces in the late fifties. All these advances of communist territorial control – like those against the Baltic States in 1939–40 – were across common borders, hence the concept of contiguous revolution. They were noteworthy in that they succeeded.

The major failure territorially was the invasion of South Korea by the North in 1950. Here is not the place to discuss the military aspects of the operation, though the propaganda aspects of the Chinese military successes were undoubtedly considerable in Asia at the time. The costs in man-power were heavy and the drain on the Chinese economy considerable. Despite this no ground was gained.

The Korean war may well have been an adventure of its own, with special circumstances that did not apply elsewhere as far as contiguous revolution was concerned. It could rather be considered as a part of the second type of war then being waged by the communists, which might be called 'leapfrog revolution'. This sums up the type of outbreaks at various points in South-east Asia from 1948 onwards. In Burma, Malaya, Indonesia and the Philippines at about this time wars broke out with communist-led insurgents fighting the government forces. In Burma and Indonesia this civil war was relatively short-lived. In the Philippines it continued for years until the rebels were finally eliminated as an effective force. It was fiercest in Malaya – then a British colony – where its effective support was the Chinese, who received their aid from Peking rather than from Moscow. By the end of British rule in Malaya these communist rebel forces had lost their vigour, though they still had a nuisance value in a number of districts.

During this period, all these leapfrog revolutions received the full and open support of the whole communist propaganda system. They were presented as noble campaigns against reaction. In the Marxist context they were considered as just wars, because they were being fought for 'national liberation'. On the other hand, the actions being taken by the threatened governments were illegal and unjust, the communists had long since declared that they were never guilty of aggression or imperialism, because they were communist. Aggression and imperialism were manifestations of capitalism. Communism was opposed to capitalism, therefore it was opposed to and incapable of aggression.

This was the theme in the communist Press and over the radio. It was picked up by all the communist fronts, each of which in its own way gave its support to the guerrillas. This was particularly the case with the World Federation of Democratic Youth and its lesser partner the International Union of Students. In February 1948 they organized jointly a South-east Asian Youth Conference in Calcutta. The overt part of this conference did not attract much attention at the time, but it has long been considered as the cover behind which Asian and European communist experts got together to plan the leapfrog revolutions which followed several months later in Burma, Malaya and Indonesia.

Concurrently with this front conference was held the Second Congress of the Indian Communist Party, also in Calcutta. This adopted a policy of violence which showed itself in strikes and revolts in various cities and provincial centres, with an attempt to overthrow the Hyderabad provincial government in the Telengana district. One of the background features of the 1949 World Youth Festival organized by the World Federation of Democratic Youth and the International Union of Students in Budapest was the petition among delegates in support of the Telegana revolt, organized against a background of denunciation of the Nehru régime as imperialist agents. In 1950 this abortive campaign of violence was abandoned by the Indian communists and the international propaganda in favour of it ceased abruptly.

While the leapfrog revolutions were being tried out unsuccessfully in Asia, the main communist campaigns in Europe were political, aimed at turning the people against their own governments, their governments against each other and Western Europe against the United States. Within the individual countries of Western Europe the national communist parties were adopting 'united front from below' tactics in their approaches to the non-communists left, except in those few cases – such as the Nenni Socialists in Italy – where they could get unity from above. During the period of the Labour Government in Britain (1945–51) they concentrated on attacking the Labour leadership from without, having been effectively prevented any formal participation in the Labour movement by the straightforward defensive weapon of proscription, which barred members of the Labour Party joining communist or communist front bodies on the Party's proscribed list. Similar measures taken by most of the major unions prevented any member of the communist party from holding executive office.[1]

This period saw the beginning of the decline in popular support for the European communist parties, following their wartime high-spots. As this decline of the overt parties set in, so did the activities of the covert communist fronts step up at the international and national level. We have already discussed these in general terms. Here we put them into the context of time.

In 1945 and 1946 the main international communist fronts aimed at special groups were set up by respective international congresses. They almost all had considerable non-communist

[1] The list of proscribed organizations published by the Labour Party is given in Appendix III. It should be remembered that in Britain this list also includes fascist organizations. Similarly in the U.S.A. the official *Guide to Subversive Organizations and Publications* covers fascist as well as communist organizations, though in both cases few fascist bodies are listed because few exist. In the case of the British trade unions a few were communist-dominated in the late 40's and early 50's and the smaller ones still continued so into the 60's. But in 1961 the most notable of the communist-run unions, the Electrical Trades Union, had an internal purge which dramatically swept the communists out of power, despite extensive rearguard actions.

support at this stage, though in every case but one they were in fact safely under communist control from the beginning. In 1945 the World Federation of Trade Unions (W.F.T.U.) and the World Federation of Democratic Youth (W.F.D.Y.) were both founded by Congresses held in London, a factor exploited to the full in their propaganda ever since. In the same year the Women's International Democratic Federation (W.I.D.F.) was formed in Paris: in this last case it had few non-communist member organizations of any size and never received any support from the major international or national women's organizations of Western Europe or North America.

In 1946 the following fronts were formed, all with non-communist support: the International Association of Democratic Lawyers (I.A.D.L.), the International Union of Students (I.U.S.), the World Federation of Scientific Workers (W.F.S.W.), the International Organization of Journalists (I.O.J.). The World Federation of Teachers' Unions (F.I.S.G.) was also formed in 1946, but it has never had much non-communist support and is really a Trade Department of the W.F.T.U., with a professional rather than a trade aspect.

In 1949 the World Peace Council (W.P.C.) was founded by a Congress held concurrently in Paris and Prague, the latter being for those delegates from communist countries who could not get French visas in time. The initiative for it had been taken some months earlier, in the autumn of 1948, by a Congress of Intellectuals for Peace held in Wroclaw (Breslau). In its turn the W.P.C. – known for a time in its early days as the Movement of Partisans for Peace – organized an International Economic Conference in Moscow in April 1952. The organizing committee for this continued in existence until 1956, first as the Committee for the Promotion of International Trade (C.P.I.T.) and later as the International Committee for the Promotion of Trade. It was wound up in 1956 after abortive attempts to organize a second world economic conference, but its activities are still continued by a number of national committees, of which the most active in the non-communist world is the British Council for the Promotion of International Trade.

Another offshoot of the W.P.C. is the International Medical

Association, founded at the World Congress of Doctors organized under W.P.C. auspices in 1954. In 1957 the W.P.C. set up the International Institute of Peace in Vienna, to act as a cover when it was expelled by the Austrian authorities as a threat to the neutrality laid down for Austria by the 1955 Peace Treaty. Also in 1957 the W.P.C. saw another of its brain-children established in a home. This was the Afro-Asian People's Solidarity Council in Cairo, born at a W.P.C.-backed Asian peace conference organized in Delhi in 1955 as part of the communist plan to capitalize on the Bandung Conference of Asian governments which was taking place at the same time. Last of the offshoots was the Permament International Committee of Mothers, conceived by the W.I.D.F. in 1955. Like its parent body, it has so far not enjoyed non-communist support on any scale.

Passing mention should be given to the International Federation of Resistance Fighters (F.I.R.), formed in 1951 out of the International Federation of Former Political Prisoners of Fascism, itself founded in 1947 in Paris. This again has had little non-communist support and operates almost entirely in Europe.

The main international fronts were founded during this first Stalinist period and their very monolithic nature soon brought about the wholesale resignations of the non-communist members. This was noticeably so in 1948 with the W.F.T.U., the W.F.D.Y., the I.U.S. and the I.A.D.L. The first three lost members through the disillusion created by their violent attacks on the Marshall Plan, the European Defence Community, the creation of the German Federal Republic as a full political body in Western Germany and all other attempts to attain the political and economic recovery of Western Europe. The W.F.T.U. in particular came under strong criticism for the way it tried to organize dock strikes in France and West Germany. The I.A.D.L. came under fire from Western lawyers for the way it condoned political arrests and trials in Eastern Europe, while the I.U.S. lost much support because of its failure to take any action over government reprisals against students in Czechoslovakia at the time of the 1948 coup in Prague.

Disillusion with the four bodies specifically brought about the formation of new, non-communist organizations. In 1949 the

International Confederation of Free Trade Unions (I.C.F.T.U.) and the World Assembly of Youth (W.A.Y.) were founded by the West European and North American bodies which had resigned from the W.F.T.U. and W.F.D.Y. In 1950 the disillusioned Western student unions formed the Co-ordinating Secretariat of National Unions of Students (Cosec) as an alternative to the I.U.S., followed some time afterwards by the International Commission of Jurists as the non-communist alternative to the I.A.D.L. Disillusion in the ranks of Western journalists came by 1949, when the British president of the I.O.J. resigned, saying – as did other such Western officers of other fronts – that it had become 'in effect, a branch office of the Cominform'. The disillusioned set up the International Federation of Journalists as a democratic alternative.

During all this time these organizations were claiming vast increases in total membership. The W.F.T.U., for instance, has stated the following totals over the years: 1945 – 62 millions, 1949 – 72 million, 1956 – 88 million, 1959 – 95 millon, 1961 – 119.5 million. During this period there were no significant additions from the non-communist world, so the additions must have come from the Communist Bloc. Though no breakdowns are given only about fifteen per cent of W.F.T.U. membership is from outside the communist world – some 12 million members against the 55 million of the I.C.F.T.U.

In 1945 the W.F.D.Y. claimed 40 million affiliated membership. Despite the resignations of almost every non-communist affiliate the claim had risen to 70 million, by 1954 to 85 million, and by 1959 to 87 million. Here again the bulk of the rise is from the Communist Bloc, particularly from China. In 1946 the I.U.S. claimed 1,500,000 student members. Despite the resignations of 1948–50, this figure had risen to 5 million by that latter year and 6 million by 1953. Only in 1954 did the claim start to fall, being then cited as 'over 5 million'. By 1956 it had dropped again to 3¼ million.

Such were the basic situations as they developed in the mass communist fronts. By the end of the 40's they had lost their non-communist veneers and their usefulness as instruments of communist policy was considerably diminished. New organizations were being formed which competed directly in the fields where they had expected to work unhindered, competing without the need to toe the Stalin line of the moment.

Against such a background of declining influence came the formation of the World Peace Council[1] in April 1949. This had many advantages. Firstly, its declared concern was peace in all its aspects. As such it had the potential to attract those who might be scared off by the more specific activities of the existing sectional fronts. Its spread of interests was its advantage. Much of its work could be hived off to the other fronts, which in their turn would be represented at its meetings. It was developed in a deliberately nebulous way. It is made up of individuals and representatives of organizations, both international and national. It makes no claims to arithmetical membership. Such claims as it does make are to those signing its various world appeals and these figures are astronomical. The first and most famous, the Stockholm Appeal of 1950 for the banning of atomic weapons, collected millions of signatures from the world over. The Warsaw Appeal, which followed later the same year and called for a Five-Power Peace Conference, collected a claimed 600 million signatures. The Vienna Appeal of 1955 repeated the Stockholm message and collected 650 million signatures. Other campaigns of this nature were also run and the W.P.C. claimed the credit for 'forcing' the Western powers to negotiate, when the Soviet Union finally agreed to meet them at Geneva in 1954.

Other early activities of the W.P.C. included the convening of the Moscow Economic Conference in April 1952, the launching of the Germ Warfare propaganda campaign (discussed fully in Chapters 9–11) a month earlier, the organizing of successive peace congresses, which later became rather more informal and better camouflaged 'meetings', the setting up of regional organizations and ancillary bodies, the most important in recent times being the Afro-Asian People's Solidarity Organization in Cairo. Right at the beginning, it instituted annual International Peace Prizes worth £5,000 each for literary, artistic, film or scientific contributions to peace. These are quite distinct from the Soviet Government's Stalin Peace Prizes (renamed Lenin Peace Prizes from 1956

[1] Now more usually known as the World Council of Peace (W.C.P.).

onwards) which have been awarded in their time to nearly all the W.P.C. leaders.

Thus in the World Peace Council we can already see the beginning of flexibility in the communist propaganda approach, even before Stalin's death. This flexibility was showing itself in small ways elsewhere. In 1952, for instance, the International Union of Students reversed its previously unyielding attitude on national student unions becoming associate members, enabling them to take part in its practical activities without becoming committed to its political policies. In the Marxist sense this concept was meaningless and had been rejected as such by the I.U.S. leadership for some years. The change of tactic came several months before Stalin's death, though it was too late to be an effective method of holding non-communist affiliations. The remainder of the West European national unions left in 1952 and 1953 and only a handful of new bodies took associate categories.

At the same time as the international fronts were changing their patterns of action, the national Communist Bloc friendship societies were developing. In most of Western Europe there already existed various kinds of Soviet friendship society, such as the Society for Cultural Relations with the U.S.S.R. in London, the Scottish-U.S.S.R. Society and its English brother, the British-Soviet Friendship Society. Similar friendship societies were formed in the late 40's to cover the various countries of Eastern Europe, particularly Poland, Czechoslovakia and Hungary. They organized delegation visits, film shows, exhibitions and tours by choirs, dance ensembles and individual artistes. Membership subscriptions were low and considerable subsidies were received from the embassies and legations of the communist countries concerned. As far as the communist friendship societies in Britain are concerned – and these were and still are typical of the general run – they usually sported a sponsoring list of eminent names from the arts and professions, while having established members of the Communist Party in control of the actual day to day running of the societies' affairs, but keeping discreetly out of the limelight. This was as true in the early 60's as it was in the late forties.

It is important to remember that these friendship societies of the 40's and 50's only operated outside the Communist Bloc. Immediately after the war there was a Czechoslovak-British Friendship Society active in Prague, supported particularly by the large number of Czechs who had fought in the West during the war and who had returned with British wives. But this was closed down by the Czech authorities early in 1950, at about the same time as they had closed down the British reading-rooms which until then had been run by the British Council in Prague and Bratislava. Similar reading-rooms were also closed down in the other parts of Eastern Europe where the British Council had until then been allowed to run cultural activities on a limited basis.

The prime function of the friendship societies was to generate a positive support of communist policies in the countries concerned. This was noticeably so in the case of the Soviet friendship societies, which laid great stress on economic and social successes in the U.S.S.R. In this considerable use was made of the Great Constructions of the Stalin era, such as the grandiose plans to plant huge tree belts across the great plains of the southern Ukraine and Siberia and, to dig 1,400 miles of canal across the deserts of Turkmenia.[1] Delegation visitors returning from Russia at this time were full of these programmes and what they promised for the future as part of the fulfilment and overfulfilment of the economic plans laid down by Stalin.

Typical of the world-wide presentation of these new Soviet Construction schemes was that given to a meeting attended by a thousand people at Battersea Town Hall, London, in January 1952. Dr S. M. Manton, F.R.S., discussed the biological aspects of the projects while the physicist Professor J. D. Bernal, F.R.S. – presented as having made a special study of Soviet building and engineering during three visits to the U.S.S.R. – spoke on the engineer and Nature.

'All the schemes,' Professor Bernal declared confidently, 'will be finished, if there is no war, by 1957. When they are, the additional food and power they will produce will put the Soviet Union once and for all out of reach of any fluctuations of climate, and will provide such riches as will ensure a peaceful transition to

[1] This Grand Turkmenian Canal project faded out in 1954. It should not be confused with the far more modest Kara Kum canal of a decade later.

communism, where each gives according to his ability and receives according to his needs'.[1]

This meeting was organized by the Society for Cultural Relations with the U.S.S.R., which supported it with a special exhibition, which was afterwards put on national loan, together with a selection of supporting films from the U.S.S.R. The S.C.R., as it has always been known, plays the cultural Box to the more political Cox of its partner the British-Soviet Friendship Society.

This political background was set in 1953 for the S.C.R. by its President, D. N. Pritt, Q.C., who has for long played a leading role in such international communist fronts as the I.A.D.L., of which he is also President, and the World Peace Council. In the Spring 1953 number of the S.C.R.'s *Anglo-Soviet Journal* he wrote an obituary on Stalin in the name of the Society and its members.

What, he asked rhetorically, did members of the S.C.R. – with their particular interest in cultural relations – owe to the great Joseph Stalin? It was their privilege, he answered, to record gratefully the new concept Stalin had given to the dignity of man. Thanks to Stalin's work and that done under his inspiration, man's personality was no longer cramped. After elaborating on this point, he concluded with a dedication on behalf of the members to the 'conscious, purposeful humanism' which Stalin had brought into their lives, and through which they might hope to build for themselves and others, a world of peace and growing culture.

This was the message of the communist *Agitprop* throughout the world into the early 50's. How the system changed and developed in the decade which followed will be discussed in the next chapter.

[1] In March 1962 Khruschov scathingly dismissed what he called 'the so-called plan for the transformation of nature'.

CHAPTER SIX

# The New Look

Though there were initial hesitancies during the interregnum of the collective leadership period in the Soviet Union which followed the death of Stalin in March 1953, the mid-50's saw the new, more buoyant phase of the Soviet-led international communist propaganda get under way. Greater and more flexible use was being made of all media of communication, both at home and abroad: radio, publications, delegations, tourism, cultural exchanges, diplomatic approaches. To these forms of propaganda by the spoken and written word was added the fundamental new form of propaganda by action, economic aid. No more and no less than before, this opening up of the communist system in its relations with the rest of the world was a controlled function, an adaptation of tactics to suit a new series of situations arising from the death of a hitherto deathless omnipotent.

Some of these situations could be foreseen, some could only be dealt with as they arose. Foreseen was the expectation of the non-communist world that a thaw would set in following Stalin's death. Equally foreseen was the same expectation from within the communist world itself. Unforeseen was the reaction to the thaw when it came. In this chapter we shall concern ourselves with the general trend of communist propaganda techniques for non-communists as they developed in the post-Stalin 50's and early 60's. In Chapter 7 we shall turn to the unforeseen factors brought about by the rise of China, the concept of polycentrism and the challenge to Moscow as the vanguard of the world communist revolutionary movement.

Throughout the whole period we are discussing, the most striking demonstration of communism's increasing use of the propaganda weapon is the rapidly-expanding use made of international radio broadcasting. We have already noted in passing that as far back as 1933 the Soviet Union had introduced regular German-language broadcasts over the long-wave Moscow transmitter. Short-wave transmitters were added in 1934 and by 1942 Moscow and Kuibyshev short-wave stations were on the air 400 hours a week in seventeen foreign languages. The installations were severely damaged during the war, but they were given priority rebuilding and by 1948 they were putting out 334 hours a week in thirty-one languages, directed at all parts of the world.

By this time the Soviet radio facilities were being joined by those of Eastern Europe and Communist China, the latter from a station in communist-held Yenan. In that same year Radio Pyongyang began broadcasting North Korean programmes to South Korea. Various clandestine communist stations were also on the air by that time. Only Hungary, Eastern Germany and parts of what was then French Indo-China held by communist Viet-minh had still to take the air internationally: it was 1954 before Radio Hanoi took the place of spasmodic clandestine Viet-minh stations and became the voice of the newly-formed communist North Vietnam.

In all some 600 hours a week in thirty-six languages were being broadcast internationally by the Communist Bloc transmitters in 1948. By the beginning of 1961 this total had risen to over 3,200 hours in fifty-six languages, a more than five-fold increase in broadcasting time over the span of a dozen years.

In 1950 the Communist Bloc was broadcasting 1,100 hours abroad weekly. At the same time the combined overseas transmissions of the BBC and the Voice of America was slightly greater than 1,150 hours. By 1955 the Communist Bloc transmissions had risen to 1,900 hours weekly and the B.B.C.–V.O.A. total to 1,500 hours. Nineteen-fifty-six saw a great if temporary upsurge in the V.O.A. transmissions but the Communist Bloc output of 2,100 hours weekly was still well ahead of the B.B.C.–V.O.A. total of 1,600 hours. By 1960 the Communist Bloc had reached 2,900 hours while the B.B.C.–V.O.A. fell short of 1,200 hours. In making these comparisons only the British Broadcasting Corporation and the Voice of America are taken into account as they have the biggest international audience of the Western transmitters. Such transmitters as Radio Free Europe and Radio Liberty are not included as they are solely concerned with audiences inside the Soviet Bloc.

WEEKLY HOURS OF INTERNATIONAL BROADCASTING BY COMMUNIST BLOC RADIO STATIONS 1948–1960

| | *8/48* | *12/54* | *12/60* |
|---|---|---|---|
| U.S.S.R. | 334 | 623 | 997 |
| Eastern Europe | 178 | 764 | 1066 |
| Communist China | 16 | 116 | 687 |
| Far East Orbit | 11 | 35 | 271 |
| Clandestine | 70 | 137 | 182 |
| TOTALS | 609 | 1675 | 3203 |

*Notes:*

1. Figures represent total transmission time, including repeats, as no exact differentiation between original programme hours and repeat transmissions is available.
2. U.S.S.R. figures include output of Radio Moscow as well as other U.S.S.R. stations originating external broadcasts.
3. Communist China's output includes broadcasts to Taiwan and Quemoy.
4. The Far East Orbit radios are those at Pyongyang, Hanoi, and Ulan Bator.
5. Figures are rounded.

WEEKLY HOURS OF INTERNATIONAL BROADCASTING BY COMMUNIST BLOC RADIO STATIONS, 1960

| | U.S.S.R. | Eastern Europe | Communist China | Far East Orbit | Clandestine | Total |
|---|---|---|---|---|---|---|
| TO | | | | | | |
| Western Europe | 256:00 | 442:15 | 63:00 | – | 128:10 | 889:25 |
| Eastern Europe | 58:15 | – | – | – | – | 58:15 |
| Yugoslavia | 29:45 | 38:55 | – | – | – | 68:40 |
| Europe (total) | 344:00 | 481:10 | 63:00 | – | 128:10 | 1016:20 |
| Near East and South Asia | 264:50 | 288:25 | 70:00 | – | 24:40 | 647:55 |
| Africa[1] | 42:00 | 19:50 | 35:00 | – | – | 96:50 |
| Far East | 119:00 | 6:25 | 410:55 | 270:50 | – | 807:10 |
| Latin America | 56:00 | 80:10 | 31:30 | – | – | 167:40 |
| North America | 108:00 | 105:00 | 56:00 | – | 7:00 | 276:00 |
| Other[2] | 63:05 | 85:00 | 21:00 | – | 22:30 | 191:35 |
| WORLD TOTAL | 996:55 | 1066:00 | 687:25 | 270:50 | 182:20 | 3205:30 |

[1] An additional 66:30 hours per week, exclusive of Arabic, were partially beamed to Africa by the Bloc.

[2] Target area not specified; to compatriots abroad outside the Americas.

Such are the bare figures which highlight the dramatic increase in Communist Bloc broadcasting for abroad. They are elaborated statistically in the tables adjoining which give an idea of the directions in which this tremendous technical propaganda exercise has been made. Over the years since 1948 there were marked fluctuations in the direction of the campaign. Initially Western Europe was subjected to the most concentration, with some increase in attention to North America. Following the break with Tito, broadcasts specifically intended for Yugoslavia were increased out of all proportion to the size of the target. In the two years following Stalin's death, there was a reversal of policy from feuding with Tito to wooing him and this was reflected in the Soviet Bloc broadcasts for the area. In 1948 they totalled 24 hours weekly. They were up to 77 hours in 1949, 143 hours in 1950 and 193 hours in 1951. In 1949 a clandestine 'Free Yugoslavia' transmitter was brought into operation against Tito. By 1954 this station had been closed down, at the same time as the general broadcasts were falling, declining to 60 hours by 1958. In that year there was a reversal of the mitigated approach, which showed itself by a small increase in radio propaganda to 68 hours weekly in 1959, at which rate it remained into 1962.

In one sense Yugoslavia was and still is a special case. Following the death of Stalin there was increasing interest by his successors in areas farther afield, particularly Asia, from 1955 onwards. It was this year which saw the beginning of the spectacular increases in output from Peking radio. From 1948 to 1954 the weekly total had risen from 16 hours to 116 hours, representing only seven per cent of the world communist output. In 1955 the Chinese figure rose to 157 hours, rising still more sharply to 512 hours in 1949, representing eighteen per cent of the world communist total. By the beginning of 1961 it was higher still at 687 hours, twenty-one per cent of the total output.

After the Suez crisis of 1956, greater attention was paid to the Near and Middle East, together with Latin America, though in relative terms these areas received only moderate attention. The biggest expansion was that for Africa. Broadcasts to this continent started in 1956 with 3½ hours weekly. In 1959 this had reached 51 hours and in 1960 the figure almost doubled to 97 hours weekly. To these should be added for 1960 a further 66 hours intended for other areas, but beamed also to Africa.

Early in 1960, Radio Moscow started regular broadcasts in Swahili, the first African language to be used on a schedule basis. These broadcasts were doubled in 1961 and have been followed by other African languages such as Hausa and Somali, as well as the lingae francae of English, French and Portuguese. Arabic transmissions are mainly intended for the Mahgreb countries and the U.A.R. but they too can be heard south of the Sahara.

By the beginning of 1961, more than one-third of the communist broadcasts were from the combined transmitters of the East European stations at 1,066 hours weekly. Second came the U.S.S.R. with 997 hours, third China with 687 hours, fourth the other Asian communist stations with 271 hours[1] and lastly the clandestine stations with 182 hours weekly.

Though the clandestine transmissions represent a relatively small part of the total output, they are important because they are intended for special targets and because they are not acknowledged by any of the communist countries. They usually appear when the communists consider a situation in an area calls for extreme measures, transcending accepted diplomatic procedures and language. In such a situation a radio station with an appropriate name is suddenly heard over the air from an undisclosed spot. Claiming to speak in the name of the people, it criticizes the existing régime in deliberately violent terms and may well call for the overthrow of the government in the name of democracy and freedom. When its purpose is done, it disappears.

The oldest of the clandestine communist radios is that for Spain, which started in 1941 as *Radio España Independendiente* (R.E.I.). In 1948 it was the only clandestine station surviving from the war and it has continued its violent anti-Franco broadcasts into the 1960's. It has naturally taken advantage of all open signs of internal discontent, such as the strike situations in June 1959 and again in May 1962.

Two clandestine stations were started for Western Europe in 1950. One for France (*Ce soir en France* and *Ce matin en France*,

[1] These do not include Mongolian international broadcasting, which started in 1961.

according to the time of day) lasted for five years and specialized in speeches by leading French communists. The transmission for Italy (*Oggi in Italia*) was still on the air in 1960, despite official Italian protests in 1955 and again in 1958, claiming interference in Italian elections. Another programme for Western Europe started in 1956 with the *German Freedom Station 904*, which began broadcasts to the German Federal Republic in August 1956, immediately following the banning of the communist party there. In October 1960 this was supplemented by a programme for the West German armed forces, the *German Soldiers' Station*, part of a general drive directed from East Germany, aimed at causing disaffection in the Federal German Army. In addition to these radio transmissions, two illicit publications and printed appeals were distributed on a large scale to the home addresses of reservists as well as serving officers and men.

*Radio Free Greece* was operated by the Greek Communist Party in exile from 1947 until 1956, when East European diplomatic approaches to Greece started. Last of the European clandestine stations is *Radio Free Portugal*, a product of the 1960's which in April 1962 broadcast the text of a call by the Portuguese Communist Party to the youth of Portugal to rise against the war in Angola.

Attacks on the Shah's régime in Iran have been made intermittently by overt Soviet stations and for a while they were supplemented by the clandestine *Azerbaijan Democratic Radio*, which developed the overt broadcasts in vituperative forms. These attacks on the Shah and his government of the day were in Persian, Azerbaijani and Kurdish and openly supported the suppressed communist Tudeh Party, while inciting the people on the Iran-Soviet borderlands to revolt. The station ceased in August 1953. In April 1959 its place was taken by the present clandestine *National Voice of Iran* radio, which dwells on the theme that the Shah has sold out Iran to the foreigners. Originally in Persian, Azerbaijani was added later.

The *Voice of Truth* is in Greek and Turkish for the Middle East, starting in March 1958 and taking a line similar to that of the now defunct *Radio Free Greece*. At about the same time in 1958 a clandestine station directed at Turkey was begun with the name

*Bizim Radyo* (Our Radio). It directed its attacks not only against the Turkish régime, but also against American activities and policy in relation to Turkey. In January 1964 when the new crisis in Cyprus started the *Voice of Truth* alleged Turkish aggression against the Greek population while *Bizim Radyo* alleged the Turkish community was being threatened by the Greeks.

Apart from the clandestine Viet-minh transmitters which operated during the war in the then French Indo-China – and which ceased operations in November 1954 after the Geneva agreement – there has been only one clandestine station from communist sources for Asia. This was *Radio Free Japan*, which started in May 1952 and went off the air in January 1956, by which time the Communist Bloc were trying to normalize relations with Japan. This relaxation of pressure by suspending the clandestine broadcasts was accompanied by more substantial overtures, including the repatriation of Japanese nationals and an increase in trade.

These clandestine transmissions were directed against the nationals of other countries. More overt, but in a sense part of the same process, were the broadcasts from certain stations directed at emigrant colonies from the Communist Bloc in other parts of the world.

These transmissions for exiles – whether old-established or post-communist – have always been part of a general propaganda drive either to get them to return to their homelands or to persuade them by cajolery or threats to support communist policies in the new lands of their choice. In Latin America especially there were set up during the late 40's and 50's national networks of *émigré* clubs and social groups for Communist Bloc exiles, run with the backing and financial aid of the communist diplomatic missions concerned. In Western Europe this was particularly noticeable among the Polish groups, which had settled before the war in north-west France, and the similar post-war Polish groups in Britain. For some years after 1948 the Polish embassy covertly financed on a lavish scale such a social club in London, the *Polskie Towarzystwo Kulturalno-Spoleczne*, which distributed Warsaw and local Polish newspapers and magazines around the Polish communities in Britain, organized local Polish football leagues, ran film shows of the latest

SOVIET BOOK PRODUCTION FOR ABROAD 1956–60
(Books of 50 pages or more)

| *Languages* | *No. of Titles* | | | *No. of Copies* | | |
|---|---|---|---|---|---|---|
| | *1956* | *1958* | *1960* | *1956* | *1958* | *1960* |
| German | 151 | 173 | 221 | 16,990,100 | 12,667,300 | 18,488,500 |
| English | 240 | 258 | 373 | 7,743,250 | 11,560,600 | 14,602,600 |
| French | 118 | 117 | 178 | 2,260,500 | 2,329,500 | 5,491,500 |
| Bengali | 1 | 17 | 29 | 20,000 | 217,500 | 125,000 |
| Spanish | 33 | 32 | 87 | 248,000 | 149,700 | 735,500 |
| Hindi | – | 19 | 37 | – | 146,800 | 185,400 |
| Arabic | 7 | 13 | 38 | 83,915 | 81,500 | 211,600 |
| Finnish | 43 | 25 | 30 | 424,400 | 55,500 | n.a. |
| Persian | – | 7 | 14 | – | 44,600 | 48,500 |
| Urdu | 5 | 9 | 26 | 59,500 | 38,000 | 60,000 |
| Dutch | – | 5 | 5 | – | 28,400 | 20,000 |
| Swedish | 8 | 4 | 6 | 39,500 | 17,000 | 40,000 |
| Esperanto | – | 1 | – | – | 10,000 | – |
| Japanese | 2 | 2 | 3 | 3,100 | 9,500 | 12,500 |
| Kurdish | – | 4 | 6 | – | 4,000 | 5,500 |
| Norwegian | – | 1 | 1 | – | 2,500 | 2,500 |
| Italian | – | – | 1 | – | – | 10,000 |
| Serbo-Croat | 4 | – | 2 | 17,000 | – | 10,000 |
| Portuguese | – | – | – | – | – | – |
| Greek | – | – | – | – | – | – |
| Turkish | – | – | – | – | – | – |
| Indonesian | – | – | 4 | – | – | 34,500 |
| Farsi | – | – | 2 | – | – | 4,500 |
| Farsi-Kabul | – | – | 2 | – | – | 1,700 |
| Tamil | – | – | 3 | – | – | 10,900 |
| Tagalog | – | – | 1 | – | – | 3,000 |
| Punjabi | – | – | 1 | – | – | 1,200 |
| Amharic | – | – | 1 | – | – | 500 |
| Burmese | – | – | 4 | – | – | 8,000 |
| TOTALS: | 613 | 687 | 1,075 | 27,892,265 | 27,371,900 | 40,113,400 |

*Notes:*

1. The German publications include those for distribution in Eastern Germany: there is no breakdown showing how many go there.
2. Though no books were published in the years chosen in Portuguese, Greek or Turkish, single titles of each in prints of 6,000, 2,000 and 1,000 respectively were published in 1959.
3. Details for 1957 and 1959 have not been given as they only demonstrate the general trend as shown here. The totals are as follows: 1957 – 701 titles and 29,301,400 copies; 1959 – 830 titles and 30,596,660 copies.
4. These figures do not include the large numbers of titles in the original Russian and other languages of the Soviet Union which are exported to countries outside the East Bloc.

Polish titles and arranged for *emigré* children to go for holidays in Poland. Following the deportation by the British authorities back to Poland of several of its organizers it had virtually ceased by the mid-50's, confining its activities primarily to acting as a rest centre and hostel for the crews of Polish ships calling at the port of London.

Together with the rapid increase in radio propaganda the output of the printed word developed proportionately. It is not possible to give any quantitative assessment of the propaganda output intended specifically for foreign consumption before 1956, but the picture since then is clear, as the details given in the table opposite show. In fact this is only part of the whole picture, but – representing Soviet output as it does – it is the major part. Taking books of fifty pages upwards only, and thus excluding large numbers of pamphlets, we see that the number of titles published for abroad rose from some 600 in 1956 to well over 1,000 in 1960. The number of copies in this period rose from nearly 28 million to well over 40 million.

From the figures available for 1954 and 1955, for instance, 830 titles for foreign readers were published in 1954 and 912 titles in 1955, with a total of 29·7 million and 21·1 million copies respectively. But these were for all publications, including pamphlets, so the actual book production would be considerably lower.

Such statistics as these confirm what most of us know from the evidence of our own eyes. Communist printed propaganda is widely and lavishly distributed. At this stage we are only concerned with that printed in the communist world for distribution outside. Indigenous communist publications are not taken into account, though in their localized influence they are often more effective than the general material put out for overall consumption from Moscow, Peking and other centres.

In the qualitative sense the death of Stalin was followed by an all-round improvement in the presentation of communist propaganda. Until 1953 the publications from Moscow in particular were rendered ineffective as much by their dullness as by their enforced adulation of Stalin. The English-language publications were written or translated in such a heavy way as to be almost unreadable. Relatively few Russian books were permitted for export and the magazine subscription list for foreign readers of Soviet publications was confined to the Moscow Central Press, and not to every title of these. In effect there was an export ban on any publication which might reveal from its reportage of local affairs something about the daily life of Russians under Stalin. The same applied to scientific journals, which were almost all restricted in their circulation abroad. At the same time, of course, there was complete censorship of all foreign publications entering the Soviet Union and the East European countries (after about 1948–9). This control outwards and inwards was vested in the respective book import-export organizations such as *Mezhdunarodnaya Kniga* in Moscow.

The export controls for Soviet books began to ease from 1954 onwards, when the Soviet republican newspapers in the local languages and in Russian were put into the export catalogue. The 53-page periodicals export catalogue for 1955 had expanded to a larger-paged volume of 276 pages by 1962. The expanded list for 1955 was still less than 400 titles, against over 3,300 titles in 1962. But even at this, the 1962 list of periodicals permitted for export did not include any local newspapers, even such widely-quoted ones as the Moscow evening paper *Verchernaya Moskva* or the daily *Moskovskaya Pravda*.

From now on there was a corresponding expansion in the distribution of Communist Bloc prestige magazines, a partial list of which is given opposite. They became steadily more polished and subtle in their presentation of the communist case and by the early 1960's their prices had dropped considerably. Outstanding in this respect were the monthly *Soviet Union* and the weekly *Peking Review*. *Soviet Union* was originally a rather large and cumbersome colour magazine. The postal subscription for it in the United Kingdom up to 1957 was fifteen shillings, itself a cheap price for a lavish monthly. After this date it was reduced to a more manageable size and the quality of writing and pictures used in it were improved. At the same time the subscription fell to ten shillings a year, with a twenty-five per cent introductory reduction for new subscribers taking out two years at a time. This reduction applied to three other such Soviet magazines for abroad.

The *Peking Review* is quite different in its concept. It is a weekly news magazine and review of current affairs which began in 1957 and which is airmailed from Peking to any address in the world. The United Kingdom subscription is twenty-four shillings annually. This would not be sufficient to pay normal airmail charges.[1]

As the list of Communist Bloc publications for abroad shows, there is every opportunity taken to put over the Party line in the manner appropriate to different publics. In every country where they maintain diplomatic posts, the Communist Bloc countries publish their own news sheets and periodicals locally as part of their normal information services. These in their turn are supplemented by the local communist party and front publications, such as those listed in Appendix II. Though the indigenous publications are usually sold at commercial rates, the Bloc embassy publications are free or very cheap. The *Soviet Weekly* published by the Soviet Embassy in London was recently *raised* in price to fifteen shillings a year for postal subscribers, at which price it just covers the mailing charges of this well-produced twelve-page tabloid newspaper in two colours.

One reason for the improvement of communist propaganda materials in the mid-50's was the provision of new printing works at that time and the emphasis put on the whole question at the Twentieth Party Congress in 1956. The printing plant expansion embarked upon after this Congress was expected to add 100 million volumes a year to Soviet book output.

The mid-50's mark the beginning of what could be called the Outward Bound period in communist personal relations, particularly as applied to the Soviet Union.

The first Soviet tourists to go outside the Communist Bloc visited Britain in 1954 as part of an exchange scheme. More and more parts of the Soviet Union and Eastern Europe were opened up to foreign visitors as the 50's advanced into the 60's. This freedom of movement was relative to the excessive restrictions of Stalin's day, when tourism as such in the Communist Bloc did not exist. Even in 1963 large areas of the Soviet Union remained forbidden to foreign visitors without special permits. In 1961 several thousand motorists from Western Europe had driven themselves

[1] Similarly low subscription rates are charged for the main Russian-language newspapers. Thus *Pravda* is airmailed to foreign subscribers for 365 days a year at a total cost of under £2.

to Moscow and other major Soviet centres west of the Urals, travelling along a limited number of major trunk roads off which they could not stray. These individual tours were permitted under stringent controls (an official Soviet interpreter had to be carried, for instance, at the motorist's expense). A similar programme prepared by Intourist for 1962 was cancelled without any warning early in that year and all private touring of this nature by West Europeans was forbidden. Coach tours were restricted to certain routes. There were some relaxations in 1963.

Onerous though these restrictions were in absolute terms, the increased opportunities for tourism inwards and outwards of the Soviet Bloc represented a relative step forwards in terms of propaganda. A major weakness of Stalin's closed system was removed. Non-communist reactions in many cases helped increase the propaganda impact. For instance, in 1963 visitors to Moscow still returned home emphatic that they had *not* been followed by the secret police, deducing from this that communism had changed out off all recognition. This impression was heightened because the visitors noted that Russians smiled at them and were glad to see them. From such simple personal acts, the impressionable visitor to the Communist Bloc is prepared to build up a whole new concept of peaceful coexistence to suit what he chooses to interpret as the communist world outlook.

By 1962 tourism in many ways was back in essence to delegation travel. For Communist Bloc tourists there was in any case little alternative to the delegation system, for few left their own countries on visits other than in groups. In fact, the Soviet references to the increase in exchanges use the sense of tourism as inclusive of all kinds of delegation visits, whether inwards or outwards.

Apart from administrative ease and economies of cost, delegation travel offers the advantages of greater control of individuals within the group by a relatively small number of key officials. This had been a notable feature of communist organized delegations for a number of years, with a mass of non-communists supervised – often without any of them knowing it – by one or two Party officials in commanding, though unobtrusive, positions.

If the 1960's saw continued restrictions on tourists, it was within the framework of a greater freedom of movement for everyone than was the case ten years earlier. At the same time, however, a phenomenon of the tail-end of the Stalin period came to the fore again after some years of relative obscurity. This was the campaign on the domestic front for continued vigilance against Western espionage and the intrigues of imperialist agents in disguise.

In the late 40's and early 50's this vigilance campaign had focused upon the main classes of foreigners functioning at that time in Eastern Europe – Western diplomats, businessmen and journalists. Between 1949 and 1951 there were a number of show trials in Eastern Europe – a British and a French diplomat in Poland, an American businessman in Hungary and an American journalist in Czechoslovakia – which were widely publicized throughout the Bloc at the time as warnings to the populace of the risks of speaking too freely to Westerners. In all the countries concerned laws had been promulgated which made the passing of normal economic or political information to a foreigner an indictable offence against the State, both for the informer and the informant.

These laws have never been repealed in Eastern Europe. They were introduced in the Soviet Union in 1959 and 1960, at the same time as a fresh vigilance campaign was started, this time warning against spies disguised as tourists. This campaign has been particularly strong in the Soviet Union, but it has also been carried on in the rest of Eastern Europe.

Between 1960 and 1962 there was a new series of show trials. This time the majority of them were in the U.S.S.R., though a number took place in Poland and Bulgaria, involving expatriate Poles visiting the homeland in the one country and a French exchange teacher in the other. The Soviet show trials were of small fry – two Dutch sailors, two middle-aged German tourists, American students.[1] All in their own ways were accused of taking photos of military installations and obtaining information illegally to pass on to Western intelligence agencies. All were found guilty, though not all behaved according to the expected pattern of show trials: one of the defendants was adamant to the end that he had not indulged in any espionage and that his actions were quite innocent. Nineteen-sixty-three saw a British businessman jailed on charges of

[1] I exclude the U2 trial of 1961 from this list because it is a special case.

espionage in the Soviet Union, while the American Professor Barghoorn – a Soviet affairs specialist from Yale visiting the U.S.S.R. as a tourist – was arrested in October that year and only released after the personal intervention of President Kennedy.

As a decade previously, the actual facts of the cases were of no consequence. What was important was for the people in the Bloc to understand that it was personally dangerous for them to mix too freely with foreigners. In Stalin's time they were curious to meet the few foreigners who came their way. Ten years later they were equally curious to meet the many thousands of foreigners they saw on the streets. Whereas the job of communist propaganda was to paint the best picture for the tourist to see when in the Communist Bloc, at the same time it was policy to prevent any great contact between the citizens and the visitors, in case mutual curiosities revealed too much.

From the mid-50's onwards the Communist Bloc in general, and the U.S.S.R. in particular, began to take an increasing part in what might be called normal international activities. Their diplomats emerged from their shells and joined in the accepted rounds of diplomatic life, Communist Bloc delegations took part in all manner of conferences,[1] they entered sporting and cultural events on an increasing scale, while student and university exchanges proliferated. Communist Bloc films were shown at every possible festival of international note and in this way they were introduced to an ever-widening world audience.[2] With the removal of the heavy hand of Stalin, the quality of Soviet film-making rose and through it of Soviet propaganda, as did the quality and propaganda

[1] At times their participation caused some puzzlement for instance, a high-level Soviet delegation attended an Industrial Editors' Conference in Chicago in 1916 under the impression that it was a meeting of leading industrial and economic experts. In fact, it was of editors of company house journals!

[2] Communist films were first shown at international festivals in 1950, but it was not until 1955 that they started to win awards. In 1961 the Communist Bloc won 42 of the 204 awards made at non-Bloc festivals. Czechoslovakia, Poland and the U.S.S.R. have established themselves as the main Bloc contenders at these festivals which give them excellent opportunities to advertise the communist system, to woo the emerging nations and to increase the sales and audiences of communist films throughout the world.

value of films from other communist countries, notably Poland, Czechoslovakia and Hungary.

This new flexibility gave considerably greater scope for effective action abroad of the communist propaganda apparatus, which now found itself confined only by the Party line of the moment. The stands at the trade fairs became showplaces of communism in construction, particularly the Soviet Pavilion at the Brussels World Fair in 1958 and the Soviet Trade Exhibition in London, 1961. By 1962 Soviet participation in international trade fairs had expanded to include the following events: Leipzig, Poznan, Brno, Zagreb, Accra, Lagos, Budapest, Conakry, Tripoli, Khartoum, Izmir, Nicosia, Damascus, New York, Washington, Minneapolis, Hanoi and Rio de Janeiro.

In 1952, it will be remembered, the World Peace Council organized an international economic conference in Moscow, which had the theme that East-West trade was essential to raise the living standards of Western Europe. Typical of the propaganda on this theme was a pamphlet for foreign consumption, published in Moscow in 1952, under the title *International Trade and the Improvement of the Standard of Living of the West*. The writer – M. Alexandrov of the Moscow Institute of Economics – reminded his readers that before the Second World War, Eastern Europe exported a great deal to the West, particularly food and other primary products. Projecting this past into the present, Alexandrov summed up the Moscow argument for the West:

At the present time Western Europe is in a position to export still larger quantities of commodities like timber, furs, certain kinds of ore, oil products, coal, wheat, rye, butter, meat, sugar, eggs, etc. On the other hand, the vast peaceful construction that is going on in the Soviet Union, the European People's Democracies and in the Chinese People's Republic opens up the possibility of placing big and profitable orders with the industries of the Western countries for equipment of the innumerable construction schemes stretching from the South China Sea to the Danube. Nor are there any business considerations that can hinder an increase in the export from the Western to the Eastern countries of the products of the consumer goods, food and other industries. Even if trade with Eastern Europe were brought back to the pre-war level – and in view of the steady improvement in the conditions of life of the people in the East European countries this could easily be exceeded – Great Britain could increase her exports of cotton goods by 50 per cent and worsteds by 24 per cent. It would enable France to increase her exports of medicaments by 20 per cent, dyes, pencils and paints by 30 per cent, cotton yarn by 54 per cent, perfumes and soap by 9 per cent, canned fish including sardines by 36 per cent, etc.

These persuasive arguments were presented against a background of increasing economic autarchy in the Communist Bloc, which was being deliberately converted into a self-contained economic unit with the Soviet Union as the arbiter of which country should trade with which. As time went on there were fewer agricultural products to export to the West and official economic policy as laid down in Moscow left no foreign exchange for the import of what were considered non-essentials.[1]

The whole purpose of the campaign which revolved around the Moscow Economic Conference and its aftermath was to combat the Western embargo on the export of strategic goods to the Communist Bloc, particularly at the time of the war in Korea. The communists could make these impressive shipping lists – which grew in length and size after Stalin's death – because they knew nothing would result. Moscow made sure of this by making orders for non-strategic goods conditional on the West's acceptance of the parallel orders for strategic goods.

When Stalin died the Moscow Economic Conference died with him, though its continuing organization, the International Council

[1] Speaking for the benefit of trade unionists at the Conference itself, V. M. Kuznetsov, secretary of the Soviet trade union movement, declared that the Soviet trade offers could provide 100,000 jobs in Italy, 200,000 in Britain, 100,000 in France, 100,000 in West Germany and 100,000 in Japan. In fact, West European imports from the East actually declined between 1952 and 1953, while Western exports only rose by $50 million. Despite Soviet offers to buy several million pounds worth of British textiles and many resultant telegrams and promises of jobs for Lancashire workers British textile exports to the U.S.S.R. totalled $100,000 in 1952 and in 1953. In 1954 and 1955 the figures were too small to be recorded. Trade with China in 1952–3 was better, but even here it was not as rosy as predicted. Promised orders for £30 million of British goods by China in 1953 failed to materialize, while Switzerland – which did not take part in the Moscow Conference – enjoyed as large an increase in exports to China as any country. Belgium, which was very active in Moscow, only increased sales to China by $800,000, though Belgian imports from China rose by $3 million.

for the Promotion of International Trade, lasted into 1956. The concept of internal Bloc self-sufficiency was not abandoned, instead it was elaborated with the introduction of the international division of labour concept. This came about first with the revision of the Soviet economic plans following Stalin's death. As these were adjusted, so were those of the East European countries. By 1962 there were definite moves towards national specializations in the main branches of industry by the East European countries, working under the general direction of the Moscow-controlled Comecon organization.

By this system, foreign trade continued to be residual rather than an integral part of communist economic policy, so much so that it received only passing mention in the Soviet seven-year plan approved in January 1959. In absolute terms, however, the foreign trade of the Communist Bloc rose considerably from less than $11,000 million in 1950 to some $25,000 million by 1960. This represents eleven per cent of world trade, but even then only equals the low sum of $25 per head of population in the Communist Bloc, compared with well over $100 of foreign trade per head of population outside the Bloc. Some of this increase in trade with the outside has been at the expense of intra-Bloc trade. This was running at eighty per cent of the total in 1950 and by 1960 it had dropped to seventy per cent. But this still remained very high compared with the pre-war proportion of ten per cent.

The Soviet Union switched its economic attentions from Western Europe to other areas almost as soon as Stalin had been embalmed. By 1954 a new economic drive had been launched, directed initially at non-communist Asia and the Middle East, but extending itself to the African continent from 1957 onwards. This drive was largely in the form of credits and specific aid projects, rather than in normal export-import terms. The offers were directed generally to the newly-emergent nations and the terms were usually of a barter nature, repayment and interest being in terms of the recipient country's exportable surpluses.

According to statistics published in Warsaw in 1961, between 1953 and 1961 the Communist Bloc granted or promised to the under-developed countries of Asia, Africa and Latin America credits totalling close to $4,000 million at the official rate of exchange. The greatest proportion went to Asia ( $2,460 million), with nearly $970 million to Africa and about $540 million to Latin America. Of individual countries, India received $900 million, the United Arab Republic $625 million and Indonesia $375 million.[1]

Initially, this communist economic aid was concentrated on large-scale projects with a basically propaganda value: steelworks, power-stations, dams, radio and television transmitters, complete collective farm complexes, sports stadia. These projects have both economic value and considerable visual impact. They represent the new export versions of the Great Constructions of Communism. By the beginning of 1962 the total of communist aid to the developing countries had risen to $6,500 million of which $2,000 million was of a military nature. Of the $4,500 million economic aid, it is estimated that $3,000 million is accounted for by these large-scale economic-propaganda projects. Initially the speed of agreement on economic aid between the individual Communist Bloc countries and the recipients was not matched by actual deliveries, with only about a quarter of the money allocated being spent by late 1961. But the pace in 1962 was showing signs of increasing as surveys were completed and more and more projects were started.

Whereas two-thirds of Western economic aid is in the form of grants, the Communist Bloc credits are usually as loans, often good only for buying goods and services from the donor country, although at a low interest rate of two and a half per cent, these Bloc credits have a relatively short duration of twelve years, against Western credit periods of up to thirty or even occasionally forty years. Western interest rates can be as high as five per cent, but many have no interest at all. There were signs in 1962 that the interest trends were reversing themselves, with a new Soviet loan to Tunisia being at three per cent against American considerations of reducing their charges on future credits.[2]

[1] To put these Communist Bloc credits into perspective, the United States alone in one year – 1959–60 – spent about $2,860 million on economic aid, of which $710 million went to India, $400 million to Latin American countries and $320 million to Africa.

[2] The negative aspects of Soviet economic aid – such as dumping – are not considered in this context.

With the increasing realization of the possibilities of propaganda by diplomacy, Communist Bloc leaders began travelling outside the Bloc from the mid-50's onwards, contrary to the policy of Stalin, who only ventured outside on one occasion, when he attended the Teheran Conference with Roosevelt and Churchill in 1944. In 1954 the Chinese premier Chou En-lai visited Delhi to sign the 'five principles' treaty of friendship and non-interference in each other's internal affairs between Communist China and India. From 1955 Khruschov and his henchmen of the day visited Yugoslavia to try to heal the ideological breach, toured south-east Asia twice, visited Britain and France, then the United States (Khruschov going on to Communist China straight from Washington). In the autumn of 1960 Khruschov made a series of widely-publicized speeches to the United Nations General Assembly and the following year he met President Kennedy in Vienna.

In their turn, other East European leaders made more modest tours overseas, while return visits were made to Soviet Bloc capitals by Western leaders such as the German Chancellor Adenauer to Moscow in 1955 and the then American Vice-President Nixon to Moscow and Warsaw and the British Premier Macmillan to Moscow in 1959.

In 1955 admission to membership of the United Nations was granted to fifteen states. Up to this time, Soviet attitudes to the U.N. were conditioned by two main subjective factors. Ideologically, the United Nations and its agencies were considered inimical to the communist world outlook by their very supra-political nature. The United Nations concept of collective security was an objective one, in the sense that the collective security it envisaged was not based on any specific political dogma. The communists, too, believed in collective security, but were subjectively opposed to what they considered the class enemy, capitalist system. By its very nature, the United Nations tolerated if it did not actively strengthen the capitalist system. For this single reason, the Communist Bloc had no ideological purpose in giving it any support.

Tactically, in the original United Nations organization, the Communist Bloc knew that it was always in the minority at voting time. Since it could not support many of the proposed U.N. actions – particularly in the Security Council – it made itself more unpopular by using its right of veto over and over again. This was as true after Stalin's death as it was in his time.[1] But with the influx of new members from 1955 onwards, the Soviet Union realized that the potential balance of power was changing, possibly in its favour. From this time on the Communist Bloc members of the U.N. and its agencies began to take more active roles, particularly in the plenary sessions with their opportunities for unlimited propaganda. While Communist Bloc speakers became prominent at business sessions of committees and agencies from which they had been absent for five years and more, their countries were paying little more than nominal attention to the practical work of the United Nations agencies, much of which they still boycotted for ideological reasons. Thus the 1960 pledges for the U.N. technical assistance programme showed that Canada, France, West Germany, India, the Netherlands, Sweden, Britain and the U.S.A. each contributed more to this scheme for helping the developing countries than did the U.S.S.R. India gave the equivalent of $2·5 million, Sweden $3 million and Britain $8 million in convertible currencies. The U.S.S.R. gave $2 million in roubles, which meant that the money could only be spent in financing study visits to the Soviet Union or the provision of Soviet technicians and equipment to help the recipient countries.

But in terms of votes gained, the Communist Bloc saw increased possibilities for manœuvre in the United Nations General Assembly that was including more and more representatives of developing countries. By the time of the 1961–2 General Assembly, the Soviet Union could tot up the voting figures and reckon

[1] The hundredth Soviet veto was cast in the Security Council on June 22nd, 1962. The first Soviet veto came on February 16th, 1946, a year after the U.N. was founded. On an average, the Soviet veto has overruled the majority will on the Security Council at about every tenth meeting. Up to the time of the hundred veto, Nationalist China had made use the veto once, Britain twice, France four times and the United States not at all. About half the Soviet vetoes have been used to block the admission of new members. Among nations whose membership of the U.N. had thus been delayed for a time were the Irish Republic, Italy, Austria, Finland, Jordan, Ceylon, Nepal, Japan, Libya and Mauritania.

matters to be much more in its favour than they were ten years previously.

With the increasing use being made by communist propaganda of the more normally accepted means of international communication, the communication fronts underwent considerable changes in the late fifties. For one thing, they were affected by the events of 1956 – the Khruschov secret speech at the Twentieth Party Congress, the workers' revolt at Poznan and the Hungarian uprising. The Congress speech made a mockery of all the Stalinist dogma which had been as basic to the major fronts as it was to the actual communist parties. The World Federation of Trade Unions in particular was put in a dilemma by the Poznan revolt, while the Hungarian uprising again brought uneasiness to all the fronts. The one specially affected was the World Federation of Democratic Youth, which had to be evacuated from its headquarters in the Hungarian capital to the safety of Prague.

At the time of the Hungarian events all fronts kept quiet, refraining from protest against the communist-organized counter-actions. This failure on their part to make even token protest against communist repression once more revealed their partisan nature, for which some came under fire from their own members. In this their already waning influence as mass organizations has hastened and a changed role for them became essential.

The World Peace Council became more indirect in its activities, withdrawing into the background and organizing its meetings through other *ad hoc* bodies, set up for specific purposes. From 1957 it had no permanent home of its own and operated through another front, the Institute for International Peace, in Vienna. The other bodies continued their activities in a minor key, with the World Federation of Trade Unions continuing as the most important. It concentrated on training potential allies from among trade unionists from the emerging countries, either through its own courses in their areas or by taking groups of them to its own training school in Budapest, or to those run specially for Asians and Africans in East Germany, Czechoslovakia and Poland.

Similar work was continued among youth students by the World Federation of Democratic Youth and the International Union of

Students, paying particular attention to specialist seminars and meetings. The International Organization of Journalists also organized courses for Asian and African journalists.

Important changes came about in one major organ of communist propaganda which has so far not been mentioned, the World Youth Festivals. These are organized jointly by the W.F.D.Y. and the I.U.S. through an International Festival Committee set up afresh for each Festival. Known in full as the World Festivals of Youth and Students for Peace, eight had been held between 1947 and 1962, each beginning at the end of July. The first was in Prague, then followed Budapest (1949), East Berlin (1951), Bucharest (1953), Warsaw (1955), Moscow (1957), Vienna (1959) and Helsinki (1962). According to official claims 20,000 participants from 67 countries went to Prague, 10,000 from 80 countries to Budapest, 26,000 from 104 countries to East Berlin, 29,000 from 111 countries to Bucharest, over 30,000 from 115 countries to Warsaw and 35,000 participants from 131 countries to Moscow. These Festivals were all held in communist capitals, of which Moscow was the ultimate. With the switch to a non-communist venue, the Festivals became more modest and only 18,000 from 112 countries took part at Vienna. At Helsinki there was an original target figure of 21,000 participants, but this eventually settled down to some 12,000 people from abroad. All these totals excluded visitors to the Festival from within the host country.

The first three Festivals, those of Prague, Budapest and East Berlin, were heavily Stalinist and anti-Western in tone. On the one hand they lavished praise on the achievements of the Soviet Union and the personality of Stalin, on the other they attacked every aspect of Western policy and intentions. The virulence of this propaganda became modified at Bucharest in the summer of 1953, four months after Stalin's death, and by the Warsaw Festival of 1955 the theme had changed to that of peaceful coexistence. There is little doubt that the more relaxed atmosphere of the Warsaw Festival had its influence on some of the communist delegations, particularly that from the host country and Hungary, as was shown by the students of both countries in the autumn of 1956, as well as in Czechoslovakia, where students staged short-lived anti-government demonstrations.

Though the events of 1956 had their influence in youth and student circles, these did not affect attendance at the Moscow Festival of 1957, which attracted a large number of young people curious to see the Soviet Union for themselves at relatively low cost. By now the Festival emphasis was on Asia, Africa and Latin America; the anti-capitalism of the previous Festivals, though still present, was more subtle. On this occasion there were two major groups of Americans taking part, one of which was independent of the Festival organization. Members of this latter group were very active in political debate, one person going so far as to be successful in reading the U.N. Report on Hungary aloud in the Red Square. From subsequent Soviet Press reports, this Festival had a disturbing influence on a number of Soviet youth circles.

These Festivals had proved increasingly expensive to run. The Moscow event was covered – it was stated officially – by a 40 million rouble lottery, equalling 10 million dollars at the official exchange rate. This did not take into account the costs borne by the other communist countries, who all helped to pay the expenses of selected foreign participants. Czechoslovakia alone raised over 20 million crowns (nearly $3 million at the official rate of exchange).

Perhaps because of the stir they caused within the Bloc countries, perhaps because of their cost, the Festivals after Moscow were reduced in scope, with a changed location. Vienna was chosen in part because it is an old-established conference centre, in part because Austria is officially a neutral in relation to the communist countries and Western Europe. But even the Vienna Festival was expensive at $4·5 million. There was greater scope for critics of the Festival and its backers to have their voices heard and they took the opportunity. This brought about retaliatory action by strong-arm members of the Festival guards and supporters, the resulting violence offsetting much of the usual brilliant veneer given by the cultural and sporting events. At these the highlighted troupes and teams from the communist countries presented a shimmering spectacle of communism in non-ideological garb.

At all the previous Festivals, the populace had turned out *en masse* to see what to them was a nine-days wonder. Such was not the case at Vienna nor at Helsinki, for both the Austrians and the Finns regarded the Festivals as alien and expressed their feelings in a boycott of the events. In both cases, the Festivals were organized against the opposition of the majority of the national youth and student organizations of the host countries, obtaining their support only from the communists and their allies.

One target group of the communist fronts came into greater prominence by the 60's – women. The Women's International Democratic Federation and the women's organizations in the communist countries started to increase their activities among women's circles in the emerging countries. The Bureau of the W.I.D.F. held an enlarged meeting in Bamako, capital of the Mali Republic, at the end of January 1962, while delegation exchanges between Communist Bloc and African women's organizations increased, China being particularly active.

At the same time as the international fronts became modified, so an aspect of the friendship society movement changed. In individual countries the societies found much of the work they had been doing in the early fifties no longer necessary, with the Communist Bloc carrying out cultural social and economic activities by more normal means. The main job of the friendship groups under these conditions was to organize delegation exchanges.

From 1959 onwards their work was supplemented in the communist countries themselves by the establishment of reciprocal friendship groups. Some of these linked themselves with West European countries, but their main interests lay in Asia and Africa; this was in part linked with the formation of the Afro-Asian Solidarity Movement in 1957. The Soviet groups were soon united into the Union of Soviet Societies for Friendship and Cultural Relations, with a similar co-ordinating body set up in China. Smaller groups exist in all the other communist countries. Such Communist Bloc groups in their turn help generate the formation of complementary friendship societies in the emerging countries, like the Ghana-Soviet Friendship Society and the Nigeria-Soviet Friendship Society. In general the main purpose of the friendship groups set up in the communist countries is to arrange for delegation exchanges and to organize meetings and demonstrations on appropriate anniversaries,[1] either at regular intervals or as the occasion demands, as was the case with the demonstrations and meetings following the murder of Lumumba.

The initial set-back to communist propaganda made by the 1956 events was soon put right by the launching of the first sputnik in October 1957. The space flights which followed, gave a positive dynamism to the communist propaganda drive. The sputniks were used to demonstrate the inventive and creative power of the Soviet system, while the astronauts were presented as examples of the new Soviet Man – and, with Tereshkova in 1963, the new Soviet Woman. Since the whole subject was and continues to be news-worthy in its own right, Soviet propaganda could hardly go wrong in its presentation of this new theme of the conquest of Nature by Man.

Externally, the sputniks and the astronauts have been used to show the superiority of Marxism-Leninism and scientific socialism. Internally this campaign has been supplemented by a no less vital anti-religious theme, to demonstrate the absence of a God and the overwhelming superiority of science based on materialism, not metaphysics. At its crudest the line has been that neither Gagarin nor Titov saw any sign of God when they were shot up into the heavens, therefore God does not exist.

Gagarin, Titov and the other cosmonauts became world-wide propaganda symbols, each of them making extensive international tours inside and outside the Bloc during 1961 and afterwards. When in Bloc countries they were presented as good Party members. When in non-communist countries they represented the forward-looking Soviet citizen. With both roles they were great successes. As such they were the personification of the new Soviet

[1] The main anniversary dates celebrated by the communist fronts are as follows: February 21st, Day of Solidarity with Youth and Students Fighting Against Colonialism (W.F.D.Y./I.U.S.); March 8th, International Women's Day (W.I.D.F.); March 21–28th, World Youth Week (W.F.D.Y.); April 14th, Day of Aid to Spanish Youth (W.F.D.Y./I.U.S.) April 24th, World Youth Day Against Colonialism and for Peaceful Coexistence (W.F.D.Y./I.U.S.); June 1st, International Children's Day (W.I.D.F./P.I.C.M.); October 1st, Teachers Charter Day (non-political F.I.S.E.); November 10th, World Youth Day (W.F.D.Y.); November 17th, International Student Day (I.U.S.).

image the communist leaders wished to have accepted by the rest of the world.

But this positive image was no more sufficient for communist propaganda purposes in 1962 than it was in 1952 or 1932. It still had to be accompanied by what can best be called the use of the negative example. The accent had to be on attack all the time. The enemy – and communist terminology persists in using military phrases – must be unmasked and his evil intentions exposed. He must never be allowed any good intentions. Any positive approaches he makes must by their nature be regarded as suspect.

Thus on June 12th, 1962 a new film by the Soviet director Sergei Gerasimov was previewed in Moscow, with the full hit treatment in the Soviet Press. With its title *Men and Beasts* it took the memory back a decade to the notorious *Silvery Dust* xenophobia of the bacterial warfare propaganda period.[1] According to the Moscow reports, Gerasimov had been working for years on the script, based – we are told – on a real-life story of a Soviet officer, wounded in the war and taken prisoner, who later wandered from country to country as a displaced person: 'The person passes through the horrors of fascist torture chambers and experiences in full measure the anguish of being separated from home. He returns to the Soviet Union to find his old friends and become a part of Soviet society,' ran the story as recounted in the *Soviet News* published by the Soviet Embassy in London. 'Discussing his film with a *Tass* correspondent', it continued, 'Gerasimov said the main idea was the clash of morals of the two worlds – the bestial morals of capitalist society and the morals of Soviet humanism, the refusal to accept the "world of beasts" by a man reared in Soviet society.'

This general anti-Western propaganda was divided into subgroups, of which the most important was anti-Americanism. Typical of the cruder versions of Soviet Anti-Americanism is that put out from time to time by Moscow broadcasts to Africa, such as that in Swahili in May 1962 telling how an old negro was put into a cage as a side-show by a white-owned funfair in America.[2] Second

[1] See Appendix Va.

[2] Appendix Vb gives another example of the use in 1962 of anti-American xenophobia.

only to anti-Americanism comes the campaign against West Germany and the so-called German revanchism. Memories of the Nazi German past are never allowed to rest and in this campaign full use was made of the Berlin issue, both for purposes of political manœuvre and for straight propaganda uses. The new variation of the German question developed from 1960 onwards with the concept of West German imperialism in Africa and Asia. This was linked with another new concept, that of neo-colonialism, to attack Western economic aid in general and West German aid in particular as a new variation of the old-style imperialism.

As one 'anti-' campaign loses its force, so another takes its place. By June 1962 Khruschov had gone back full circle to the Moscow Economic Conference of 1952, with his demands that another such world conference should be held. This time he was not concerned with lifting the embargo on strategic exports to communist countries, but with undermining the progress in Western Europe of the Common Market negotiations and the prospects they held for a European Economic Community that might rival his own Comecon.

At the same time an old hand at propaganda for the communist system, Wilfred Burchett,[1] was writing in the Moscow international weekly *New Times* of June 20th, 1962, a long story alleging that American forces were using chemical warfare in South Vietnam. This referred to South Vietnamese attempts to clear guerrilla hiding-places in the jungle with aerial spraying, but the whole point of Burchett's article was to show the Americans up: 'Using Asians as victims for tests of new weapons fits an all too familiar picture which stretches from Hiroshima to the present nuclear-weapons tests in the Pacific.' This theme was taken up again on a wider scale in the spring of 1963 by both Moscow and Peking.

Ten years previously Wilfred Burchett had been a correspondent with the communist forces in North Korea and as such had written extensively along these same lines about the bacterial warfare campaign. The omission of any reference to this previous

[1] For some years a Moscow resident and a stringer for a number of well-known Western papers and journals, Burchett in 1961 and 1962 was co-author of two British paperbacks on the astronauts Gagarin and Titov.

experience in his *New Times* article of 1962 was notable, since he was writing about what is essentially the same subject.

The use of the negative example is not only propaganda for non-communists. It is also used in intra-Party circles against opponents of the current line. Such an 'anti-' campaign within the ranks was against revisionism and sectarianism, deviations to the right and to the left. By 1960 these internal deviations were a major problem for world communism, bringing with them schismatic ideas of fundamental importance, and the rise of Peking as a rival centre to Moscow.

# PART THREE

# *Outlook for the Sixties*

## CHAPTER SEVEN

# *Epicentres Multiply*

So far we have discussed the communist propaganda system internationally as a whole, treating it very much as a unity. In Stalin's day this was the case, as we have seen. But since the mid-50's this monolithic characteristic has disappeared. From time to time I have referred to Moscow as the epicentre of world communist activity, a seismic parallel which reflects the volcanic nature of international communism. But the 60's are very different from the 50's and Khruschov is not the same man as Stalin. Moscow is no longer *the* epicentre, for it has been joined by Peking, which at the same time rivals as it complements the Soviet capital.

The Chinese communists came to power on the mainland in late 1949, a few weeks before the gigantic celebrations of Stalin's seventieth birthday. Right from the beginning, Mao Tse-tung and his followers did not perform the servile genuflections before the Soviet leader that was so noticeable in other national communist chiefs of the day.

This was made quite clear by an article on Stalin's birthday, circulated on December 19th, 1959, by the official New China News Agency and written by Chen Po-ta, then Mao's Minister of Information. After citing Mao on Stalin as the leader of the world revolution, Chen described how Mao had 'developed Stalin's theory on the Chinese Revolution in the course of the concrete practice of that revolution' and ended by pointing out that 'Comrade Mao is Stalin's friend and comrade-at-arms'. In short Chen talked of Mao in relation to Stalin much as Stalin had talked about himself in relation to Lenin: as the intellectual equal of his teacher.

If we look at the history of Sino-Soviet relations from the mid-20's onwards we see that on more than one occasion Moscow gave Mao the wrong tactical advice and that more than once

Soviet opportunism saw Stalin backing Chiang Kai-shek, and ignoring Mao Tse-tung. Though he received Soviet military equipment aid towards the end, Mao had reason to regard his victory in China as achieved alone, even though it was won with the backing of a friendly Soviet Union. The Red Army could have been ready in the background if necessary, but the need did not arise.

So Mao, like Tito in Yugoslavia, could look upon his revolution as a native product. Like Tito in 1948, Mao in 1949 could feel independent. At the time this superficial similarity between the Yugoslav and Chinese revolutions led many to believe that Tito and Mao had much in common, that Mao was another kind of Titoist. Yugoslavia, indeed, was one of the first countries to recognize Communist China diplomatically, but Tito's overtures were rebuffed and it was not until 1955 that Peking responded with an exchange of diplomats.

Mao's communism never developed along the lines taken after 1948 by Tito. Yugoslavia developed economic relations with the West and at one time adopted a neutral line politically, to the extent that it took steps together with other, newly-emergent countries to form a third group of world powers. Internally, economic and organizational structural changes were made which abandoned the more doctrinaire Yugoslav communist forms taken over originally from the Soviet system. Communist China, on the other hand, introduced increasingly tough measures internally within the first five years of the régime. These differences were recognized by Mao, who continued to treat the Yugoslavs coolly, when Khruschov once more made peace with Tito. To Mao Tito has remained a political opportunist, an arch-revisionist.

During the early period of the communist régime in China, the main emphasis was on internal consolidation, both economically and politically. The country had been ravaged by war for more than twenty years, there was general discontent and the new régime had to be sure of its own security.

This did not prevent Mao from entering the international arena. Within a year of gaining power, he was embroiled in the Korean war and his propaganda machine was soon to help set in motion the bacterial warfare campaign – the first major occasion on which a Chinese propaganda theme for the outside world was disseminated.

By late in 1950 Peking had started a fortnightly magazine in English for overseas reading, *People's China*. This was published until 1957, when it was replaced in English by *Peking Review*, an airmailed weekly: *People's China* was joined by a number of other periodicals in a wide variety of languages, particularly Asian languages.[1] Peking's output of publications for foreign consumption does not yet rival that of the Soviet Union, but it is impressive both in quantity and quality, coming from a country which still possesses only limited typographical and foreign editorial facilities. We do not have the detailed knowledge about Communist Chinese book production for abroad that we have about the Soviet output and it would appear that this Chinese programme is somewhat more modest in circulation.

But if Chinese testimony means anything, certain types of Peking literature have a noticeable impact. On December 10th, 1961, an article in the Peking *People's Daily* declared: 'All oppressed nations and people will sooner or later rise in revolution and this is precisely why revolutionary experience and theories will naturally gain currency among those nations and peoples and go deep to their hearts. That is why pamphlets introducing guerrilla warfare in China have such a wide circulation in Africa, Latin America and Asia, and are looked upon as precious things even after they are worn and come apart and the print has become illegible through rubbing. The influence of ideas knows no state boundaries. No one can prevent the dissemination among the people of what they need.'

These pamphlets on the Chinese revolutionary experience were being circulated in Asia from 1949 onwards, usually from printing presses outside China with India as a major source. They were later published from Peking in more elaborate and substantial forms. A Peking story, which had an obvious basis in fact, was widely spread that the successful army commanders of the communist Viet-Minh in the Indo-China war had Mao's works on tactics in their knapsacks.

The official New China News Agency (Hsinhua or N.C.N.A.)

[1] These publications and their languages are listed in Appendix I.

had spread its network throughout the Communist Bloc, Asia, and Europe by the middle 50's: by 1962 it was well established in Africa and Latin America. The major exception was the U.S.A.

Chinese communist broadcasts for overseas began modestly in Yenan – Mao's operational base – in 1948. At this time Yenan was broadcasting 16 hours weekly out of a total Communist Bloc transmission time of 600 hours. By 1958 the Chinese were broadcasting 438 hours weekly out of a total 2,530 hours and by the beginning of 1961 had risen half as much again to nearly 690 hours out of 3,200 hours total Communist Bloc broadcasting for abroad. These Chinese figures exclude programmes for the Nationalists on Taiwan and Quemoy.

So by the beginning of the 1960's the Chinese communists were broadcasting propaganda abroad at no less than two-thirds of the Soviet rate of just under a thousand hours weekly. Four hundred hours from Peking were broadcast to the Far East generally, the remainder being fairly evenly spread between the other areas of the world, with the smallest transmissions (32 hours weekly) going to Latin America. Previously Africa (14 hours weekly in 1959) had been considered the least important target area for Communist Chinese transmissions. By 1960 the rate had more than doubled to 35 hours weekly and by mid-1961 the Chinese rate was equal to that of the U.S.S.R. with 56 hours weekly to Africa, out of a grand Bloc total of 170 hours.

By 1960 Communist Chinese stations were broadcasting in some two dozen languages, of which the most important were the Chinese languages and dialects beamed to listeners in the Far East (and later – in Cantonese – to Africa).

The written and broadcast words were supplemented by the mid-50's with the whole range of personal contact propaganda. The major organization carrying this work was the Chinese People's Association for Cultural Relations with Foreign Countries. The A.C.R.F.C. was formed in 1954 by the following sponsoring bodies: China Peace Committee (originally known internally as the Chinese People's Committee for Peace and Against American Imperialism, but called the Chinese Peace Committee in propaganda for abroad); the All-China Federation of Literature and Arts Circles; All-China Federation of Scientific Societies;

All-China Federation of Trade Unions; All-China Federation of Democratic Women; All-China Federation of Democratic Youth; All-China Students' Federation; China-India Friendship Association; China-Burma Friendship Association; Chinese People's Institute of Foreign Affairs.

In 1958 the President of the A.C.R.F.C. reported: 'During the past year, according to incomplete statistics, we received 151 groups of foreign guests, numbering about 1,264 persons coming from forty-eight countries. We also dispatched delegations and representatives totalling 57 groups, consisting of about 710 persons, to twenty-six countries . . . We also dispatched classical and modern art troupes to foreign countries to stage performances. In addition, there were held commemorative services for the world's cultural giants, exhibitions and screening of films, the publication and exchange of books, periodicals and other materials. These activities were not only of a greater volume compared with the past, but were also greater in scope and richer in content. All these activities have produced marked effects on and contributed greatly to the propaganda of our country's peaceful foreign policy.' In September 1959 – the tenth anniversary of communist power in China – the New China News Agency reported that over the past ten years 1,500 foreign cultural delegations and groups from 122 countries had visited China, including sports teams from thirty-three countries; 400 groups had gone abroad from China in this period.

Communist Chinese friendship associations in non-communist countries came into existence from the beginning of 1950 onwards. Within ten years such groups were known to exist in twenty-five non-communist countries, with indications of them in another nineteen countries. Sometimes the title replaced 'friendship' with 'cultural' but their purpose remained common, that of building up support for Communist Chinese policies and acceptance of the communist régime on the mainland as the *de iure* as well as the *de facto* ruler of the Chinese people.

These societies – like their opposite numbers backing the other communist countries – were given the task of promoting the communist Chinese interests by a wide variety of means. As they have developed they now import and show films produced in China;

prepare exhibitions of Chinese art, drama and handicrafts; sponsor group and individual visits to China and lecture tours in Chinese by returned travellers; arrange receptions for visiting Chinese delegations; publish and distribute mainland propaganda materials and organize friendship celebrations on official communist holidays. Outside Chinese circles abroad these activities are particularly intended for the intellectual.

Of special interest in China has been the formation of Peking-based friendship groups with specific areas, Africa and Asia. First was the Asian Solidarity Committee of China, formed in February 1956, following the W.P.C.-organized Asian Countries Conference held in New Delhi in April 1955. Following the establishment in Cairo of the Afro-Asian People's Solidarity Organization at the end of 1957, the Chinese committee changed its name to the Afro-Asian Solidarity Committee of China.

In April 1960, China followed the lead of the U.S.S.R. and set up the Chinese African People's Friendship Association, of which the most important undertaking in its first two years of existence was the extensive four-month tour by a friendship delegation to eight West African countries. The delegation's comprehensive report on this tour was broadcast to Africa in Swahili in ten instalments.

More recently formed, in April 1962, is the Asia-Africa Society of China, which has the task of promoting 'academic research in China on the political, economic, religious and cultural development of the Asian and African countries and to increase China's exchanges with them'. In October 1963 a China-Japan Friendship Society was formed.

As with other communist countries, China became more interested in foreign students towards the end of the 50's. As early as 1951 Peking was offering university courses to small numbers of students from the rest of Asia, particularly India, while an Asian Student Sanatorium was set up outside Peking in 1953 solely for the benefit of non-Chinese students. By the mid-50's there were several hundred students from other communist countries in various Chinese university centres, studying on an exchange basis. The numbers from non-communist centres are not known. But it was through the East European students in China that the impact of the Hungarian uprising of 1956 was felt directly in Chinese intellectual circles later that year and in 1957, following Mao's so-called 'Hundred Flowers' directive which was misinterpreted in the universities as a sign of a more liberal approach to culture. During the early period most of the non-communist world students in China came from Asia. By the 60's increasing numbers were there from Africa, particularly Somalia.

While this propaganda through culture was being developed, Communist China was also building up her propaganda by deeds, to match that of the remainder of the Communist Bloc. At the same time as Peking was seeking fraternal economic aid from the European communist countries, Mao's envoys were offering their goods and services to Asia and later to Africa. A transmitter was built on a fraternal basis for Cambodia; a railway was surveyed and built by Chinese technicians in the Yemen. Trade pacts were entered into with all China's neighbours, with Europe and later with the newly independent countries of Africa.

In one sense all this activity complemented that initiated by Moscow. In the early days of communist rule in China it had often been explained in Party circles that the Soviet communist experience gave the lead for revolutionary work in the capitalist countries of Europe and North America. At the same time the Chinese experience served the revolution in the colonial areas. By this argument the two propaganda networks of Moscow and Peking supported each other in the non-communist world. Where the message from one source might prove unacceptable, that from the other would succeed. This was particularly valid in areas where colour was important. Here the Chinese had the advantage over the white Russian, the more so as Peking could depict Mao's regime as having liberated China from Western colonialism.

Inevitably, however, the dividing line between complementary and antagonistic propaganda became difficult to define. By virtue of historical developments – both of China in relation to the world as a whole and of the Chinese communists in relation to the communist movement internationally – the time was bound to come when Mao would challenge Stalin's successors, just as there is good reason to believe that he would have challenged Stalin if the Soviet dictator had lived longer.

After Stalin's death Mao sat alone (apart from the ideological outcast Tito) as the sole survivor of those leaders who had fought successfully right through a revolution. Furthermore, he had fought successfully in the face of ill-timed policies decided in Moscow. Looking back over events leading up to the victory of 1949, Mao could find little for which he could really thank the Kremlin, other than ideological backing. After 1949, when he wanted massive economic aid from his communist neighbour, he only got it at a heavy price in repayments. At the same time as the Chinese were having to pay their way with Soviet aid, they watched other, non-communist and bourgeois governments – such as those of Mr Nehru and Colonel Nasser – given preferential treatment by Moscow, on easier terms. This question of Soviet aid for what were often anti-communist régimes was one of the factors bringing about the Sino-Soviet dispute.

This wooing of the national bourgeoisie in the developing countries started, as we have seen from the previous chapter, about 1955. Until this time Moscow dogma had seen all non-communist régimes in Asia as being lackeys of the imperialists. In the 40's and early 50's Mr Nehru and other leaders of the former British colonial territories were subject to repeated communist propaganda attacks both from within their own countries and from the international movement generally.

The doctrinal change dates from the Bandung Conference of Asian nations in the spring of 1955, in the summer of which Mr Khruschov made a well-publicized tour of India. Communist China was invited to take part, but the U.S.S.R. was excluded from Bandung on the grounds that she was not an Asian power. This argument was sustained despite Moscow's claims on behalf of the Soviet Central Asian republics. Realizing that the Bandung Conference represented a new grouping in world politics, Khruschov – then coming into power following his defeat of the Malenkov group – introduced doctrinal changes which modified the old 'two camp' concept. He brought in the concept of 'positive neutralism', that is neutralism in world politics which did not aid imperialism. In this way Moscow was able to classify, almost overnight, the former imperialist lackeys into positive neutralists.

The most important of these positive neutralists was India,

which in the years to follow became the biggest non-communist recipient of Soviet economic aid. At the time of Bandung, India also signed the Five Principles agreement with China, which pledged non-interference in each other's internal affairs. Despite this apparent link of friendship between these the two greatest Asian powers, it was obvious that Communist China regarded India as a potential rival in Asia. India offered a different political social and economic system which was at least of equal interest to other developing countries. So the Soviet help for India was looked upon in Peking as help for the ideological enemy.

Following the Chinese incursions into Indian border areas and the final invasion of Tibet in 1959, Sino-Indian relations became strained at the same time as Soviet-Indian relations improved still further. By the autumn of 1962 the Five Principles of 1955 had been reduced to words on a useless piece of paper, with India refusing to renew the Treaty with China until the border questions had been solved and Chinese troops had withdrawn: the Chinese for their part refused to give way.

In contradistinction, however, Peking had taken careful steps to enter into amicable negotiations with her other southerly neighbours, Burma, Nepal and Pakistan over the border question. With them there were no incursions by Chinese communist troops and the demarcations were drawn up at the conference table. Peking gave its support to Pakistani claims on Kashmir, knowing full well that the Soviet Union supported the Indian claims. This was as much a rebuff to the U.S.S.R. as it was to India.

In the mid-50's the main ideological cause of dispute was the changing Soviet attitude to the national bourgeoisie in the emerging countries. The revelations about Stalin given by Khruschov to the Twentieth Party Congress in Moscow in February 1956 had its obvious repercussions in China, as well as elsewhere in the communist world. In the early days, it will be remembered, Peking supported the Hungarian revolution. It was only when the Chinese leaders realized that the revolt was against the established order that they changed their line and condemned it as an unwelcome manifestation of what Mao later called 'antagonistic contradictions' within communist society.

But Mao supported Gomulka in Poland at that time in the new

Polish leader's doctrinal battle with Khruschov. Gomulka's demands for more freedoms in Poland were seen by Mao as a form of 'non-antagonistic contradiction', which could be supported. This support was underlined in 1957 by the Chinese premier Chou En-lai. At the same time Mao published his directive 'let a hundred flowers bloom', which was taken in Chinese intellectual circles as a sign of greater liberalism. Mao's directive was intended as a safety valve, but the spate of criticism it let loose in the summer of 1957 came as an abrupt reminder that a little freedom generates demands for still more and the ideological valve was tightened up again very quickly

In late 1957 the U.S.S.R. launched her first inter-continental ballistic missile in the shape of Sputnik 1. This in its turn strongly influenced China's international thinking, for it gave the Communist Bloc the basis of a great new military weapon. The sputnik was launched on the fortieth anniversary of the October revolution, which was followed by the first Moscow Conference of Communist Parties, attended by Mao himself among the other world communist leaders. All was outward harmony at this conference and Mao even wrote some couplets in praise of it.

But the Chinese communists did not benefit from it to the extent they wished. In particular they did not get the help they wanted to become an atomic power. Mao called a Congress of the Communist Party of China in 1958 and from this Congress stemmed the Great Leap Forward and the establishment of the system of communes. It was the communes question which heralded the second ideological split between China and the U.S.S.R.

The Great Leap Forward was Peking's grand gesture of economic defiance. The commune was the ideologically advanced system of group living and working on which the Leap Forward was to be based. Both were given tremendous publicity in China and abroad as proof that Chinese communism worked. By 1960 the admissions of serious mistakes were being made and by 1962 the process was reversed, with the industrialization schemes halted in order to cope with the far more pressing agricultural problems.

The communes were in themselves a great ideological challenge to Soviet communism and the collective system. It was on this theme that Soviet propaganda began indirect attacks on Chinese policies, with articles in the Moscow Press explaining in detail that communes were nothing new; that the Soviet Union had tried them many years before and had found them unworkable.

In January 1959 the Soviet Party held its 21st Congress in Moscow, ostensibly to endorse the new seven-year plan. Internationally its main purpose was to heal the breach with China with the announcement of a new Sino-Soviet economic agreement. Later that year, Khruschov paid a second visit to Peking (his first had been in 1954) but only after he had toured the U.S.A. and had met President Eisenhower at the series of Camp David conferences. Whether intentional or not, this was seen by Peking as consorting with the ideological enemy – that Khruschov should visit Mao immediately afterwards only made the situation worse in Chinese eyes.

Matters started to come to a head a few months later in the summer of 1960 at a meeting of communist leaders convened for the Rumanian Party Congress that year. In August 1960 Soviet technicians were being withdrawn from China and Soviet aid began to dwindle, with China turning to the West for purchases of grain and machinery. In cutting off economic relations with a country with which it was having diplomatic and ideological differences, the Soviet Union was repeating its earlier treatment of Yugoslavia. Within a matter of months Moscow was to do the same again with Albania, which in its turn had to get help from elsewhere, mainly former political enemies in the West.

In November 1960 the Chinese made a bid at the Moscow Conference of Communist Parties for equal ranking with the U.S.S.R. They succeeded to the extent that the Soviet Party decided to reduce its own status to that of the 'vanguard' in the world communist movement. The Conference was held in conditions of curiously open secrecy – though everyone knew it was going on, nothing was officially admitted. The Declaration published at the end was a compromise document, which could be interpreted as desired.

It was at this stage that the third ideological difference between the Soviet and Chinese Parties became clear. This was on the concept of peaceful coexistence, reformulated – as we have seen – by the Moscow Declaration as a tactic to be used by communists in the fight against capitalism. Peking's presentation of the Moscow Declaration deliberately omitted references to the use of peaceful coexistence as a weapon and stressed the direct revolutionary approach.[1] It was this championing of revolutionary extremism in Peking's world outlook which continued to dominate the dispute with Moscow, though other factors came up as time went on.

From 1959 onwards the Chinese sought alliances within the world communist movement. In April 1960 they published considerable material on the ninetieth anniversary of Lenin's birth to show that Chinese communism followed in the path of Lenin himself. This was widely distributed in translation abroad. But from January 1961 onwards Moscow had gained ideological control of the only organ of world communism, the *World Marxist Review* published from Prague.[2] In this January 1961 number it published Khruschov's assessment of the Moscow Conference and his further attack on revisionism of the right and dogmatism and sectarianism of the left. The source of left-wing sectarianism was left unstated, though all knew it to be China.

There was little outward sign of direct trouble between the two communist powers. Instead the dispute was transferred to third parties. Molotov was made a personal whipping-boy by Khruschov and after the 1960 Moscow Conference this role was taken on internationally by Albania, which in 1961 began a series of lengthy ideological slanging matches with the Soviet Union. From then onwards the interpreters read 'Mao' for 'Molotov' and 'China' for 'Albania'. In this way the two great powers gave themselves ground for manœuvre and retreat without either of them losing face before the lesser members of the communist movement, or indeed in the eyes of the world at large.

The open propaganda duel between Peking and Moscow was conducted in ideological terms of a highly esoteric nature, meaningless to the onlooker. Peking, it will be remembered, devoted

[1] Thus the Chinese ideological journal *Red Flag* of December 1960 changed a vital sentence of the Moscow Declaration. This referred to 'the struggle for peace, national independence, democracy and socialism' but in *Red Flag* it became 'the struggle against imperialism and for world peace, national liberation, democracy and socialism'.

[2] In January 1963 the Chinese edition of the *Review* was discontinued, and later the Korean edition.

much space in 1960 to the heritage of Lenin and how Mao and the Chinese communists were carrying on that heritage. This was followed later in the Chinese ideological Press by attacks on 'Bernsteinian revisionism' and 'Kautsky deviations', delving into the history of Marxist philosophy to attack Soviet policies in the international field. When Khruschov began to make fresh negotiations with the Kennedy administration early in 1962, Peking started yet another anti-American campaign, directed personally against President Kennedy. Perhaps with the knowledge of this Chinese hostility the Soviet Leader in May 1962 told a visiting American journalist that though he would like to invite President Kennedy to Russia, he had to bear in mind that the Soviet people still remembered the U2 spy-plane shot down over the U.S.S.R. in 1960, the incident which brought with it the cancellation of the Paris Summit Meeting that summer.

For its part, the Soviet Press was equally oblique though in a different manner. From 1960 onwards, for instance, the usual Moscow Press editorial eulogies on Communist Chinese anniversaries were omitted. The Moscow weekly *New Times* in its first number of 1962 published a long article on Peking which talked about the father of Chinese nationalism Sun Yat-sen but made no mention whatever of Mao Tse-tung. When in March 1962 the Peking *People's Daily* called for moderation in economic planning, it was republished prominently in *Pravda*, though only after a lapse of five days. On an earlier occasion *Pravda* had used the quote technique to attack the Albanian leaders directly, by reprinting a criticism from the Danish communist paper *Land og Volk*. In this way it extended technique more normally used in the communist Press to attack Western policies by selective quoting from Western sources.

The intra-Party polemics were extended to radio broadcasts from late 1961 onwards, the initiative being taken by Moscow, which began regular broadcasts to China in Kuoyu, the communist-promoted standardized version of Mandarin, which is most widely understood in China. By early 1962 these Soviet broadcasts were polemical, attacking the Albanians and the Yugoslavs, frequently by name, and condemning them as dogmatists or revisionists.

Peking Radio started special transmissions for the Soviet Union at the end of February 1962, confining itself to fairly innocuous programmes dealing with news of the day and background feature talks. In 1960 the Russians stopped the distribution in the U.S.S.R. of the Sino-Soviet Friendship magazine *Druzhba*, the main organ of Chinese news and views in the Soviet Union. The Chinese also stopped the circulation in China of the equivalent Soviet paper. While the U.S.S.R. had its Kuoyu radio service in operation by this time, the Chinese had no such means of ensuring that their voice was heard over the border. The Peking Russian language transmission from February 1962 seemed to have been a precautionary step by the Chinese to provide themselves with a means of countering Soviet broadcasts.

In March and April 1962 there was talk on both sides of a possible break, with *Red Flag* asserting that China would not be afraid of it. In Hungary the Party theoretical journal also took up the issue, declaring that a split was preferable to confusion. In April Khruschov began fresh overtures to Yugoslavia, which within a year was to be once more officially listed by Moscow as a member of 'the socialist camp'.

By 1962 the Sino-Soviet dispute was being felt throughout all the communist front organizations. It had first erupted behind the scenes at the Council meeting of the World Federation of Trade Unions in Peking in June 1960, but without any public references to the differences at the time. It was another eighteen months before the dispute became fully noticeable in the fronts. In December 1961 the World Council of Peace met in Stockholm to begin the organization of a World Congress for Peace and Disarmament, to be held in Moscow in July 1962. This Congress was openly opposed by the Chinese delegates.

Throughout 1962 and 1963 the Sino-Soviet split dominated the major fronts. At the Afro-Asian Writers' Congress in Cairo, February 1962, the Chinese objected to proposals to send greetings to the W.C.P. and were publicly rebuked for this by the Soviet delegate. At the actual Moscow Peace Congress in July the Chinese continued to use the sessions as platforms for their own national liberation themes. So by the beginning of 1963 the World Peace Council was turning into a Sino-Soviet brawling ground, while its international standing had already been weakened in quite another way when its delegates were refused representation at the Oxford Conference of Non-Aligned Peace Movements held in January 1963, on the grounds that it was an aligned body. Some months later a meeting of the W.C.P. scheduled for Warsaw in June was cancelled at the last moment. A meeting that autumn was once more a platform for disagreement.

The World Federation of Trade Unions has been equally burdened by the dispute. It had to face a clash over the Common Market, which was supported by some of its members, but rigidly opposed by the Chinese. This issue was only side-tracked by a policy of agreeing to disagree. More important than this, however, was the Indonesian proposal in May 1963 to convene an Afro-Asian Workers' Conference in Djarkarta later in the year. This Indonesian proposal had the full support of the Chinese. In retaliation the W.F.T.U. called its affiliates in Asia and Africa to a consultative meeting in Prague at the end of July to conduct what it called 'a broad exchange of opinions'.

Such bodies as the World Federation of Scientific Workers, the World Federation of Democratic Youth and the International Union of Students suffered in their own special ways, as well as the International Organization of Journalists and the Afro-Asian People's Solidarity Organization. The Scientific Workers Seventh General Assembly at the end of 1962 was hampered in its resolutions by the extreme anti-imperialist views of the Chinese: the impasse created was only resolved by the Chinese absenting themselves from the final session. The W.F.D.Y. and the I.U.S. both brought discredit on conferences organized in Algiers and Tunis in the spring of 1963 because the Sino-Soviet dispute pushed out matters of immediate African concern. This also irritated African delegates to the Moshi, Tanganyika, conference of the Afro-Asian People's Solidarity Organization in February 1963.

For a long time the International Organization of Journalists had been trying to convene a 'unity' meeting with non-affiliated national journalists' organizations. It had hoped to get fresh support in this from a Conference of Afro-Asian journalists held in Djarkarta in April 1963, organized by the Indonesians with strong Chinese support. The meeting was held but the I.O.J. and the Russians were only given observer status and so played no direct role in setting up the Peking-orientated Afro-Asian Journalists' Association, with affiliates in forty-eight countries. Following this success, Peking in the summer of 1963 proposed that as a follow-up a conference should be held of journalists from Africa, Asia and Latin America.

For its part the I.O.J. acted more conservatively, organizing a Third World Meeting of Journalists in September 1963 on board the Soviet liner *Litva*, cruising in the Mediterranean. Officially organized by an I.O.J. offshoot, the International Committee for the Co-operation of Journalists, the conference paid brief visits to Algiers, Tunis, Tripoli and Alexandria and its shipbound nature ensured a greater control by the organizers.

At the end of June 1963 the Women's International Democratic Federation held a Congress in Moscow which again brought the Sino-Soviet animosities into the open. Despite the triumphal appearance in the Soviet delegation of the woman astronaut Tereshkova – it almost seemed as if she had made her space flight especially for the Congress, so close was the timing – the meeting was a failure as a symbol of solidarity, with the Chinese and Russians making accusation and counter-accusation. Moscow won the day, but at the expense of weakening yet another of its fronts.

Indeed, by mid-1963 it appeared that the Chinese were intent on setting up their own system of communist fronts. This was strongly suggested by the new Afro-Asian workers' and journalists' organizations, as well as by the proposal to set up a Chinese Regional Centre of the World Federation of Scientific Workers. In the early 1950's a Peking-based Asian and Pacific Peace Liaison Committee was set up as a W.C.P. regional centre. This also became a useful outlet for the Chinese views on national liberation and peace.

Up to the beginning of 1963, the polemics within Party circles had continued without direct references to the two main protagonists. Then Moscow proposed a conference with Peking to resolve current differences and this was eventually agreed for July 1963, after an initial postponement by the Russian side. But before this could take place the Chinese put their cards on the table with a detailed restatement of their line in an open letter to the Soviet Party on June 16th. This stressed the revolutionary role of world communism and underlined previous Peking attacks on Yugoslavia, stating in clear terms that 'anybody (who) does not pursue the correct Marxist-Leninist line and policies, does not defend the unity of the socialist camp but, on the contrary, creates tensions and splits within it, or even follows the policies of the Yugoslav revisionists, tries to liquidate the socialist camp or helps capitalist countries to attack fraternal socialist countries, then he is betraying the interest of the entire international proletariat and the people of the world'. Following so closely on Khruschov's well-publicized *rapprochement* with Tito and the re-admission of Yugoslavia to Moscow's list of socialist countries, this could only be seen as a direct attack on Moscow's policies.

Peking distributed this letter all round the world within a matter of a week or two. But Moscow refused to publish it in the Soviet Press at the time as being 'inexpedient'. Its publication then, it was stated a month later, would have required a public Soviet reply, which would have led to more polemics, with a resulting worsening of relations between the two parties. It was not until July 14th, 1963, that the letter was published in the Soviet Press, together with the official Soviet reply restating the Moscow line that peaceful coexistence was better tactics for the 60's than revolution. By this time the Moscow Conference of Soviet and Chinese Party representatives had been held and adjourned indefinitely without agreement.

By this time, too, the Soviet, British and United States Governments had met in Moscow and come to an agreement banning nuclear explosions on land, under the sea and in the upper atmosphere. This in itself was a direct ideological rebuff to the Chinese, for it meant that Moscow was prepared to negotiate with the ideological enemy in the face of all Peking's accusations of betrayal.

So 1963 saw the challenge to Moscow as sole centre of world revolution come fully into the open. Ten years after his death Stalin's monolith was split asunder. No longer is there a single driving force for the communist movement, but two. Both have the same expressed aim, the establishment of the communist system throughout the world. Their differences lie not in their ultimate objective, but in the manner of its attainment.

CHAPTER EIGHT

# *What is to be Done?*

Communist propaganda as an instrument of totalitarian expansionism has one vital specification – it is world-wide in concept and in operation. With relatively few exceptions, the propaganda campaigns of any one moment can be traced from country to country, from community to community. In mid-1962, for instance, the European Common Market was being attacked by Western communists as an anti-Soviet political device which would only weaken the individual countries belonging to it. In Africa and Asia the same Common Market was being attacked by communists as an economic weapon against Afro-Asian advancement. The two lines of attack were linked by direct Moscow propaganda in its denunciation of the Common Market as part of the imperialist plan to build up a unified Europe politically and economically in opposition to the Communist Bloc.

At this same period the Soviet Union was pressing its disarmament proposals hard on every occasion, notably at the World Peace Congress organized during July in the Soviet capital by the World Peace Council, with the support of well-wishing, non-communist adherents. In these circles disarmament of the Great Powers was urged as a means of lessening world tensions.

In more militant Party circles, the Soviet disarmament proposals were presented in a very different light, summed up by an article 'The Struggle for National Liberation and Disarmament' in the June 1962 *World Marxist Review*. The writer, a North African Party militant, Abdelkader El Ouahrani, summed up the significance of the Soviet stand thus: 'When we speak of general and complete disarmament we primarily have in view the disarmament of Big Powers, the powers possessing modern arms, not the peoples fighting for freedom. This is not because general and complete disarmament does not concern them, but because weapons possessed by the national-liberation armies would at a stretch suffice merely for the "strictly limited contingents, agreed for every country, of police (militia), equipped with small arms, designed solely to maintain internal order and protect the personal security of citizens', as envisaged in the Soviet disarmament plan. That is why there are no grounds for saying that complete disarmament would weaken the oppressed peoples. People who argue along these lines approach the disarmament problem too narrowly, and their attitude, favouring the arms race, is not only mistaken. In a way it even plays into the hands of the imperialists.' Earlier in this article Abdelkader assured his fellow Party members that the communist supporters of disarmament were no pacifist dreamers, thinking of peace at any price. They saw the disarmament issue as one of the essential strategies of communism today.

The problem for us is to assess communist propaganda at any one time; this poses a fundamental problem, one that is capitalized to the full by Moscow and Peking.

This is well illustrated by the bacterial warfare campaign discussed later. Accusations against the Americans were made and their general theme was accepted as truth by large numbers of people. This acceptance cannot be measured statistically, but those of us who look back to that period 1952–3 will remember the opinion often expressed that even if the Americans had not used germ warfare in Korea, they were quite capable of doing so. Remembering specific incidents connected with this campaign, it is significant how many times responsible scientists were to forget their whole academic training, indeed their academic instincts, and back claims that could not stand up to the slightest scientific investigation.

For ordinary people the problem was their inability to sift the evidence for themselves: either it was not there, or they did not feel competent to study it. For the scientists involved the problem was more complex. In many cases they could not be bothered to study the matter, or they preferred to have their minds made up for them. They preferred to be governed in their emotions and actions by the mob-thoughts in their heads rather than by their intellects.

This mob-emotion in the individual expresses itself as antipathy, rather than in any positive way. This negative fixation has been well exploited by the communists ever since the end of the war, with their carefully controlled programmes of anti-Americanism in all parts of the world, programmes which on many occasions have descended to pure xenophobia. Where other nationalist issues are stronger, so the communist line is switched. In Eastern Europe the fear of German revanchism – however ill-founded – is constantly kept alive. Similarly in Western Europe the jackboot is a commonplace placard symbol of anti-German sentiment.

It was under these circumstances that in June 1962 a Welsh miners' gala in Cardiff was reportedly told by a leading M.P., Miss Jennie Lee: 'The biggest single tragedy since the end of the war was rearming Germany. I am critical of the Soviet Union in some respects, but I have profound sympathy with the warning they have given on the price we may have to pay by them (Germany) starting a third world war.' This sentiment is typical of much muddled thinking conditioned by constant communist allegations of German revanchism as an active precursor of a third world war.

Examples such as these can be extended to cover every field of international activity, with a regular flow of communist accusations of bad faith against the West, of imperialist plottings against the well-being of Asia, Africa and Latin America. Our problem is to put these accusations into perspective.

In assessing communist propaganda, we must first assess ourselves. We must be quite sure in our own minds what we mean when we use those words which flow so freely off the tongue – freedom, democracy, equality, fraternity, peace. We must be just as sure of ourselves when we resort to those equally glib adjectives reactionary, undemocratic, fascist, anti-popular, repressive. When weighing the communist use of such words, we must remember the esoteric double-talk meanings given to them in Party parlance. For the communist, freedom, democracy, equality, fraternity and, above all, peace can only come when communism is firmly established throughout the world. Whatever forces oppose communism, they are by their very nature reactionary, undemocratic, fascist, anti-popular and repressive. When we study the communist viewpoint, we must consider it in terms of these double values.

This puts the onus of self-discipline as firmly on ourselves, as it does on the communists. There is one fundamental difference.

The communist has a discipline demanded of him by the Party and system to which he belongs, and which he is expected to support in every way possible. The non-communist must go it alone. He must be clear in his own mind because he feels the need within himself, not because he has been so instructed. He must replace propaganda by understanding, catchwords by thought. There is no propaganda for freedom, the two are inimical.

Because such a duty is self-imposed, it is all the more difficult to carry out. It is human nature to want to be positive. This can be a weakness as much as a strength. After more than fifteen years of a Cold War begun by the communists as part of their campaign of attrition, everyone is tired of the whole subject. After fifteen years, we are beginning to forget how it all started. The Zhdanov directives, the Berlin blockade, the progressive seizures of power throughout Eastern Europe, all these were contributory factors to the Cold War, which would not have started but for Moscow's expansionist activities and the threats they represented. But – unless we are directly involved – memories are short: we are only human and want the hatreds of the 50's transformed into amiabilities for the 60's.

Under such natural and emotional conditions, self-discipline is all the more necessary. The short memory of mankind is a vital weapon in the communist armoury. Throughout all the Soviet violations of solemn agreements in the 20's and 30's, through the period of Moscow's territorial and ideological expansion in the 40's, during the suppressions of revolt and disaffection in the 50's, the communist leaders have gone ahead with their plans in the face of world opinion, reckoning that mounting indignations would soon subside and that, as one crisis overtook another, so the past would quickly be forgotten.

We should remember how communist propaganda has been helping this process by the use of the negative example, the technique of masking one's own shortcomings by constantly drawing attention to those, real and imaginary, of the opponent. It is not sufficient for communism's dynamism that it should simply extol its own virtues and successes: for the propagandist that is a relatively minor task, even now.

Far more important is the exposure of enemies. The enemies of communism are as varied as the peoples of the world, so there is no end to the attack. As fast as one enemy is considered vanquished, so communist propaganda must seek out fresh targets for its shots.

We have seen how in the 40's the attack was on American aid for Europe under the Marshall Plan: by the 50's it was switched to colonialism. But this decade was marked by the peaceful transition to nationhood of many colonial countries, in defiance of all communist dogma. So in the 60's a new doctrine of neo-colonialism was formulated, by which all forms of Western aid were condemned outright as representing economic imperialism in another form.

In the 30's the Nazis in Germany headed the anti-Comintern pact and their war against the Soviet Union from 1941 onwards was presented by Hitler as a holy crusade against communism. This has been used ever since by communist propaganda to equate anti-communism of all kinds with nazism and fascism – a smear tactic which has proved particularly effective in vaguely socialist circles, where critical appraisals of communist policies and actions can be relatively easily countered by implications that the critics were mouthing the hysterical outbursts of Hitler.

This theme was projected on a grand international scale in the 40's and 50's by representing American political and military leaders and their administrations as the neo-Nazis. This thesis has often been used by the communists to argue that for them to make concessions to America on vital issues would be the same as making concessions to Hitler. In the 60's, the concept of American imperialism and German nazism became combined into a third, that of West German imperialism, as represented by West German economic relations with the developing countries.[1]

For the communists, it is essential that their potential opposition be kept divided. They are therefore fundamentally opposed to any defensive alliance, whether it be S.E.A.T.O. in South-East Asia,

[1] At the same time the Communist Bloc actively pushed the claims of its own East German member, the German Democratic Republic. Few countries outside the Bloc have recognized Eastern Germany diplomatically, preferring their contacts with the Federal German Republic in the West, which had so much more to offer them economically. This preference for West German aid is a major reason behind the communist attacks.

C.E.N.T.O. in the Middle East or N.A.T.O. in Western Europe. All such groupings must be presented in communist propaganda as aggressive in intention and action. By the same basic approach, actions by supra-national bodies such as the United Nations can only be backed when they are considered likely to help further the communist cause. Because Trygve Lie initiated the U.N. action in Korea, he incurred the hostility of the Communist Bloc and his re-election as Secretary General was effectively opposed by the Soviet Union. His successor, Dag Hammarskjöld, came under communist fire himself, following his actions with the U.N. Committee on Hungary after 1956, and in 1960 the Soviet Union blocked his re-election as Secretary General, proposing that a three-man *troika* be set up in his place. If carried out this move would have given the communists an effective veto on any action proposed by the *troika* majority which did not suit them.

The major group resistant to communism is that of religion. Communism by its ideology is militantly atheistic, as it showed by its suppression of religious activities in Russia in the early years of the Revolution, but religion has continued to function despite all the restrictions imposed on it. In the late 50's and 60's Moscow started a new anti-religious drive, with the accent on better propaganda with less open coercion.[1] This drive within the Bloc boundaries is complemented by one of a quite different nature, directed against religious groups outside the Bloc. In this external drive, the communists make systematic use of religious organizations and personalities to support their international campaigns of the moment, particularly those concerned with peace.

The communist attack on religion within the Bloc is all-embracing, being directed against Christians, Jews, Muslims and the rest without discrimination. If individual religious leaders come into conflict with the Party or the State, they are publicly pilloried as corrupt creatures greedy for power, counter-revolutionaries and spies working for imperialism and fascist reaction. Everything is done at the show trials of such churchmen to reduce their standing in the eyes of the people from one of moral leadership to one of criminal corruption.

[1] In 1963 A.P.N. became directly involved in this propaganda drive.

Similarly in the trade union world, the communists must constantly attack the institutions they do not control, by all means at their disposal. Thus in the late 50's the successes of the International Confederation of Trade Unions in Africa was such that Moscow instigated – not for the first time – a campaign of forgeries in Africa in 1960 as part of its plan to discredit the I.C.F.T.U. as 'the new vehicle and machinery of imperialist control and stranglehold of the African continent', to quote the words of one such forgery entitled *The Great Conspiracy against Africa*, in which was published the supposed secret annexe to a British Government Cabinet Paper on Africa.

Such attacks on countries, religions, trade unions and others likely to provide opposition to communist local, national and international policies are essential features of communist activities. Their logical extension became operative in the summer of 1962 when attacks began on anti-communism itself, continuing on and off into 1964. This 'anti-anti-communism' had two aspects. Within Party circles anti-communism was condemned as counter-revolutionary. For this ideological reason, Party members were told, they must actively oppose any signs of anti-communism and not allow it to go unanswered. At the same time, in non-communist circles, anti-communism was condemned as being against the spirit of peaceful coexistence. The communists wanted to coexist peacefully with non-communists, ran the argument. The dangers of a third world war came from those who would not trust the good intentions of the communists and their leaders: the Cold War was being deliberately carried on by the anti-communists for their own despicable ends; by its very nature, therefore, anti-communism was one of the greatest barriers to peace and understanding.

Soviet propaganda launched the new decade of the 60's with the formation of the press agency A.P.N. *Novosti* under the motto 'information for a world in need of mutual understanding'.[1]

[1] In May 1962 an Indian paper, the Bombay *Free Press Journal*, took to task the way in which *Novosti* implemented its motto 'information for a world in need of mutual understanding' when discussing a *Novosti* booklet circulated in India by the Soviet Embassy. The booklet, entitled *The Ghost Returns*, was a criticism of West Germany. What was the message of mutual understanding in the booklet, asked the *Free Press Journal*: 'It is provocative material against West Germany. It is not con-

For its part, the non-communist world leaves no doubt in the minds of everyone that its fundamental interest in world peace is based on the existence side by side of a wide range of political and social systems.

Communists also desire to avoid world war, but this they do not believe possible except under a world-wide communist system.[1] Towards this goal, as we have seen, they are expending considerable resources against established systems, some of which work reasonably well while others are ready for modification and change. The communists must always attack, as the best means of defence. Being continually on the offensive, they reckon to prevent people – within and outside the Bloc – from considering communist programmes too deeply. This is an essential task for the Party apparatus at every level and in every part of the world.

A century ago, writing in the *New York Tribune* in April, 1853, Karl Marx took a look at the international scene. 'The ignorance, the laziness, the pusillanimity, the perpetual fickleness and the credulousness of Western governments,' he declared, 'enabled Russia to achieve successively every one of her aims.' In modern terms the bitter commentary of Marx brings before us once more our own weaknesses.

But communism also has its own weaknesses. It is based on the utilization of the masses and its propaganda is directed accordingly. By its very nature it cannot brook opposition for long; it cannot afford to make fundamental concessions. This is something that no propaganda technique can hide in the long run.

[1] To this end they see national liberation in a limited light. As an article in *Soviet State and Law* No. 7, 1962 stated in legalistic terms: 'the national sovereignty of the Socialist countries knows none of the aloofness and nationalist inclinations of individual countries as it admits where necessary of the subordination of the interests of the individual country to the more important, international interests of the entire Socialist Commonwealth'.

---

ceived in the spirit of "mutual understanding". It is vicious and venomous. It can only help promote hatred.' The paper went on to ask: 'Is it correct for a foreign diplomatic mission in India to carry on malicious propaganda and political vendetta against another country with which we have friendly relations?'

PART FOUR

# *A Propaganda Case History: Bacterial Warfare*

CHAPTER NINE

# *Sending the Message around the World*

Of the many hate campaigns waged by communist propagandists in the post-war years, the most highly organized, closely concentrated and virulent was that generally known as the germ war, or more formally the bacterial warfare campaign of 1951–3.

Whereas the other anti-Western propaganda was general in its concept – anti-colonialism, ban-the-bomb, peace drives and five-power-pact appeals, colour bars and racialism – the bacterial warfare drive was quite specific in its intention. This was to brand the United States contingent of the United Nations forces in Korea as war criminals, deliberately resorting to bacterial weapons against the armed forces and the civilian population of North Korea and North-east China.

These were not the only atrocity allegations made by the communists against the Americans.[1] As will be discussed later, the Peking and Pyongyang Press and radio made every imaginable accusation, ranging from vague generalizations to complete statistical details. These accusations were made only to be shelved and replaced by fresh horror stories. They started as an organized stream in 1951, developing into 1952, when they were almost entirely supplanted by the bacterial theme, which continued right past the armistice into the United Nations debates of the autumn and winter of 1953, when an effective stop to the campaign came, not from Peking or Pyongyang, but from Moscow. The campaign officially ended in 1953, but this is not to say that it then ceased to have any effect – this indeed is the crucial test of all propaganda.

[1] Although the forces fighting for South Korea were under United Nations command, the communist propaganda was specifically anti-American in its content and so it will be less confusing in dealing with this particular aspect to refer to American or United States forces, only bringing in the U.N. when particular mention of it is made.

Undoubtedly the accusations against the Americans had significant influences at the time, but how long afterwards did these influences continue?

The bacterial warfare (B.W.[1]) was waged with all the resources of the world-wide communist propaganda machine that could be put to work. The theme was simplicity itself and needed no subtlety; it could be played as a piece of straight xenophobia or as a study in pained intellectual distress.

It is of particular interest to the student of propaganda: first of all, it was specific and so demonstrates how many variations are possible on a single theme; secondly, it was conducted not only in terms of breadth, but also of depth. Unlike any other such campaign before or since, the subject was pursued in great detail, right to the laboratory bench. Thirdly, the campaign involved a large number of people. Indeed, so large was the number – hundreds of what might be called direct participants, not to mention thousands of others involved indirectly – that the accusations acquired tremendous force and credibility, because it seemed impossible that so many responsible people should deliberately lie as part of a concerted plan.

The immense detail of this anti-Western campaign makes it a profitable exercise in propaganda which will show us just how people may find themselves involved in the communist apparatus without ever being aware of the part they play. Such people may be housewives or scientists, they may be members of communist society or bourgeois intellectuals of the West.

Many of the events that were puzzling at the time are now somewhat clearer with the passing of the years. For many people germ warfare is something long forgotten, at least in their conscious memory. The Korean campaign as such is rarely referred to by communist propagandists nowadays, though the subject in general is quite often stirred up, but as a case study in purpose and technique it is as fresh as it ever was. The only difference is that the propagandists of today have learned from the mistakes of a decade ago.

The war in Korea broke out on a Sunday in June 1950, with the

[1] The scientifically correct term is micro-biological warfare but I am using that by which the campaign was commonly known.

South quite unprepared. The North Korean forces advanced rapidly southwards, their armies vastly superior in numbers and equipment. An appeal to the United Nations from South Korea against this aggression was backed by a Security Council demand that the North should withdraw its forces and accept mediation. This was ignored and the South then appealed directly to Washington. Based in part on the Security Council resolution, President Truman told the South that he would send in not only arms, but also American forces. In the fortuitous absence of the Soviet member, the U.N. Security Council approved the American action and invited other U.N. members to follow suit in furnishing: 'Such assistance to the Republic of Korea as may be necessary to repel the armed attack and to restore international peace and security in the area.'

From this time on the U.N. action in Korea – and the debates on it in the U.N. itself – was led by the Americans in dynamic style. In the three years which followed, the brunt of the fighting was borne by American soldiers and airmen, with other epic parts played by British and Turkish forces and smaller contingents from other U.N. member countries.

At this early stage another important step was taken by President Truman, outside the U.N. framework. Since American forces were involved on the mainland of Asia, he decided to 'neutralize' the island of Taiwan (Formosa), held by the Nationalist Chinese forces of Chiang Kai-shek, who only the previous autumn had been driven off the Chinese mainland by the victorious communist armies of Mao Tse-tung. This policy of neutralization meant that the U.S. Navy was given the job of preventing communist occupation of the island, at the same time as it prevented Chiang launching a large-scale attack against the mainland.

Within a few weeks of their attack the North Korean forces had occupied all but a small part of the South. But the arrival of fresh American troops and equipment saw the situation change. On September 1st the North's last great offensive was beaten back. Within three weeks the South Korean capital of Seoul was recaptured and the whole of South Korea cleared.

With South Korea won back, the U.N. Commander-in-Chief, General MacArthur, considered that apart from clearing up the war was over. On October 1st he broadcast to the North Korean forces demanding their surrender; but the North did not capitulate, and left the U.N. in a quandary. Should they advance and destroy the aggressors, even though they were now in their own territory? Or should they just stand guard on the frontier? There was considerable debate inside and outside the United Nations on these crucial issues, linked as they were with the general desire to limit the war and to prevent it spreading farther in Asia. Then on October 7th the General Assembly voted to establish a 'unified, independent and democratic government of Korea'. With the North Korean refusal to surrender or to negotiate, this could only be done by the U.N. forces occupying the North as well as the South, to supervise the political organization.

On October 8th the U.N. forces crossed the 38th Parallel and advanced northwards, to occupy the capital, Pyongyang. No action was taken either by Peking or Moscow in support of the North.

But already the Chinese communists had given the warning that if the Parallel were crossed, they would not remain impassive. As the U.N. forces advanced they started to meet Chinese troops fighting with the North Koreans. Within a few days the fact was confirmed by Peking and on November 6th the Chinese intervention was reported to the United Nations Security Council by General MacArthur. The next day Peking radio put out the first story that Chinese 'volunteers' in their thousands were in Korea. Still the U.N. forces pressed on, reaching the Yalu river border between Korea and China on November 21st. Here it was that an offensive was announced by General MacArthur which if successful would to all intents and purposes finish the war by Christmas. But almost before it had begun, it clashed with a counter-offensive on a heavy and well-planned scale by the Chinese in large numbers – 450,000 according to General MacArthur's estimate. With this open entry of a Great Power on the side of the North the political as well as the military situation was radically changed.

Militarily the U.N. forces were forced to retreat. Pyongyang was recaptured by the North and Seoul was reached and taken once more by the communists. Politically the controversy over China's aggression lasted a month in the United Nations. Eventually Communist China was branded as an aggressor by the General Assembly, though the vote was by no means unanimous.

The Chinese advance had cost them dearly in lives and the first few weeks of 1951 saw their impetus slacken and turn into retreat. By March the advancing U.N. forces had recaptured Seoul and in April they were back at the Parallel once more. Here they dug in and repulsed communist counter-attacks. By this time the U.N. forces had complete superiority in the air and savoured the expectation of victory. While this was going on, MacArthur had been relieved of his command for political indiscretions and his place had been taken by a more cautious man, General Bradley. His objective was no longer to drive the communists out of North Korea, since to his mind the war could be ended when the Chinese realized that aggression had failed. This was the situation in June 1951.

Then on June 23rd, a year after the war had started, came the first sign of its end. The Soviet delegate to the United Nations, Mr Malik, gave a radio talk, one of a U.N. series. Almost in passing, he dropped a comment that the time had come for a settlement of the Korean question, discussions should begin for an armistice and the opposing forces should withdraw to either side of the Parallel. It was in this almost off-hand manner that the Soviet Union returned to the centre of the Korean stage in the U.N., having previously left things to China, returning in the guise of the peace-maker, although it was to be more than two years before the armistice actually took place. It is at this point that the bacterial warfare campaign began to pick up.

The first signs that bacterial warfare charges were to become a major factor of communist propaganda were not of any significance at the time they showed themselves, rather they were a relatively small part of a much wider series of attacks accusing the United States forces of all manner of atrocities against the civilian population of North Korea. By their very nature these atrocity charges were quite remarkable, covering as they did every category of crime and inhumanity against the defenceless. Yet within eighteen months they were dropped, as soon as they had served their immediate purpose of building up a xenophobic image of a gook-hating G.I. crashing his way across Asia.

It is worthwhile considering these initial charges, which were so very pointed in their statistics of suffering. They can best be summarized from the report of an international commission organized by a leading communist front, the Women's International Democratic Federation, from its headquarters in East Berlin. Composed of seventeen women 'delegated by different women's organizations, some of them members of the W.I.D.F. and some of them not', the delegation prepared its report, 'in accordance with the evidence members saw with their own eyes and with statements given to them by eye-witnesses and officials in Korea'. The report was made in May 1951 'somewhere near Pyongyang' and dealt mainly with events at the end of 1950 and the first weeks of 1951, the period when fortunes swayed north and south of the Parallel, following the entry of the Chinese into the war. The areas surveyed by the commission were those which had felt the sweep south of the communists and the return north again of the U.N. forces, prior to the uneasy stabilization at the Parallel itself.

At the one extreme the commission presented mass murder, for instance: 'members of the commission established that in the whole province of Whang Hai 120,000 had been killed by the occupying armies, in addition to those killed by aerial bombardment. In the town of Anak, 19,092 people had been killed by the U.S.A., British and Syngman Rhee forces.' At the other, the same sub-group of the commission told of an eleven-year-old girl who came from a village 32 km. from Anak, who stated: 'She was in the fourth class at school when the Americans came to her village and she was put into prison with her parents. After twelve days her father was crucified and thrown into a river. The child's mother was a member of the Party of Labour (the North Korean Communist Party) and the child told commission members that for this her mother had had her head and her breasts cut off. The same child's sister was buried alive. The child herself is now in a school for orphans, and on learning from her teacher that the commission was visiting the district asked to be allowed to give evidence.'

Another typical passage of the report quoted the evidence given by a woman of the deaths of her son and six grandsons, adding:

'We thought that the Americans were Christians, gentlemen. We did not think that they would kill people with such brutality.' This disillusioned reference to violated Christian principles was repeated time and time again, with the corollary story of a widow bereft of her family who '. . . before the Americans came had been a Christian and went to church regularly, but she could no longer believe anything'.

This atrocity report was widely published by the W.I.D.F. and its associated bodies in the summer of 1951, with the *Cominform Journal* bringing it out as a special supplement in mid-August, when the truce talks were under way. The examples given are a small part of the whole; their purpose was obvious in its simplicity. The popular image of the U.N. soldier as the big-hearted man who could always find a sweet for a child and a helping hand for a woman had to be destroyed. Confidence in the Church and religion generally could also be undermined at the same time. Full capital was made out of the undoubted savagery between Koreans from the North and South, facing each other in a bitter civil war, and bedevilled by political considerations decided way beyond their own borders.

No one could ever claim that the commission itself was impartial, the W.I.D.F. background was too obvious for that. Certainly it was not a commission of investigation in the sense that it wanted to look dispassionately into the allegations against the U.N., to assess the extent to which they were true or false, minimized or exaggerated. The investigators' job was simply to set the story down and tell it to the world. This they did on their return to their different countries, in lecture tours, pamphlets and articles in the sympathetic Press. In the communist countries there was wide publicity given to their stories, though elsewhere more concern was felt for the success of the truce talks and an end to the conflict itself.

This commission was in Korea from May 16th to May 27th, mostly in the region of the capital Pyongyang. On May 8th, a week before they arrived, the North Korean Foreign Minister had sent an official protest to the United Nations charging American troops with spreading smallpox in December 1950 and January 1951. This was reported in the Soviet Press on May 10th and in the Chinese papers on May 11th. On May 13th the Soviet government paper *Izvestia* linked the smallpox charges with previous allegations of bacterial warfare preparations in the U.S.A. and the alleged protection by the Americans of Japanese army scientists branded as war criminals by the Russians two years earlier, charges to which we shall return later in more detail.

This official protest formalized a number of reports which together indicated a growing interest in the bacterial and chemical warfare theme in communist propaganda. In February 1951 a Soviet broadcast to Germany told how workers in Hamburg had been overcome with mustard gas when unloading some American ships. On March 5th Peking radio alleged that chemical attacks had been made by U.N. forces on three dates, February 23rd and 26th and March 3rd. Two days later the Peking *People's Daily* asserted that this incident was no accident since: '. . . the American use of poison gas in Korea coincides with the report from Germany that mustard gas had been sent to Hamburg from America.'

The next day the Moscow *Literary Gazette* picked up the theme of chemical warfare with the first of many attacks on the use of napalm as a weapon of war. March 14th saw a Peking Red Cross protest to the League of Red Cross Societies: '. . . to take action to prevent the atrocity of using poisonous gas by the American imperialists in their war of aggression in Korea.' This was reprinted by *Pravda* and a few days later Peking reported that the evidence of 'poisonous shells' had been collected and photographed, while publishing a Chinese eye-witness account of an alleged American chemical warfare attack.

Almost immediately *Pravda* came out with another report from Peking sources that the U.N. Commander-in-Chief, General MacArthur, was '. . . engaged in large-scale production of bacteriological weapons for use against the Korean army and people.' This theme was picked up by the *Cominform Journal* later in March and on April 3rd the Bulgarian Red Cross protested to the U.N. charging the Americans with using chemical warfare, with a similar protest from the Rumanian Red Cross on May 4th, following a Peking report that the Americans in Korea were carrying out bacterial experiments on Chinese prisoners.

Variations on this last story were to persist for many months. They had as their basis an American landing-craft equipped with laboratories for research into bacterial diseases, which was sent to Korea for anti-epidemic work in general and specifically to check the large number of Chinese prisoners-of-war in the south for plague, smallpox and other epidemic diseases they could have brought south with them, diseases made all the more virulent by the destruction of war. As the germ charges increased a year later, this landing-craft was to become a symbol for communist propagandists of the Americans' complete disregard for human values, reducing their Chinese prisoners to the role of experimental animals.

In May 1951 the *Cominform Journal*'s Political Notes column was quite blunt in its theme of the moment. Under a cartoon showing a stern Chinese volunteer pointing to the gallows awaiting a cringing and bloody-handed MacArthur with severed women's heads hanging to his belt, the commentator Jan Marek left no doubt in his readers' minds:

'The words of righteous wrath and indignation in the Declaration of the Government of the Korean People's Democratic Republic addressed to the United Nations Organization resounded throughout the world. Addressing world public opinion on behalf of the Korean people heroically fighting for freedom against the American aggressors, the Government of the K.P.D.R. demands the arrest and trial of MacArthur, former Commander-in-Chief of the U.S. intervention troops in Korea, his successor, General Ridgway, and the other participants in aggression who are guilty of grave crimes against humanity.

'It has been proved irrefutably that on the basis of captured secret documents of the General Staff of Syngman Rhee's army and on the basis of evidence furnished by captured American soldiers that the U.S. aggressors are preparing for bacteriological warfare, that they dropped poison bombs from aircraft and used poison shells against the North Korean troops. They infected with smallpox the population in the provinces from which they had been driven out by the troops of the K.P.D.R. As established by medical experts, U.S. troops, before retreating from North Korea, spread smallpox among the population, seeking thereby to infect with disease the troops of the People's Army and the Chinese volunteers.'

Marek went on to refer to an epidemic in a number of provinces in the North, reaching 3,500 cases and over by April 1951, of whom ten per cent died. He claimed there were no epidemics in areas that had not been occupied by the Americans, a claim of little value when it is remembered that virtually the whole of North Korea had been occupied by U.N. forces just before the Chinese entered the war.

In Sofia a few weeks later the Women's International Democratic Federation held a council meeting at which Korea was a major subject for debate. The Chinese Vice-President of the Federation, Liu Tsin-yan, urged in a speech the need '. . . to stop the bacteriological warfare and the criminal activities of the American troops in Korea'. But this appeal found no echo in the resolutions passed by the meeting on June 22nd and 23rd, 1951.

Nor, indeed, was anything said about bacterial warfare in the report of the W.I.D.F. investigating commission, which had been there in Korea a few days after the official charge had been made by the North Korean Foreign Minister. Yet the commission members must have been told something about it. The Austrian representative Eva Prester at least was informed, for she made bacterial warfare charges in a pamphlet of her impressions published in Vienna on her return later that summer.

So in this summer of 1951 bacterial warfare charges were raised, and then dropped. The smallpox charges coincided – it now seems certain – with an epidemic. Indeed, it would be surprising if there had been no such epidemics with the country as devastated as it was. Here is not the place to speculate why the charges were not carried on, though it is noteworthy that a Chinese attempt at the Sofia W.I.D.F. meeting came to nothing just two days before the Soviet spokesman at the United Nations put forward his proposal for truce talks, a proposal he did not want over-shadowed at that moment by a new anti-American propaganda drive from Peking or Pyongyang.

This is not to say that nothing more was said in the months following about bacterial warfare. References were made with increasing frequency, but all as part of the general atrocity picture, made up as it was of indiscriminate bombing charges, deceptive looking toys that were booby traps in disguise, rape, murder and infanticide. Everything, in short, that could build up hatred and mistrust of the Americans and the U.N. forces.

One theme began to repeat itself, that of the Americans using Japanese bacterial warfare specialists – this was Soviet in origin, dating back to the end of 1949 and a show trial of Japanese war criminals in the East Siberian provincial centre of Khabarovsk. This trial was all but ignored by the West at the time it was taking place, largely because foreign correspondents were not allowed to cover it. But it began to take on a fuller significance towards the end of 1951 in Korea, a significance that was developed to the full a year later.

These occasional references and their overtones continued into 1952 without becoming specific. In the second half of February 1952 the campaign started in earnest. It began quietly, on February 18th, 1952, when Moscow Radio's Korean Service declared in an anonymous commentary *Alertness is a Weapon of the Korean People*: '. . . in order to dissolve the solidarity of the Korean home front, the American interventionists are sending spies and destructive elements into North Korea in secret for the purpose of obtaining military secrets, poisoning wells and spreading smallpox and typhus bacteria in various places.' It added the further allegation that: 'one of the most villainous methods practised by the American interventionists is the sending of lepers secretly into North Korea.' In themselves these charges were nothing new, for at various times over the previous months one or other of them had been made – all except the leper charge, which was to be levelled at a later date against the British. So commonplace were they in the Korean context that even the next phase seemed at first to be of no significance. This was a New China News Agency report relayed at dictation speed for local papers by the Peking home service programme, which stated that the Americans were resorting to germ warfare in Korea '. . . in contravention of international law . . .' and went on to mention seven alleged attacks between January 28th and February 17th in which American aircraft were said to have spread large quantities of germs of various kinds on the communist front and rear positions. This Peking broadcast was more specific, but it merely seemed to be playing a variation on a well-established theme.

It was on the next day, February 22nd, 1952 that the North Korean Foreign Minister, Pak Hen Yen,[1] made a formal statement accusing the Americans of using bacterial warfare in North Korea. This was the signal for the full-scale attack; Pak's statement ended with an appeal '. . . to the people of the whole world to check the outrages of the interventionists'. Two days later a supporting statement was made in Peking by the Chinese Foreign Minister, Chou En-lai, which again ended with the call to '. . . the world's peace-loving people to take steps to put an end to the frenzied, criminal acts of the United States Government . . .', adding the assurance that, '. . . the Chinese people, together with the people throughout the world, will struggle to the very end to halt the frenzied crimes of the United States Government . . .'.

The official North Korean protest alleged that from January 28th, 1952 onwards, '. . . the American imperialist invaders have been systematically scattering large quantities of bacteria-carrying insects by aircraft in order to disseminate infectious diseases over our front line positions and rear . . .'. On January 28th, it went on, three types of infected insects had been dropped, resembling black flies, fleas and ticks, over areas to the south-east of Ichon. On January 29th further enemy aircraft had scattered large numbers of flies and fleas over the Ichon area. On February 11th, enemy aircraft dropped large numbers of paper tubes and paper packets filled with fleas, spiders, mosquitoes and grasshoppers in the Pyongyang area. On February 13th enemy aircraft scattered large quantities of flies, fleas, mosquitoes and spiders over the Kumhwa area. This was followed on February 15th by quantities of bacteria-carrying flies, spiders and other insects over the Pyongyang area, with further scatterings the next day over areas east of the Pukhan river. Lastly, on February 17th further flies and fleas were dropped north of Pyongyang:

'Bacteriological tests show that these insects scattered by the aggressors on the positions of our troops and in our rear are

[1] There are various forms of transliteration of Korean names. Those adopted here may not be quite correct, but they are the easiest to remember.

infected with plague, cholera and the germs of other infectious diseases . . .'. The statement concluded that: '. . . this is irrefutable proof that the enemy is employing bacteria on a large scale and in a well-planned manner to slaughter the men of the Korean civilians. . . .'

The protest went on to recapitulate various points already familiar, that the American forces were using Japanese war criminals – 'running dogs of American imperialism and known to the world as arch-schemers of bacterial warfare' – and that communist prisoners were being used by the Americans for B.W. experiments.

The crux of the whole matter was given in the summing up: '. . . like the other outrages engineered by the American imperialists during the Korean armistice negotiations, the use of bacteriological warfare brings out the naked criminal character of American imperialism in all its heinousness. But whatever violent means it employs, American imperialism will never attain its ends in Korea. Nothing but the most vehement opposition of the peace-loving peoples and utter bankruptcy of its aggressive schemes is in store for it. . . .' The protest ended with an appeal '. . . to the people of the whole world to check the outrages of the interventionists and to investigate and to define the international responsibility of the organizers of the use of bacteriological weapons. . .'.

The supporting protest of the Chinese foreign Minister, Chou En-lai, recapitulated the thesis: '. . . that this is not the first time that American imperialism has used bacteriological weapons in its war of intervention in Korea . . .'. Chou cited the data already given as '. . . further proof that the United States Government is continuing planned and premeditated warfare in a completely inhuman manner . . .', but taking the accusation a considerable step further by identifying the U.S. Government '. . . as the first war criminal in the world today which in pursuance of its aggressive war does not scruple to use bacteriological weapons in violation of all international conventions. . .'.

Chou En-lai went even further in his accusations of bacterial experiments on communist prisoners of the U.N. Whereas Pak Hen Yen had been content with making the general point, Chou declared: '. . . hundreds and thousands of the captured personnel of the Korean People's Army and the Chinese people's volunteers have been victims of experiments with these bacteriological weapons. . . .'

'. . . And now,' he continued, 'American imperialism is using these tested bacteriological weapons to slaughter the peaceful people of Korea. If the people of the world do not resolutely put an end to this crime then the calamities befalling the peaceful people of Korea today will befall the peaceful people of the world tomorrow. The criminal act of American imperialism in waging bacteriological warfare has thus proved that American imperialism is the most dangerous foe of the Chinese and Korean peoples and the peaceful people of the whole world. . . .'

Chou, like the North Korean, Pak Hen Yen, drew the conclusion that the Americans were using germ warfare side by side with delaying tactics in the armistice negotiations. 'It must be pointed out,' he said, 'that the American imperialists were forced to conduct armistice negotiations after receiving shattering blows at the hands of the heroic Korean People's Army and the Chinese people's volunteers during the war of intervention which they launched in Korea. Nevertheless the American imperialists refuse to acquiesce in their own defeat. In the negotiations, they resort to all sorts of shameless tactics to obstruct the progress of the negotiations on the one hand, and callously conduct brutal germ warfare on the other. They attempt by these means to prolong and extend the Korean war and achieve their aggressive designs to destroy the People's Republic of China and undermine peace and security in the Far East. The Chinese people are determined to smash and inevitably will smash the shameless machinations and criminal acts of American imperialism. American imperialism will not only fail to attain its criminal end but will without doubt ignominiously pay the penalty for its crimes before the just wrath of the peaceful people of the whole world. . . .'

Chronologically Chou En-lai's statement as Chinese Foreign Minister came on the heels of more generalized protests from Peking. These were made on the previous day, February 23rd, by the Red Cross Society of China – which was to take an active role in events to follow – and in an editorial of the Peking *People's Daily*, which referred to the resolution on disarmament contained in the appeal to the United Nations by the communist front World Peace Council in Vienna in November 1951.

The *People's Daily* – the official Chinese Communist Party organ – appealed to the peoples of the world '. . . to rally at once for the sake of civilization and justice and to halt the appalling crime of American aggressors in carrying out large-scale germ warfare in Korea . . .'. Invoking the W.P.C. Vienna resolution as applying to the new situation the editorial proclaimed that it called for '. . . the unconditional banning of all types of atomic, bacteriological and chemical weapons, poison gas, radioactive weapons and other means of mass annihilation and for the denunciation as war criminals of the government to employ them first. . . .' In fact, the Vienna resolution in question did not mention branding the first government to use weapons of mass destruction as war criminals, but the propaganda point was made.

Within two or three days protests from communist-organized bodies in China and North Korea were rolling in. They included the All-China Federation of Labour, the All-China Federation of Democratic Youth, the All-China Democratic Women's Federation, the Chinese People's National Committee in Defence of Children, the All-China Association of Societies of the Natural Sciences, the All-China Association for the Dissemination of Scientific Knowledge, the All-China Students Federation, the Chinese Peace Committee, and the Korean Federation of Trade Unions. These protests repeated points made in the North Korean and Chinese Government statements, modifying the common theme to the organizations concerned. Thus the women's organization's protest declared that, 'the American aggressors' bloodstained paws are menacing the whole of mankind, especially the lives and security of women and children . . .', while a joint protest from youth organizations made their point in a different style: '. . . youth and students throughout China will not tolerate this arch-crime of the American aggressors; we will continue to strengthen the movement to resist American aggression and aid Korea, actively support the Korean People's Army and the Chinese people's volunteers, make efforts to study military science, strengthen our national defences and smash all criminal schemes of the American aggressors until they are willing to accept a just and reasonable Korean armistice agreement . . .'. In this way the new B.W. theme was linked with other major propaganda programmes of the moment, thus maintaining a continuity of effort.

Reaction in the Soviet Union and Eastern Europe was slow at first. The Soviet Press published the statements of Pak Hen Yen and Chou En-lai, but without comment. It was not until March 5th, 1952 that any signs emerged, when the Polish Red Cross protested to the International Red Cross requesting emergency measures to prevent the recurrence of these criminal acts. But the international communist fronts had been busy. On February 29th the World Federation of Trade Unions made its first protest. On March 4th – within a fortnight of the first whisper of the new campaign over Moscow Radio and eleven days of its announcement from Peking – it was stated in *Pravda* that a commission of investigation was on its way to Korea from the International Association of Democratic Lawyers, a communist front operating from Brussels. This was the first of the much publicized investigations sent out to Korea and North-east China in the next few months.

March saw the pace heat up considerably. In their turn the communist fronts took up the protest theme: on March 7th the Women's International Democratic Federation; on March 8th the International Union of Students and the well-known French communist scientist and President of the World Peace Council, Frédèric Joliot-Curie, his own voice expressing itself side by side with that of the W.P.C.; on March 12th it was the turn of the World Federation of Democratic Youth.

On March 14th Mr Malik, the Soviet delegate, raised in the U.N. Disarmament Commission the question of prohibiting the use of bacterial weapons by the U.S.A. in Korea and China, bringing it up again and again on March 14th and 19th, April 9th and 24th and May 9th, 13th and 28th, 1952. During this period Peking and Moscow started to send out the first of a large mass of documentation to communist organizations throughout the world.

It was in mid-March that the protest meetings in China and the Soviet Union began. These were organized by such bodies as the Chinese Committee for Peace and against American Aggression in Korea (referred to as the Chinese Peace Committee in propaganda intended for non-communist readers abroad) and the Soviet Peace Committee.

On March 14th, 1952 the Soviet Press reported widespread protest meetings, the main one being held in the Tchaikovsky Hall, Moscow, attended by '. . . representatives of public organizations, trade unions, scientific literary and artistic workers of the capital of the Soviet State . . .', in order to express '. . . their wrathful protest against the monstrous crimes of the modern cannibals who are striving to wipe out the peoples . . .'. One of the main speakers was Prof. N. N. Zhukov-Verezhnikov, an eminent Soviet bacteriologist and a Vice-President of the Academy of Medical Sciences as well as being a presidium member of the Soviet Peace Committee.

Speaking as a scientist, Dr Zhukov declared: '. . . the American imperialists have perpetrated a new crime. They have carried out a bacteriological attack on the Korean People's Democratic Republic'. He went on: '. . . mention must be made of those who are the executors of such orders. I have in mind those bacteriological specialists by whose hands the bacteriological weapons have been made which are today being used with the help of hundreds of aircraft against women, old folk and children in Korea and China. These people call themselves scientists and specialists. Their Wall Street masters have given them the titles of professors, doctors and generals. But in reality these people should for ever be known as criminals, as the mortal enemies of mankind, as deadly foes of science. . . .' Finally, he declared: '. . . may the names of all those who have a hand in this crime against mankind and science be for ever branded in the memory of mankind . . .'.

This speech is doubly significant, in itself for its whole tenor and in the speaker for the important role he was to play in later events. Dr Zhukov-Verezhnikov was no ordinary Soviet scientist expressing the abhorrence of the man-in-the-street. He was a man with a vested interest in the whole subject of the bacterial warfare charges, both going backwards into recent history and forwards into the events of the next six months. But this was not to become apparent until the middle of the summer, by which time his Moscow speech had been consigned to the files.

From this time onwards more and more reports began to appear in the East European Press. The Hungarian communist daily *Szabad Nep* started to give its own correspondent's reports from March 11th. This correspondent was one of Hungary's best journalists, Tibor Meray, and his detailed on-the-spot accounts of various B.W. incidents in Korea were widely publicized abroad, to the extent of being published later in 1952 in a special English-language book. Meray's accounts are particularly valuable, and will be referred to in more detail later.

Immediately after the first of the Soviet mass meetings, Istvan Rusznyak, President of the Hungarian Academy of Science sent a protest telegram to the American Academy of Science. He was chairman at the Congress in January 1952 of the Hungarian Microbiological Society which among other things came to the scientific conclusion: '. . . that America was using bacteriological weapons . . .'. So it was little surprise that Rusznyak's protest should make a demand of the American Academy in which '. . . we emphatically ask you and all American scientists in the name of progress and morality to protest against this outrageous deed and to put a stop to this crime which is being perpetrated by scientists in the name of America . . .'.

In Budapest on March 19th a rally demanded in the name of all the 1,600,000 residents of the city that the United Nations should hold a public trial of those responsible for bacterial warfare in Korea. On March 25th in Prague a similar meeting was held of the faculty members of the Charles University and other scientific institutes. The next day there followed a mass meeting of 3,000 in East Berlin. On the same day a protest was made by the Rumanian parliament in Bucharest.

In China during this period demonstrations were held at Antung (30,000 people), Harbin (150,000), Kirin (60,000), Anshan (over 10,000), Kiamusze (over 15,000), Chengteh (18,000). Tsingtao (180,000), Chungking (12,000) and Tientsin (180,000). Chinese organizations sent out appeals and exhortations to corresponding bodies in the West; entomologists and pathologists called upon their opposite numbers in Britain; a Chinese jurist called upon the support of his fellow-judges representing the countries on the International Military Tribunal for the Far East which sat in Tokyo after the Second World War; Chinese Protestants –

including the Y.M.C.A. and Salvation Army leaders still operating in Communist China – wrote to American Protestants, while the Catholic Reform Committee in Peking called upon all Roman Catholics to rise up 'in defence of world peace and human justice,' and against the American germ war in Korea.

Outside the communist countries the campaign was somewhat later in starting but the beginning of April saw B.W. a constant front-page story in the communist Press, with plenty of follow-up stories inside. For example, in Brazil B.W. was a leader in the communist Press almost every day from April 4th to 16th, the same being true of *l'Humanité* in France; in Canada the story was highlighted in the communist weekly on March 31st, April 7th and 14th; in India there were three stories in April compared with one in March. In general these papers used material put out by Moscow or Peking radio and Press agencies, or detailed the local activities of the mobilized groups and individuals, with cross-reports on the activities of groups in other countries.

Some of these groups had no national or local significance, some spoke in the names of many thousands, as were the cases in Britain of the Britain-China Friendship Association and the Electrical Trades Union respectively, or the Karachi Peace Committee in Pakistan on the one hand and the All-India Trade Union Congress on the other. Again the Burma Peace Committee was appealing on behalf of very few, but the Indonesian Trade Union Federation's Central Bureau was a powerful organization which claimed substantial backing for its protests.

The Patriarch of the Russian Orthodox Church in Moscow had protested as early as March 21st, with the Soviet Baptists following on April 1st. On April 13th, the Moslem protests came from Peking, with Soviet Moslems on May 1st, at the same time as a Chinese Christian leader appealed to members of the World Council of Churches. The next day an open letter to Red Cross Societies throughout the world was sent by the President of the National Red Cross Society of China, recapitulating the B.W. charges.

This growing list of protest was not the totality, but it shows the scope of action following the two relatively brief and factually vague statements in February of the North Korean and Chinese

Foreign Ministers. Virtually every organized group in the communist orbit had its part to play in generating mass anti-Americanism based on the bacterial warfare charges. In their turn the international communist fronts, their local affiliates and the national communist parties in the West and in the developing countries all faithfully transmitted the line, so that by May the American Association of Scientific Workers was writing to President Truman and to Mr Malik condemning B.W. and demanding measures against transgressors; meanwhile in Manchester fourteen housewives marched through the centre of the city, carrying protest banners and a petition to President Truman.

On May 5th, Peking reported the alleged confessions of two American Air Force Officers, Enoch and Quinn, who after their capture by the communists had admitted taking part in germ raids over North Korea. Their story gave a transfusion of new blood to a campaign that was beginning to suffer for lack of fresh evidence. The next few days saw the International Union of Students issue a display kit of photographs and documentation for use on college and university notice boards all over the world. A bacterial warfare exhibition opened in Peking and this formed the basis of two large illustrated pamphlets which again had world-wide distribution. Renewed protests followed the Enoch–Quinn confessions and the Peking Exhibition was the basis of many stories taken back home by friendship delegations that had been in China for the May Day celebrations that month.

*Pravda* in Moscow serialized the Enoch–Quinn confessions over four issues beginning May 6th. Ten days later it published a strange confession story of Robert Gilarol, supposedly an American airman who had dropped colorado beetles over Eastern Germany,[1] to have trained germ warfare criminals and to have been one of the first to use B.W. weapons in Korea. The story is strange in that it was not sustained, being dropped without further comment and without being taken up by other communist organs.

In one sense the World Peace Council meeting in Oslo at the end of March 1952 had set the international germ warfare campaign in motion, when it gave the delegations documentation to take back home with them. Three months later, on July 1st at a meeting in

[1]The colorado beetle episodes will be discussed as a side issue later.

East Berlin, it passed a resolution on B.W. and received a long report from the leading French communist, Yves Farge, on his own investigations in North Korea. A fortnight later another traveller – the Very Rev. Hewlett Johnson, Dean of Canterbury – returned home with his story of germ warfare as he reckoned to have seen it through his own eyes.

By this time the stories were taking on new aspects. In its July 4th number, for instance, the Soviet Navy paper *Red Fleet* told how '. . . English servicemen, particularly English sailors, were engaged directly in the spread of leprosy in the Northern areas of Korea, dropping lepers in the rear of the People's Army . . .'. This story – like that about the airman Gilarol – is peculiar in that only the Russians published it. It was first put out, it will be remembered, in the Moscow broadcast in Korean of February 18th, 1952 – the broadcast that may have triggered off the whole campaign.

It was certainly not a story for Asia, where leprosy is only too well known. It was intended for Europeans, few of whom appreciate that – terrible as it is – it is not as immediately contagious as many other diseases. It is at least three years and may be as much as fifteen years before the disease appears and many people in endemic areas can be in contact with lepers for years without becoming infected. Even the maddest of madmen would reject it as an effective weapon against humanity.

An even stranger story, which again was not repeated elsewhere, appeared in the July 1952 number of the Polish Navy monthly *Morze*. Written by a Slawomir Sierecki, it purported to deal with an American action called Operation Sea-Serpent and was based on the supposed diary of a Captain Barnes, U.S.N. The diary started in April 1952 when Captain Barnes was transferred to the submarine SS-313. This submarine, wrote Sierecki, had the job of approaching Chinese mainland waters and spreading them with plague-infected flies. A special snorkel device was fitted by which the flies were to be ejected and carried by the wind to the shore. But as the submarine neared the Chinese mainland west of Hainan it was engaged by some communist patrol boats, which dropped depth charges. The container holding the infected flies was broken and the flies were released inside the submarine.

For seven days the members of the crew died, one after the other. One evening the writer of the diary – the submarine commander, Captain Barnes – tried to escape by dinghy with another crew member. The dinghy was washed ashore empty on the beach of Hainan, with only a cap and the diary in it. That was the end of the story.

These stories were flashes in the pan, no sooner written than forgotten. But in Moscow the theme was given a dramatic setting in November 1952 with the publication of an anti-American satire *The Jackals* by the Estonian communist propagandist August Yakobson, translated from the Estonian by the Soviet Writer Publishing House and published in various languages for foreign readership by the monthly *Soviet Literature* magazine. The play was added to the repertoire of the Maly Theatre in Moscow and a year later, on October 19th, 1953, a new colour film based on the play was given its first showing in Moscow under the title *The Silvery Dust*.

Coincidentally, in Paris the French communists at this time in 1952 attempted to stage Roger Gaillard's *Le Colonel Foster plaidera coupable* (Colonel Foster Will Plead Guilty), only to have it closed down by the Paris police after the first night. With a humanity in it that was totally lacking in *The Jackals*, it dealt with the theme of alleged American atrocities in Korea and the moral dilemma of the guilty. But its crudities nowhere approached those of the Yakobson essay in xenophobia. The review of the Yakobson book as published in *Pravda* of December 10th, 1952 is given in Appendix Va because it shows the vicious nature of the narrative itself and the approval with which it was viewed officially in Moscow at the time and – as the preparation and showing of the subsequent film revealed – even a year later, after the Korean cease-fire had been signed.

Briefly, the story tells of how an American scientist wants to experiment on human beings. Because he cannot obtain a supply of Korean and Chinese prisoners from Korea, he decides to make do with some Negroes sentenced to death on rape charges, though in reality they are Peace Partisans suffering for their convictions. Every aspect of anti-American propaganda is brought into *The Jackals*, which is for that reason of great propaganda interest, because it synthesises it all into one massive exercise in political and cultural xenophobia.

*Pravda* was not the only Soviet paper to approve *The Jackals.* The *Literary Gazette* reviewed it on November 14th, 1952 with the admiring comment: '. . . the author has called his new work a dramatic satire, and the play fully justifies such a definition . . . the play of A. Yakobson is written with the red-hot pen of a dramatist-journalist. In it light, shade, love and hate are powerfully and vividly defined. . . .' Invoking the words of Gorki, the *Literary Gazette* reminded its readers: '. . . to be impartial is to be without feeling. We are people of feeling. We hate passionately and shall be partial – understand us like that! . . .'

The World Peace Council meeting in Oslo at the end of March was doubly important. In the first place it provided the necessary propaganda documentation – based on material put before it by Dr Kuo Mo-jo, the chief Chinese member of the W.P.C. and the leading spokesman of Peking's anti-American drive, and secondly it resolved to send an international scientific commission of its own to North Korea and North-east China '. . . for the investigation of the facts concerning bacterial warfare in Korea and China . . .'.

From mid-June to the end of August 1952 the six scientists forming the main body of the commission travelled several thousand miles, interviewed scores of people and dealt with many pages of documentary material. They went from Peking to Shenyang (Mukden) and Pyongyang and even made a flying visit to the edge of Inner Mongolia. In September their report was published – a 665-page volume (of which 600 pages were appendices) weighing 2½ lb. and running to 330,000 words, plus some ninety photographs and twenty maps.

In saying that the report was published in September, an important qualification must be made. Initially there was a wide distribution of a small pamphlet comprising the actual report of the commission, but without the evidence upon which the findings were based. This evidence was in the 600 pages of appendices. Wide circulation was given to the original small pamphlet version in September and October 1952. It was not until November that the main report became available from Prague and then only on a limited basis. This scientific commission report is the key to the whole campaign and as such will be discussed in detail. At this point in the chronological scale it is sufficient to note it as starting off a fresh propaganda drive in the autumn and winter of 1952.

Previous criticisms of the earlier investigation reports were often based on the non-scientific character of those making them – – lawyers, politicians, clergymen. This time the critics were answered by the claim that this latest – and certainly most important – delegation was made up of scientists, who looked at the whole subject with scientific impartiality. Furthermore, it was said, they had produced the evidence for their findings in very great detail. This point was pressed home very hard in meetings and newspaper articles from September 1952 onwards.

The publication of the report came in time for a World Peace Council meeting held in Peking in September 1952 and, more important still, for the W.P.C.'s People's Congress for Peace, held in Vienna in December 1952. The Congress set up a special bacteriological warfare commission headed by Dr Andreen, the Swedish member of the international scientific commission. A major speaker on the subject was the Chinese Professor Chen Wen-kuei, who will be referred to later for the important role he played behind the scenes of the campaign. 'Before we left Peking,' Dr Chen told the 2,000 delegates to the Congress, 'we received a report from the Epidemic Prevention Corps of the Chinese volunteers that U.S. aircraft were still waging bacteriological warfare in Korea. In October insects and infected leaves of trees were spread by them and bacterial bomb cases have again been found. In addition U.S. aircraft have continued to drop germs and other infected objects in North-east China.' He gave the warning: '. . . Germ warfare in China is only an experiment with weapons that American generals intend to use on a much bigger scale in a future great war . . .'.

Mention has been made of the original listing of alleged bacterial attacks by U.S. aircraft at the beginning of 1952. This was followed by a further series which was the basis of the investigations carried out by the scientists and which will be dealt with separately. During the summer there were no reports of further attacks, indeed nothing was said until Dr Chen Wen-kuei spoke in Vienna in December, referring to incidents that had taken place in October.

These were not mentioned again until the end of February when the New China News Agency gave a list of dates in October, November and December 1952 when attacks were said to have been made. On February 21st Chou En-lai used a Soviet Army Day speech to accuse the U.S.A. once more of 'brutal' germ warfare in Korea.

The next day – the anniversary of the original 1952 charges – Peking published two more alleged confessions of B.W. guilt from American officers, Major Bley and Colonel Schwable. Bley's deposition was dated January 21st and Schwable's December 6th and 19th. The depositions alleged that B.W. had begun in November 1951 and in May 1952 a new policy was initiated to establish a 'contaminated belt' across Central Korea.

So a new campaign began, with the line set by the *People's Daily* accusation that it was the American intention to 'direct bacteriological warfare against the broad masses of the Asian people . . .'. The next day, February 25th, *Pravda* commenting on the depositions, spoke of the danger of a new Black Death, while Moscow Radio broadcasting to Germany suggested that B.W. in Korea was merely a rehearsal for a larger B.W. in Germany. On March 6th a Chinese dispatch from the Korean front accused the Americans of using poison gas shells during January and February, repeating the accusations of exactly two years previously. On March 22nd the accusation of dropping poison gas bombs over Kangwon province five days earlier was made.

Once more open letters and appeals were issued by religious and scientific spokesmen in China to their colleagues. With the approach of the spring thaw in March 1953 Pyongyang radio alleged that American B.W. attacks were being waged '. . . even more desperately, with seven incidents in five days'. The substance of these reports was repeated a few days later by the New China News Agency. But, apart from generalized statements, specific accusations once more came to an end with the last incident reported in Mid-April by Pyongyang, though it had happened as long before as March 17th.

By this time the subject had dropped considerably in importance as far as Peking and Moscow were concerned. It was only to be raised once more and that was six months later, when the armistice had been signed and prisoners of war were being exchanged by both sides. To everyone's surprise, the repatriates from the communist side included the various Americans who had confessed to bacterial warfare charges. They repudiated their confessions as soon as they reached the U.N. lines, and later told in detail how they had been put to tremendous pressures by their communist captors until they had made them.

This repudiation was anticipated by the communist side to some extent, for they printed in advance reports that the returning P.O.W.s would undoubtedly be put under pressure by the American High Command to repudiate what they had said of their own free will while prisoners of the Koreans and Chinese!

In the event the repudiations were presented before the United Nations General Assembly by the U.S. delegate in October, 1953. On November 11th Peking fired its last shot with the publication of what it called, '. . . fresh evidence confirming the use of bacteriological weapons by the Americans in Korea and China . . .'. This was a series of depositions by nineteen American airmen obtained before they had been repatriated. In the main the 'fresh evidence' was a recapitulation of old accusations.

However, one fresh detail was given, of a startling magnitude. 'On January 10th, 1953,' the Peking statement of ten months later stated, 'a large-scale attack directly planned by Washington was launched on the Sinanju area by the Fifth Air Force. In this attack four planes from each fighter-bomber wing, four from each marine air group and two B-26 types of planes were daily to carry germ weapons. This attack, which lasted five days and at its height reached 480 sorties daily, was one of the most frenzied and savage crimes committed by the American forces in the Korean War.'

This story was distributed by Moscow as well as Peking. By its description it revealed an attack far, far greater than any other alleged B.W. raid of the Korean war. Yet it had not been mentioned earlier in the year, not even at the time the Schwable–Bley confessions had been published in the March.

Mention has been made in passing of the conduct of the campaign in diplomatic circles, particularly the United Nations. The course of this campaign in more formal circles – as distinct from that aimed at rousing popular feeling – shows how protests from the various communist governments were backed by the communist front organizations.

The first protest was the shortlived one of May 8th, 1951 by the North Korean Foreign Minister, which was addressed directly to the United Nations. This was not followed up at all by the international communist fronts, though one or two isolated references were made to its implications by individual members of the Women's International Democratic Federation.

The second and more important North Korean protest was that of February 22nd 1952 which signalled the start of the main campaign. In this the North Korean Foreign Minister appealed '. . . to the people of the whole world to check the outrages of the interventionists and to investigate and define the international responsibility of the organizers of the use of bacteriological weapons . . .'. This was backed up by a similar general statement by Chou En-lai, speaking on behalf of Communist China. A second statement was made on March 8th by Chou, making it known that '. . . members of the American Air Force who invade China's territorial air with bacteriological weapons will be dealt with as war criminals on capture . . .'. This was supported on the same day by a statement in Peking of the non-communist rump political parties still permitted on the mainland.

These warnings took no note of the official denial of the B.W. allegations made on March 4th by the American Secretary of State, Dean Acheson. Instead, that day saw the first of the communist front protests to the U.N., from the Women's International Democratic Federation. On March 5th the Polish Red Cross protested to the International Red Cross. On March 8th it was the turn for the World Federation of Trade Unions to write to the United Nations, followed by the International Union of Students on March 10th. The following day the Czech communist paper *Rudé Právo* reported that Czechoslovak microbiologists, epidemologists and public health workers had protested to the communist-front World Peace Council and to the World Health Organization.

On March 11th Dean Acheson requested the International Red Cross to investigate the B.W. charges. On March 12th, the Bulgarian National Committee in Defence of Peace protested to the U.N. March 13th saw the International Committee of the Red Cross agree to Acheson's request. More significantly, on the same day the Soviet Peace Committee held a rally in Moscow which marked the real beginning of the organized world-wide protest campaign.

In the United Nations Disarmament Commission on March 14th the Soviet delegate Mr Malik raised the question of prohibiting B.W. by U.S. forces in Korea and China. Coincidentally the Asian and Australian Liaison Bureau of the World Federation of Trade Unions protested from its Peking headquarters to the U.N. Secretary-General, Trygve Lie, and to the Chairman of the Security Council.

It did not take long for the Red Cross to come under fire. On March 19th the Peking *People's Daily* attacked the International Committee of the Red Cross as a tool of American imperialism. Notwithstanding this rebuff and its wider significance, Mr Trygve Lie on March 20th offered the help of the World Health organization to the Chinese and North Korean Governments in fighting epidemics. This offer was repeated without result on March 27th and April 3rd, 1952.

On March 24th the International Association of Democratic Lawyers protested to Mr Trygve Lie. The next day the British Foreign Minister, Mr Eden, condemned the allegations as entirely unwarranted and false, followed a day later by the rejection in the Disarmament Commission by Mr Malik of an investigation by the International Committee of the Red Cross, which he considered quite unsuited, being '... a purely Swiss national body ...'.

On April 2nd the first official North Korean protest to the U.N. was made. Speaking a fortnight later to the Communist Party Congress in London, the well-known Party figure Ivor Montagu – who had just been in China – alleged that more than 2,000 bacterial bombs had been dropped by the Americans. This somewhat startling statement was not followed up by the local B.W. campaign sub-committees set up by national peace committees following a World Peace Council directive of April 19th, 1952.

Following the attack on the International Red Cross came one on the World Health Organization. In mid-April the Chinese communist Press denounced it as '. . . one of the specialized agencies of the U.N. which jumps at the crack of the State Department's whip. . . .' The W.H.O. offer to help fight epidemics was a '. . . new twist to an old trick . . .'. If it succeeded in getting into North Korea and China it could '. . . obtain intelligence on the effects of U.S. germ weapons and whitewash American guilt by a false report . . .'. If it and the International Red Cross failed to get in, then American propaganda could '. . . maintain the pretence of 'humanitarianism' and smear the people's governments of China and Korea for 'inhumanity' and 'fabricated reports . . .'. This was the official line as laid down in *People's China* at the time. On April 23rd, 1952 the North Koreans declined W.H.O. help and said the spread of epidemics had been prevented. Six days later the International Red Cross suspended its investigating commission because it had received no replies from China or North Korea. Somewhat belatedly this withdrawal from the scene was followed the next day by an attack over Moscow Radio on the International Committee as a tool of the State Department.

The Enoch-Quinn confessions were published in May and widely circulated by international communist publications. In Peking the Chinese Peace Committee published a series of English-language booklets under the general title *Stop U.S. Germ Warfare!* while in East Berlin the German Peace Committee published a similar booklet under the title *Amerika und der bakteriologische Krieg*, for general distribution in Germany. The new line of these publications was to stress American long-term preparations and the German booklet in particular went to great lengths to trace these back to 1941 and link them with the Japanese work in Manchuria publicized by the Khabarovsk trial of December 1949.

On May 11th the Soviet news agency *Tass* published a letter to President Truman and to Mr Malik from the American Association of Scientific Workers condemning B.W. Just over a month later on June 18th Mr Malik proposed in the U.N. Security Council that the Council should appeal for the ratification of the 1952 Geneva Protocol prohibiting, among other things, the use of B.W.

The refusal of the United States to ratify this protocol, although one of the original signatories[1] was to be a target for communist propaganda for some months to come, a target all the more vulnerable because of the apparent unreasonableness of the American attitude, as communist China had formally ratified the protocol on July 13th, 1952.

The U.S. refusal was nothing new. It was based on the premise that the protocol as subsequently signed by other states, not all of them communist, was fundamentally weakened by reservations made by them. Britain and France, for instance, signed it subject to the reservations that it was binding only in relation to states effectively observing it and that it should cease to be binding if an enemy failed to respect the prohibitions laid down. Similarly, the Soviet Union and various other states made reservations regarding states which had not ratified or acceded to the protocol or who did not respect its provisions. The 1952 Chinese ratification had also made equal use of an escape clause: '. . . the Central People's Government shall undertake to implement strictly the provisions of the protocol, providing that all the other contracting and acceding powers observe them reciprocally . . .'.

The effectiveness of such protocol depended on the mutual trust of the acceding powers, a trust that was obviously lacking in Korea. If the Americans had signed the protocol in accordance with Mr Malik's proposal, they would have been accused immediately of breaking their solemn vows, in even more strident terms than before. Their refusal was presented as confirming their use of bacterial weapons. The Geneva Protocol – like the Geneva Convention when it came to the communist treatment of prisoners[2] – was only of value to the communists when it served their purpose. In September the Report of the International Scientific Commission set up under the auspices of the World Peace Council was

[1] Japan was one of the original signatories, but no mention of this was made in the B.W. propaganda.

[2] Communist China recognized the 1949 Geneva Conventions on the treatment of the wounded and sick in the field and the treatment of prisoners of war and civilians behind the lines on July 13th, 1952. This did not prevent the wholesale ill-treatment, torture and killing of U.N. prisoners during the Korean war, even during the armistice negotiations and afterwards.

widely published, with copies sent to all delegations at the United Nations General Assembly.

This led to the matter being raised in the House of Commons on October 24th, 1952, by Mr S. O. Davies, Labour M.P. for the Welsh mining constituency of Merthyr Tydfil. This was not the first occasion on which the B.W. issue had been raised in the House. In March Mr Eden's denial of the charge had been made in response to the question of a Labour elder statesman, Mr Arthur Henderson, who asked the Foreign Secretary '. . . what information he has received from the United Nations concerning the Union of Soviet Socialist Republic's official complaint that United Nations forces in Korea have been guilty of carrying on germ warfare . . .'.

Mr Davies – well known as a stormy petrel of the extreme Left of the Labour Party – was more blunt. 'I propose to say something about germ warfare in Korea,' he said. 'I know that the charge that germ warfare had been carried on there by United Nations forces is usually answered by the cry that it is not true – and that in a voice affecting horror that the United Nations should resort to such a vile practice. It is, however, well known that in the last ten or twelve years America has built up huge organizations for developing and prosecuting bacteriological warfare.'

Mr Davies developed this further and then was interrupted on the point of order that the issue, being American, did not come under any Ministerial responsibility and so could not be discussed. 'Further to the point of order,' Mr Davies demurred at one stage, 'some of us have not a shadow of doubt that bacteriological warfare is being carried out in Korea at this moment. There are British personnel engaged in the Korean war. This government is responsible for the Korean war (here an interruption) – this government assumes its responsibility within the United Nations – and surely one is entitled to raise any matter relating to the Korean war, where young British lives are being lost and being ruined at the moment.' After further points of order and a reference to the British signing of the 1925 Geneva Protocol. ('the fact that we have signed the Geneva Protocol makes it far more ignominious on our part that we have not protested against that kind of warfare in Korea') Mr Davies took up his main theme.

'Hon. Gentlemen,' he said, according to the Hansard report of the debate, 'however sensitive they may feel about it must know that the carrying on of germ warfare in Korea has now become very well known, and is backed by evidence that cannot be honestly challenged. I have to admit that the British Press in all matters relating to the abominations of the United Nations in Korea has, during the last two to two and a half years, wallowed in the most cowardly and reckless mendacities, and deliberately refused to give the people even a part of the truth of what has been going on. I am sorry to have to say that about the Press of my own country.

'I shall be asked, how do I know germ warfare has been carried on in Korea, and I shall be reminded that I have not been there. I was not at Hiroshima, nor at Nagasaki, when the atom bombs were dropped. But I happen to know that the bombs were dropped there. I did not see Hitler's gas chambers at work, but we all know they were used with dreadful consequences. We know because we have relied on the word and evidence of men and women whose integrity we have no reason at all to doubt. And evidence equally reliable, I contend, has come to us from the Far East, proving beyond all shadow of doubt that germ warfare has been carried out in North Korea and China.'

Mr Davies continued to mention such evidence as the Enoch–Quinn confessions before taking up the newly-published International Scientific Commission report, which he said '. . . has presented evidence which cannot be gainsaid, and I am fully confident will not be disputed by any competent scientist in this country . . .'.

He concluded (in the sense that his speech was interrupted by the Deputy Speaker with a reminder of the passing of time) with, '. . . the truth of the charges I have made tonight will not be contested on any factual grounds, but feeble excuses will be made and feeble questions asked, such as, for example, why did not the North Koreans and the Chinese invite the International Red Cross to investigate the charges of germ warfare? The reasons are obvious. When ghastly massacres were taking place in Nazi concentration camps, Red Cross investigators were issuing reports that all was well. Have we forgotten their report on the notorious camp at Auschwitz of gas chambers fame, that murder camp at which. . . .', and here the Deputy Speaker intervened.

At this point the Under Secretary of State for Foreign Affairs, Mr Nutting, interrupted with a question: 'May I ask him (i.e. Mr Davies), having made the accusations against the Red Cross relating to the last war, why in August 1949 the Soviet Union and its Eastern satellites all endorsed a report and signed a convention at Geneva in which there was a resolution describing the Red Cross as an impartial humanitarian body?'

To which Mr Davies replied: 'I shall answer the question when I have had time to study the conditions under which such a report was made, and not before.' He summed up: '. . . the foul business goes on, with germ warfare, bubonic plague, cholera, typhoid, smallpox, tetanus, with mass killings of men, women and children; and on, like the Gadarene swine, we go into the abyss of moral and spiritual degradation . . .'. This was the B.W. story in a nutshell. It was to be repeated in a different form by Mr Davies some months later.

Though the Scientific Commission report was widely circulated in all countries where the communist fronts operated, very few fresh protests to the U.N. or other organizations resulted. Significantly, in Britain one such front received the Commission report quite coolly – the Executive Committee of the Medical Association for the Prevention of War considered the report, but neither endorsed nor rejected it. Similarly the Association of Scientific Workers leadership were convinced neither one way nor the other after reading it.

Exactly a year after the beginning of the B.W. propaganda campaign, the two new confessions of the American Officers Schwable and Bley were published in Peking. Alan Winnington, the *Daily Worker* correspondent with the North Koreans, wrote a long dispatch on the two airmen in the *Daily Worker* of February 24th, 1953. This was sent to every United Nations delegate, the paper informed its readers. The next day the U.N. Commander-in-Chief, General Mark Clark, denied the fresh charges made as a result of the Schwable–Bley confessions.

Five days later, on March 2nd, Mr S. O. Davies raised the issue once more in Parliament by asking the Secretary of State for Foreign Affairs: '. . . when he was informed by the United States Government of their directive to introduce in Korea widespread germ warfare?' To which Mr Selwyn Lloyd, the then Foreign Secretary, replied: '. . . . the United States Government has not communicated to Her Majesty's Government any directive about the introduction of germ warfare in Korea. Germ warfare has never been used by the United Nations forces in Korea; and I believe that the allegation that any such directive has been issued is complete nonsense. . . .'

Mr Davies continued: '. . . has the Right Hon. and learned Gentleman been made aware of the report recently published by two high-ranking American officers who have served for a considerable time in Korea and are still in Korea about the use of germ warfare there, where amongst other things an effort was made to lay a cholera belt across North Korea? Surely the Right Hon. and learned Gentleman ought to make inquiries into these facts when they are known to the public although deliberately denied by this government?'

A short debate then ensued as to whether Mr Davies should produce evidence to support his unqualified accusation against the United States' '. . . directive to introduce in Korea widespread germ warfare . . .'. While on the one hand it was maintained that the rights of Members in the House of Commons allowed them to make accusations they thought fit without any compulsion to reveal supporting evidence, this was seen on the other hand as representing '. . . no limit to the fantastic and untruthful nature of any allegation any Hon. Member tries to embody in a question, because there is apparently to be no limit to charges that are entirely without foundation or which currency can be given by means of Parliamentary question? Is not the House entitled to protection?'

To which the Speaker gave the official answer: '. . . there are certain limits but, on the other hand, it is very important in this House to maintain the rights of Hon. Members . . .'. At which point the matter was closed.

In March a United Nations five-power investigating committee into bacterial warfare was proposed in the Political Committee against the opposition of the Soviet Union which continued to urge the ratification of the 1952 Geneva Protocol. In mid-April Peking renewed the B.W. charges and attacked the concept of a U.N.

impartial committee as a means of checking the effectiveness of the alleged B.W. activities. On April 23rd, 1953, the U.N. General Assembly set up a five-member investigating commission by thirty-two votes against five with four abstentions. It never went into operation and was eventually wound up.

In May there were fresh B.W. charges and in June Ivor Montagu told a World Peace Council meeting in Budapest that the British were using B.W. against the rebels in Malaya.

On July 27th, 1953 the Korean Armistice Agreement was signed at Panmunjon. A month later there was a brief report of some American artillery officer prisoners who had confessed to having fired bacterial shells, but this story was never expanded.

At the beginning of September came the main wave of repatriation, including all the officers who had signed B.W. confessions. Anticipating that they would have a change of heart on repatriation another correspondent with the North Koreans, Wilfred Burchett, warned *Daily Worker* readers in advance that their recantations should be expected and viewed with care.

In October the full background story of how the communists extorted the confessions from the American prisoners was told in the U.N. Political Committee by the American delegation. For his part the British delegate to the Political Committee roundly attacked the Soviet call for ratification of the 1952 Geneva Convention – which was still being made – as intended to distract public attention from the communist refusal of an impartial investigation of the whole B.W. charge. Early in November the General Assembly decided to take no vote on the 1952 convention demand and referred it to the Disarmament Commission, where it stayed. At which point the B.W. question in the United Nations ceased to be a live issue.

A few days later, on November 11th, 1953, came the last shot from the Peking locker with another sheaf of American confessions. But the echoes quickly died away and the main campaign ended, as far as communist propaganda was concerned. A year later there was a show trial in China when thirteen Americans were sentenced, including eleven captured airmen who should have been repatriated under the Armistice Agreement of July 1953. The sentences ranged from four years to life imprisonment for alleged espionage.[1] At the same time five Chinese were sentenced to death and five to prison. No mention of bacterial warfare was made at the trial.

Thus far we have looked at the general propaganda sweep of the bacterial warfare charges both among the public and in official circles, as transmitted by the communist fronts and others less committed. By and large we have taken the official denials at their face value without examining any evidence that may have been presented with them. We can take it for granted that such denials should have been made and made very often in a blanket form without supporting explanations.

But it is far more important for us to look at the evidence produced by the communists to back up their charges. After all this is what they asked us to do at the time. And it is an exercise which repays the effort. The fundamental evidence is that contained in the bulky report of the International Scientific Commission, for this brings together much of the material referred to rather sketchily in earlier reports of individuals such as the Dean of Canterbury and the French National Peace Committee President, Yves Farges, and of commissions such as that of the International Association of Democratic Lawyers.

There is a common factor to all these earlier reports in their circumstantial nature. None of the people giving the evidence ever saw B.W. waged themselves, they all quote the evidence of others. Some of them (as we shall see from the writings of the Hungarian journalist Tibor Meray, who visited the early B.W. sites) presented their stories with considerable emotion and powers of description.

[1] They were eventually repatriated by Peking on the personal intervention of the U.N. Secretary-General, Mr Hammarskjöld.

CHAPTER TEN

# *The Evidence*

In the early months of the B.W. campaign a Chinese People's Commission for Investigating the Germ Warfare Crime of the American Imperialists was set up in Peking, with a sub-section operating in Manchuria as the North-East China Group of the commission. Its report was published in April 1952, but although it was widely publicized in China, relatively little was made of it in Peking's overseas propaganda organs, such as the English-language *People's China*. The main emphasis abroad was given to the reports in a series of booklets entitled *Stop U.S. Germ Warfare!* published in English by the Chinese People's Committee for World Peace and Against American Aggression and distributed in part by the Chinese Esperanto League.

The commission was a large one composed of two groups. The first was socio-political in content – representatives of trade unions, youth and women's organizations, religious and other public bodies. In addition there were over forty Chinese specialists in clinical medicine, bacteriology, epidemiology, pathology, parasitology, toxicology, veterinary science and other branches. Many of these gave evidence later. The purpose of the first, non-specialist, group was to hear the evidence from witnesses in the localities they visited. The second, specialist, group was concerned primarily with checking the scientific aspects. They identified specimens, diagnosed symptoms, conducted autopsies.

While the North-East China Group concerned itself solely with events in Manchuria, the main body of the Chinese Commission operated in North Korea. One section took part in identification work with the Chinese People's Volunteer Epidemic Prevention Corps with the Chinese forces in Korea. The remainder split up into two groups, one going to the Wonsan region and the other to the central part of the 38th Parallel. In Korea over 150 witnesses were examined and 1,165 items of evidence inspected. Recordings were made of the more important witnesses, of confessions of captured agents and of statements by American prisoners of war. The whole operation was photographed and filmed.

'Based on the data and the results of the tests,' the report summed up, 'the Commission considers it conclusively proved that the U.S. Government used aircraft, shells and other methods to spread bacteria-laden insects and other infected objects in large quantities and that the evidence is irrefutable. The results of the examination of the insects and other infected objects spread by the U.S. have established that to date disease-germs of plague, cholera, typhoid, paratyphoid and dysentery have been used. We also have data proving that the American aggressors are using *Bacillus anthracis* and other pathogenic organisms. The facts prove that the U.S. Government is by these means attempting to cause man-made epidemics in order to wipe out the Korean people and the Chinese and Korean troops in large numbers and to destroy livestock and damage crops in Korea.'

The main means of dissemination charged were spraying from aircraft and dropping containers or bombs with special casings. Typical examples of the evidence listed in the commission report was that given at the beginning, summarized as follows.

Just after midday on February 11th a Chinese soldier in the Chorwon area saw three American P-51 fighters flying at about a thousand feet: '. . . the aircraft sprayed such insects as anthomyid flies, springtails and stone flies which were found scattered over the snow over an area extending 10 kms. from east to west and 5 kms. from south to north. They were even found in large numbers in places shaded from the sun. The temperature then was four degrees below zero centigrade. Many of the anthomyid flies soon froze to death. Some of those that fell in shaded places and survived slowly flew into the sunlight. . . .'

Another example from Youngwon told of how on March 26th an assistant army physician of a Chinese unit saw an American plane circle and then drop two bombs in a power dive. One bomb made a crater five inches deep, while the other landed a mile away, both of them splitting open: '. . . each created an insect-congested zone of about 200 metres in length and 100 metres in breadth, and the insects were primarily stone flies. The density averaged over 100 insects per square metre. The insects were densest inside the bomb crater. At the time of finding insects were still crawling out of the burst bomb casings. . . .'

A relatively short chapter of the Commission's report on Korea presents evidence to show that '. . . in Korea, where no plague has appeared, the American aggressors began using this deadly disease as an instrument of war, dropping carriers of plague bacillus – rats and fleas – in an attempt to achieve their aggressive aims by mass slaughter through plague epidemics . . .'. No detailed proof was produced, but generalizations were made that '. . . in areas where rats were dropped from the air by the American aggressors, a number were found infected with plague bacillus. Bacteriological and immunological tests, using such methods as staining smears, germ culturing, serological reaction, animal inoculation and pathological section have proved that these rats carried plague bacillus. . . .' The report went on: '. . . in these same areas we have also discovered victims of plague. Specimens of viscera and blood taken from the victims have proved on careful and detailed bacteriological, immunological and pathological tests, using such methods as staining smears, germ culturing, serological reaction, animal inoculation and pathological sections, that these victims were stricken by *Bacilli pasteurellae*. . . .'

Parallel evidence was given in the third chapter to prove '. . . the outbreak of genuine cholera in Pyongyang was artificial and is induced by cholera-vibrio-carrying flies disseminated by U.S. aircraft . . .'. Similarly with the sections dealing with gastro-intestinal infections, anthrax and leaf-fungus.

The final chapter, headed 'depositions of American P.O.W.s and airborne special agents' confined itself to quoting from two U.S. Army privates on what they had heard others say and one Chinese agent who was parachuted into Korea 'to investigate the effectiveness of germ warfare'.

The report of the North-East China Group was along similar lines. It established that American planes from Korea had flown over Chinese territory: '. . . in the areas over which the enemy planes intruded there were repeatedly found large numbers of flies (including such species as anthomyid flies, blow flies, non-biting stable flies, sunflies, house flies, horse flies), mosquitoes (including such species as aedes, culex, midges, etc.), spiders, springtails, ants, fleas, migratory locusts, pigmy locusts, crickets, etc. . . . Considering the areas where these were discovered in relation to the intrusions by American aircraft, the state of the distribution of these insects, the places and the season in which the insects appeared, there is not the least doubt that these insects were disseminated by American aircraft. . . .'

Parallel with this Chinese Commission was the Lawyers Commission sent in March to China and North Korea by the International Association of Democratic Lawyers, a communist front operating from headquarters in Brussels. Consisting of eight members, it was headed by Heinrich Brandweiner, then Professor of International Law at the University of Graz in Austria.[1] The others were Mme Zofia Wasilkowska, Counsellor at the Supreme Court in Warsaw; Ko Po-nien, Director of the Research Department of the People's Institute of Foreign Affairs, Peking; Mme Marie-Louise Moerens, Advocate at the Court of Appeal, Brussels; Letelba Rodrigues de Britto, Advocate at the Court of Rio de Janeiro in Brazil; Marc Jacquier, Advocate at the Court of Appeal, Paris; Jack Gaster, a solicitor and leading Communist Party member from London and Luigi Cavalieri, Lawyer at the Supreme Court of Rome, a Vice-President of the I.A.D.L.

Initially the Commission was set up by the I.A.D.L. to investigate the B.W. charges in Korea.[2] While they were there Peking alleged that B.W. was being used by the Americans in Manchuria and so the Commission's scope was extended to that area, too.

In Manchuria they heard testimonies and interviewed expert witnesses; their report follows the general line of the following specific example: On March 3rd a farmer from a village some 20 kms. from Fushun found insects leaping and crawling on the snow before his house: '. . . he informed the local authorities of his discovery and the work of collecting and destroying the insects was

[1] He later went to a teaching post in Eastern Germany.

[2] To be more precise the Commission was set up to investigate all charges of atrocities by American forces in Korea. The full report alleges a wide range of war crimes, but it is the B.W. section which was most widely reported and which concerns us directly.

organized in the following days . . .'. The insects were identified as the Collembola species which 'had been scattered in large quantities in Korea and North-east China' and which carried some sort of rickettsiae pathogen. This area was invaded by American aircraft on February 29th, that is four days before the insects were found.

In all cases the insects were reported as being found out of their normal breeding season, in unusual surroundings and usually infected. The Commission reported similarly from North Korea, with the emphasis more on the insects found on the ground than on the aircraft observed overhead. One significant incident – to which more detailed reference will be made later – was reported without any mention of American aircraft having been near: '. . . On March 5th in Pyongyang City, Chung Ku District, Quarter Nammun Ri, large and small groups of flies were found in the street spread over an area of about 1½ by 5 metres. The next day cholera broke out in the neighbouring street. . . .'

The conclusions of the Lawyers Commission report are careful to stress that '. . . it is not the function of this commission to pass a final judgement . . . Its duty is limited to an investigation of the facts and to indicate the offences against international law which in its opinion these facts disclose. If there be a defence to the crimes this report discloses, that defence must be heard by an appropriate international tribunal before final judgement can be passed. . . .'

Relatively little use was made of the Lawyers Commission report. Its evidence was highly circumstantial and – as the example quoted shows – often did not establish even tenuous connexions between American aircraft above and findings of insects and other unexpected objects below. Even before the Lawyers Commission had completed its report, criticisms were being voiced that this was a scientific matter, which should be examined by competent and impartial scientists. While the Lawyers group was still in Korea and China, the World Peace Council at a meeting in Oslo decided to set up a scientific commission. This took several weeks to organize and in the meantime a number of well-known communists and communist sympathizers – then Dean of Canterbury, Dr Hewlett Johnson; the President of the communist peace movement in France, Yves Farges; the Hon. Ivor Montagu, a leading personality of the World Peace Council and its British associate; Mrs Monica Felton, at that time chairman of the communist front for women in Britain and the Canadian clergyman and W.P.C. supporter Dr Robert Endicott – made tours of the germ incident areas. In the main they repeated what had already been said by the Chinese and Lawyers Commissions, though Yves Farges' report to a special World Peace Council meeting in East Berlin in July 1952 made special mention of a case early in April in North-east China when '. . . a large number of dead and half-dead mice and a small number of live mice were dropped by American planes . . .'. Altogether 700 were picked up and all found to be infected with plague. This incident was to assume a special importance later.

Undoubtedly the Scientific Report prepared in the summer of 1952 and published in the September was the most important of all. It was by far the most widely publicized and its findings had the greatest impact. From the point of view of propaganda analysis it also has its place because it is fully documented, so that it provides the basis for a fuller analysis of this particular campaign than any of the other material put out by the communists and their sympathizers.

According to the World Peace Council, invitations to take part in the Commission were sent out to many European, South American and Indian scientists. The invitations were issued in the name of Dr Kuo Mo-jo, President of Academia Sinica and of the Chinese Peace Committee. The main party of the Commission was made up of six people who reached Peking towards the end of June 1952. They were Dr Andrea Andreen, Director of the Central Clinical Laboratory of the Hospitals Board in Stockholm; Jean Malterre, Director of the Animal Physiology Laboratory at the French National College of Agriculture, Grignon, France; Dr Joseph Needham, F.R.S., The Sir William Dunn Reader in Biochemistry at Cambridge University; Dr Oliviero Olivo, Professor of Human Anatomy in the Faculty of Medicine at Bologna University; Dr Samuel B. Pessoa, Professor of Parasitology at the University of São Paulo, Brazil and Dr N. N. Zhukov-Verezhnikov, Professor of Bacteriology at the Soviet Academy of Medicine, of which he was also a Vice-President. A seventh member, Dr Franco Grazioso, Assistant in the Institute of Microbiology at Rome University, did not join the Commission until it was nearing the end of its investigations.

The Commission's time-table is best described in its own words: 'Having unravelled the main threads of the situation in Peking from the 23rd June to the 9th July, it proceeded to Shenyang (Mukden) where it worked from the 12th to the 25th. Accompanied by members of the Reception Committee, it then passed across the Yalu River into North Korea and held meetings in Pyongyan (subject to interruption by air-raids) from July 28th to 31st. Then returning north the Commission spent two days at a rendezvous with the captured airmen before recrossing the frontier into North-east China on August 6th. It should be recorded that the technical organization of this expedition was faultless. An earlier one, which took a shorter time, had been undertaken on the 15th and 16th July, when the Commission went by special plane, train and jeep via Chichihar and Laha to visit the localities in the Kan-Nan district which had been the scene of the dissemination of plague-infected rodents. These places are located in Heilungkiang province on the border of Inner Mongolia. Other official journeys were of a minor character.'

The language barrier was an obvious problem: 'Within the Commission itself seven languages were represented,[1] but it was found that French was the one spoken and understood by the majority of the members and this therefore became the working language. Russian, English and Italian, when spoken, were at once translated into French. On the Chinese side the fact that so many Chinese scientists speak excellent English or French was of great value to the work. But during meetings, for protocol reasons, they spoke in Chinese, interpreted immediately and often independently into French, Russian and English . . . The Commission had further the advantage that one of its European members spoke and understood the Chinese language, which was of particular value during the interviewing of witnesses, and could also read and write Chinese, which facilitated the consultation of literature and the examination of documents . . . In Korea conditions were even more

[1] The number should be six, as two of the seven Commission members were Italians. This small slip is typical of the many occurring throughout the report.

complicated, for very few Chinese scientists understand Korean, but the Commission had there the services of a remarkable linguist, Dr Ok In Sup, who interpreted freely from Korean into French, English or Chinese at will . . . A parallel check was obtained by translation into one of the European languages through Chinese and also simultaneously from Korean into Russian direct. Since frequent comparison of notes took place, it will be seen that there was not much likelihood of any mistake on points of substance.' On this basis the Commission felt it was able to understand Chinese and Korean witnesses fully.

The Commission was sure that it had penetrated the language barrier, but what about the barrier of prejudice? To what extent did it approach the investigation with a completely open mind? One member of the Commission had most certainly answered this question in a speech he had made in Moscow a few weeks previously, Dr Zhukov-Verezhnikov, the Soviet bacteriologist. In the middle of March a protest meeting against B.W. was held in Moscow at which Dr Zhukov was a star speaker. 'The American imperialists,' he declared on that occasion, 'have perpetrated a new crime, they have carried out a bacterial attack on the Korean People's Democratic Republic and the Chinese People's Republic.' He was chosen for this particular role at the Moscow meeting because at the end of 1949 he had been the chief expert witness for the prosecution at the trial in Khabarovsk of a group of Japanese military men accused of preparing for bacterial warfare against the U.S.S.R. during the last war. After a show trial closed to the Western Press, they were all found guilty and given a varying range of heavy sentences. The significance of this trial to the Korean B.W. campaign will be discussed later.

Dr Zhukov might have been excused for not having read the works of Lewis Carroll and for not remembering the court scene from *Alice in Wonderland*, in particular the succinct passage: ' "Let the jury consider their verdict," the King said for about the twentieth time that day, "No, no!" said the Queen. "Sentence first, verdict afterwards!" ' But the British member, Dr Needham, should have pondered it, for he was quoted by the *Daily Worker* in April, weeks before he joined the Commission, as saying that B.W. in Korea 'seems to be apparent from all the evidence we have'.

Dr Zhukov was not only active in Soviet scientific circles, but even more so politically and ideologically. A short while after the Moscow meetings he gave a strong warning to his Soviet fellow-scientists about their laxity in, as he put it, 'unmasking reactionary tendencies in the various branches of medicine in capitalist countries.' He was a Vice-President of the Soviet Peace Committee, a body on which he was to continue to serve for years after he had relinquished his position with the Academy of Medical Sciences.

Dr Needham was also a political man. He was President of the Britain-China Friendship Association and well known for his espousal of the various 'peace' campaigns. Dr Andreen was a leading member of the Swedish Women's Leftist Association, an affiliate of the communist front Women's International Democratic Federation. Both Dr Oliviero and Dr Pessoa were local 'peace-fighters' and up to that time only the Frenchman Jean Malterre was an unknown quantity politically. Following his return to France on the completion of the Commission's work, however, Malterre became an active campaigner on peace platforms, speaking side by side with Frederic Joliot-Curie, the then President of the World Peace Council.

It is necessary to make these analyses of the political backgrounds of the six main Commission members because the original decision of the World Peace Council was to send an 'international group of impartial and independent scientists', who would have the task of 'verifying or invalidating the allegations' levelled against the U.S. forces in Korea. The members of the Commission, it was noted at the time '. . . might or might not be connected with organizations working for peace . . .'.

The Commission spent an appreciable time in China, although only three days were spent in Korea. The last three of the ten weeks' stay were spent in preparing the report. This eventually appeared as a large volume of 660 pages weighing 2½ lb. and running to 330,000 words. In addition there were 90 photographs and 20 maps. The full title of the volume was *Report of the International Scientific Commission for the Investigation of the Facts Concerning Bacterial Warfare in Korea and China* (*with appendices*). Published in Peking but issued from the World Peace Council headquarters in Prague this black volume (referred to here for convenience as the Scientific Report) had a limited distribution by the end of November. It was never widely available.

As we noted earlier, what was issued widely was a small booklet printed on airmail paper. This comprised the 60 pages of the actual report, without any of the 600 pages of appendices. Without those appendices it is impossible to put the report into its true perspective. Without them the reader must either accept or reject the condensed version in the report proper. Yet the appendices comprise the scientific and documentary evidence put before the Commission and upon which it based many of its important conclusions.

This small booklet was issued generally in September 1952 and was given wide circulation. Critics who asked for more details were told to wait for the full volume to appear, which it did two months later, when the initial brouhaha had died down. Although this volume was not made generally available, this does not mean to say that it could not be obtained, as those who wrote for it to the W.P.C. in Prague were sent copies almost by return of post. It was also available early in 1953 from one or two communist bookshops in London, but without being put on general display.

The full report was obviously a hurried production and the English-language version shows signs throughout of slipshod translation and proof-reading. It fell into some amateurish traps, calling spiders 'insects', for instance. There were various irrelevances, such as the long dissertation given on the louse and its part played in the spreading of pathogenic germs, although the Commission itself admitted that lice were not mentioned in the reports submitted by Chinese scientists.

Again, Rocky Mountain spotted fever is a tick-borne infection with an eighty per cent mortality, which originated in a Montana valley. This was discussed in the report together with a relapsing fever found in São Paulo to demonstrate a connexion between them. It was all part of a dissertation to demonstrate that ticks are vectors of pathogenic micro-organisms – though nothing of the nature discussed was encountered by the Commission in their examination of the evidence put before them by the Chinese and Koreans.

The Commission mainly concerned itself with the reports of the earlier Chinese Commissions in Korea and Manchuria, adding that '. . . nothing of strictly scientific significance was added . . .' by the Lawyers' report. Other data examined was largely identifications and analyses of materials contained in these earlier reports.

It would obviously become tedious to detail every case considered by the Scientific Report, so this analysis will concern itself only with those actually singled out in the report for special mention.

It will be remembered that the original Chinese investigating commission – which provided the Scientific Commission with so much of its fundamental evidence – alleged that 'to date disease germs of plague, cholera, typhoid, paratyphoid and dysentery have been used' adding the further comment, 'we also have data proving that the American aggressors are using *Bacillus anthracis* and other pathogenic organs. The facts prove that the U.S. Government is by these means attempting to cause man-made epidemics in order to wipe out the Korean people and the Chinese and Korean troops in large numbers and to destroy livestock and damage crops in Korea.'

This was in April 1952; by August the Scientific Commission had reduced the list to plague, anthrax (*Bacillus anthracis*) and respiratory anthrax, cholera and leaf fungus. Dysentery, typhoid and paratyphoid were only mentioned in passing. An epidemic of encephalitis in the Manchurian centres of Shenyang and Anshan was mentioned as having 'raised the possibility that a virus had been disseminated directly by the aerosol method'. The Commission could not reach a firm conclusion on the matter, commented the Scientific Report: '. . . since it could not establish a definite relationship between the disease and the air incursions. Nevertheless the evidence is indeed disturbing and the full documentation concerning it is therefore placed among the appendices. . . .'

The original Chinese Commission Report referred vaguely to the Americans attempting to 'wipe out' the people and troops in North Korea by using B.W. Following this up the Scientific Commission stated baldly that it could not give any figures of North Koreans and Chinese killed by B.W. '. . . since it would provide the last essential data for those upon whom the responsibility lies . . .'. In any case, it summed up: '. . . the information is not necessary for the proof of the case upon which the Commission was invited to express an expert opinion. All that is necessary is to know what the Commission confirmed, namely that many human fatalities have occurred in isolated foci and in epidemics, under highly abnormal circumstances in which the trail always leads back to American air activity. It is essential that the world should take warning from what has happened and what is still happening. All people should be aware of the potentialities of this kind of warfare, with its incalculable dangers. . . .'

Three cases of plague in North Korea and one in China were picked out by the Commission for detailing in the Scientific Report. To be more precise two cases from North Korea were detailed. The third was merely given in outline, even though it involved the greatest number of fatalities and was the key case.

This incident was described very briefly by quoting from one of the documents of the International Association of Democratic Lawyers' Commission: '. . . after a delivery of fleas to the neighbourhood of An-Ju on the 18th February, fleas which were shown bacterialogically to contain *Pasteurella pestis*, a plague epidemic broke out at Bal-Nam-Ri in that district on the 25th. Out of a population of 600 in the village, 50 went down with plague and 36 died. . . .'

The Scientific Report omitted to print this Lawyers' Commission document in its 600 pages of appendices, perhaps because the Scientific Commission's reading of it was not consistent. The version as published, for instance, by the Chinese Peace Committee made no reference whatever to fleas. Instead it dwelt in detail on the finding of '. . . flies, spiders and bugs . . .', describing each group in detail. The flies had longer wings, bigger bodies and bigger heads than those commonly found in the locality; the spiders were of middle size with a little white on the body; the bugs had flat bodies and were black.

The two other Korean cases were given in much more detail. The first was in a village named Kang-Sou at the end of March 1952. A farmer went to a jar near his well early one morning after a plane had circled his village the previous night. He found fleas floating on the surface of the water in the jar. A few days later he died of nic plague and the Scientific Commission concluded that vas probably bitten by other fleas of the same sending'. 'ard laboratory test reports were produced to show that he lied of plague and that the fleas were infected with plague ria, *P. pestis*. 'Prompt sanitary measures at Kang-Sou had nted further cases.'

he second study made by the scientists was the phenomenon of ry dense mass of fleas being found in April 1952 on a bare hill- near a village named Hoi-Yang by two Chinese Volunteer rces lieutenants. Though no trace of any container could be ound: '. . . the zoning was so distributed as to indicate that they had been delivered by a container which came down rather slowly in a N.N.E. direction . . .'. The evidence for this theory was that Chinese troops stationed locally had heard a plane circling overhead at about four o'clock the same morning.

The two officers in question testified before the Commission, the one, Lieut Fang Yuan, confining himself to concurring with what his senior companion, Lieut Ts'ao Ching-fu, stated. According to Lieut Ts'ao, the mass of fleas darkened the ground and he would guess that at the densest part they numbered about 10,000 to the square yard. Hundreds of them climbed on to his boots and trousers. Neither of them felt any bites, he said, because all Chinese troops had strict orders to tuck their trousers into their boots. After they discovered the fleas, they went back to their unit, sterilized their hands with alcohol and tied up the ends of their sleeves before going out again to destroy the fleas. Finally they changed their clothes and boiled them, took baths and disinfected their dug-outs with antiseptics and D.D.T. Like other members of their unit, they had been inoculated against plague. Tests carried out showed that these fleas were infected with plague bacteria and that they were human fleas.

'The fact that they were fleas (*Pulex irritans*) parasitic on man must be emphasized,' stated the Report. 'According to what is known of the oecology of this insect, it would be impossible to find large numbers away from the houses of man. What then is to be said of the occurrence of a number of these insects estimated at many tens of thousands at one time on bare waste land remote from any human habitation? Such a witches' sabbath was certainly not called together by any natural means. More relevant was the plane which members of the Chinese People's volunteer forces billeted in the neighbourhood had heard circling over the place at about 4 a.m. on the day of the discovery. . . .'

A Chinese expert witness both on the Hoi Yang case and in general was a parasitologist, Professor Chen Wen-kuei. Considerable stress was given by the Scientific Commission to his evidence, in particular to a report he had made at the end of 1941 on a case of plague in Changteh, Hunan province, at the time he was serving with the Kuomintang's Emergency Medical Service.

The Changteh incident related to a misty morning in November 1941 when a single enemy (i.e. Japanese) plane flew very low over the town of Changteh. 'Instead of bombs, wheat and rice grains, pieces of paper, cotton wadding and some unidentified particles were dropped,' stated Dr Chen's report of December 1941 as reprinted in the appendices to the Scientific Report. Specimens of rice grains collected after the all-clear were sent to the Kwangteh hospital for testing, which 'revealed the presence of micro-organisms reported to resemble *P. pestis*'. Later examination by Dr Chen showed this to be wrong, there was no sign of *P. pestis*. But this did not prevent him summing up in 1941 and repeating in detail in 1952 that '. . . although the finding was by no means conclusive, suspicion that the enemy had scattered plague-infective material was in the mind of medical workers who saw the incident on the spot . . .'. Dr Chen did not get to Changteh until thirty-four days later, when he made his examination of the rice grains.

The importance of what at first might seem a trivial incident is that seven days after the solitary airplane flew over, a young girl went down with suspected plague, followed by four more suspected cases and one definite case of bubonic plague, all of them fatal. No fleas were found and there was no rise in the rat mortality rate, which would be expected with a plague attack, but the Commission of twelve years later went on record as deciding that plague was epidemic in Changteh during that period in November 1941 and that '. . . the cause of the epidemic was due to the scattering of plague infective material, probably infective fleas, by an enemy plane . . .'.

From North Korea the Commission turned to a much-discussed

incident in the far north-west of Manchuria, near the town of Kan-Nan in Heilungkiang province, bordering on Inner Mongolia. One morning in April 1952, the inhabitants of four villages in the administrative area of the town awoke to find themselves surrounded by large numbers of voles,[1] having heard a plane pass overhead during the night. This plane, reported the Commission, was identified by the Chinese Air Observer Corps – presumably operating near the Sino-Korean border area of the Yalu River – as an American F-82 double-fuselage night fighter. When the villagers found the voles in the morning, many of them were dead or dying and the villagers collected and destroyed 717 of them from an area around of roughly three by nine miles. Voles were found on roofs, in courtyards and even on the *kang* beds, these latter being presumed as having been carried in by cats.

Of the 700 voles only one was preserved sufficiently for bacteriological testing. This was infected with *Pasteurella pestis*. On the basis of this one specimen and the reported behaviour of many voles that were found alive the Commission concluded that all the voles were infected with plague. The fact that no human beings were infected was due in the Commission's opinion to the sanitary precautions taken after the discovery of the voles, particularly the wholesale destruction of all the 500 cats and dogs in the neighbourhood on the same day. Again the fact that no fleas were reported from Kan-Nan was considered due to the traditional flaming of the earthen floors and *kangs* of the house with dry hay and straw. 'In the opinion of the Commission, therefore, there is no doubt that a large number of voles suffering from plague were delivered to the district of Kan-Nan during the night of the 4th-5th April, 1952, by the aircraft which the villagers heard. This was identified as an American F-82 double-fuselage night-fighter.'

The Commission admitted that '. . . the principal gap in the chain of evidence consists in the fact that no container or "bomb" of any kind was discovered . . .', but resolved this mystery in its own mind by drawing attention to an article in the Japanese paper *Mainichi* which described a container and parachute made of strong paper in such a manner that it would burn away, leaving no

[1] More commonly referred to as hamsters, under which name they are widely used for laboratory testing and as children's pets.

trace after depositing its cargo of infected rats. This article was published on January 27th, 1952 – just one day, incidentally, before the alleged starting of the B.W. campaign according to the communist reckoning.

Two more sets of incidents from China dealt with anthrax. The one, referred to as the K'uan-Tien incident, concerned an episode in March 1952 outside the town of K'uan-Tien near the Yalu River in the south-east of Liaotung province. Eight American fighters were seen to pass over about half an hour after noon: '. . . they recognized them without difficulty for such intrusions were a common, almost daily, occurrence . . .'. From one of them a bright cylindrical object was seen to drop. Organized searches were immediately started and continued for several days, during which time the teams collected and destroyed large numbers of flies and spiders.

After nine days one of the schoolboys searching discovered fragments of a container in and around a shallow crater on a small island surrounded by the beds of two small rivers, at that time dried up. A large number of fowl feathers were also found in the neighbourhood. Anthrax bacilli were found on the insects, spiders and the feathers – 'highly extraordinary phenomenon' on the insects and spiders, though not on the feathers. 'In view of the above facts the Commission had no option but to conclude that insects and spiders carrying anthrax had been delivered by means of at least one container of special type from at least one American plane in the neighbourhood of this small town in Liaotung province on March 12th. . . .'

The second anthrax series was one of respiratory anthrax. Here again witnesses stated that they had seen containers dropped from American aircraft at various places on the Manchurian side of the Yalu River. Following these incidents search parties found groupings of insects or feathers which on later examination were found to be contaminated with anthrax bacilli.

At the same time there were a number of fatal cases in the areas due to respiratory anthrax and haeorrhagic anthrax meningitis. *Ptinus fur* beetles were concluded by the Commission as being responsible for two deaths, while flies and feathers were connected with another two. All four people had been active in the organized searches for insects, spiders, and feathers. A fifth case mentioned was that of a rickshaw driver in Shenyang who was simply reported to have become ill and eventually to have died of respiratory anthrax. He apparently did not take part in any campaign.

Last of the major incidents listed by the Scientific Report is one from the village of Dai-Dong in North Korea. Early one morning in mid-May 1952, 'after a night during which a plane had been heard circling round for an hour or more as if its pilot were trying to find something', a peasant girl picking herbs on the hillside found a straw package containing clams. She took some home and she and her husband ate them raw. They fell ill and by the next day were dead of cholera. Search parties went out on to the hill-sides after this and found more packages of cholera-infected clams.

The clam in question was a marine species and its presence in a hill in the middle of the countryside was described by the Commission as 'a highly unnatural phenomenon'. The outbreak of cholera itself was quite untrue to type – the season was wrong and so was the location.

The whole appearance of the packages of clams presented 'several peculiarities'. In Korea they were not usually wrapped in straw for sale and anyway they were well before season and indeed clams had not been reaching the markets at all since the Korean war began: '. . . and if anyone had gone to the trouble of laying the packages down at various places on the hillside it was hard to explain why many of the thick calcarious shells of the clams should have been broken. . . .'

But, went on the report, 'light was thrown on the sequence of events when the nature of the locality was examined.' The clams were found some 400 yards from a pumping station at the top of the hill and a thousand yards from a series of reservoirs or spring-fed ponds the water of which was drawn up by the pumping station and distributed – partly for drinking purposes – to various coastal settlements and port towns. Two nights before the clams were found, the pumping station had been destroyed by an American raid, though the pumps themselves were undamaged. Thus the clams had been dropped on the following nights to contaminate the drinking water reservoirs, but they had missed their target due to bad weather.

The choice of salt water molluscs for depositing in fresh water was seen as part of a clear plan. During their slow death in fresh water the salt-water clams would serve as natural culture mediums for the cholera vibrios, which would eventually be liberated to contaminate the drinking water. 'Thus the Commission can only conclude that American Air Force units, following a careful plan previously established, first destroyed the Dai-Dong purification plant without damaging the pumps, and then attempted to contaminate the drinking water reservoirs with cholera. The young couple who died, impoverished by war devastation, had the imprudence to eat some of the clams which had been intended as the vehicles of contamination.'

Apart from a vague and generalized reference to anthomyid flies spreading cholera, this is the only incident investigated by the Commission, which considered the evidence during a visit to Pyongyang. Yet here was another case of deaths following a cholera outbreak allegedly caused by insects dropped by American planes. It was referred to extensively in the report of the Chinese investigating commission and more briefly in that of the Lawyers' Commission, both of which provided the Scientific Commission with much of its documentation on other cases. The time-lag alone meant that the Scientific Commission could not carry out a first-hand inspection of the cases they listed, since all but one minor case occurred before they reached Peking. So all their accounts were second-hand and even third-hand.

But with the Pyongyang cholera outbreak we can read the account of someone there at the time. It is that of Tibor Meray, a leading Hungarian journalist who was special correspondent of the communist daily *Szabad Nep* in Korea from August 1951 until September 1952. A collection of his dispatches to the paper were later published in an English-language volume *Korean Testimony* by the Hungarian Peace Council. His chapter on the Pyongyang cholera outbreak of March 1952 is given here in full, for it gave the human background to these B.W. incidents in a way that does not emerge from any of the various delegation reports. It also showed the atmosphere which surrounded these campaigns:

In Pyongyang three people died of cholera on March 8th: Han San Kuk, an old man of 68, Han Kyon Sop, a boy of 6 and Han Kyon Sun, a baby of 2. They had contracted cholera from the germ-infected flies dropped by the Americans. Pyongyang, central borough, Nam Mun Ri district, second street, house number 6. This is where Han San Kuk and the two little children lived. The house is at a ten minutes' distance from the district hospital yet it took me over an hour to get there. I had already been vaccinated against cholera, but as there might have been a danger of plague, I had to don a complete set of rubber clothing: trousers coming up to my chest, a tunic with a head-dress with two slits for my eyes, black rubber boots and long gloves. Over this I put a white coat and an air-filtering mask.

We drive to Han San Kuk's house in a white ambulance car. We stop at a wide thoroughfare, it is the second street from there. The block is surrounded by a strong rope and protected by armed soldiers. The area is under quarantine, it is strictly forbidden to enter or leave it.

The physicians of the Pyongyang institute for the prevention of epidemics and I step over the rope. Here we must stop because a group of people, dressed like we are, spray our entire clothing, even the soles of our boots, with a disinfecting solution. When we leave the house a little later this process is repeated but much more thoroughly than at our arrival.

The quarantined block is a block only nominally. It is an area of the size of Liberty Square in Budapest and once it had been densely populated. Today there are but ruins and rubble, a score of bomb craters, four or five badly damaged but erect little houses and the same number of small and dark dugouts inhabited by people. This is one of the most miserable parts of tortured Pyongyang. It is densely dotted with white spots, the white of the disinfecting choride of lime applied at the foot of the ruins, around the muddy bomb craters and in the place of the burned-down outhouses.

In this hopeless-looking environment Han San Kuk's house is one of the best. It stands next to a completely burned out two-storied house built in Japanese style, it must have been a beautiful building. Between the majority of the Pyongyang houses and the village houses there is but one difference: electricity and canalization. Their form and arrangement is identical. This house is like the houses of the well-to-do farmers. It is unharmed on the inside. Only the slates of the roof are broken and part of the front wall has caved in. The hole has been closed up with boards.

Only ten days ago eight people had been living in this house. Today there are but five: Han San Kuk's son, the 36-year-old Han Sun Yon and his wife, the 33-year-old Yim Yun Bo, parents of the two dead children, and their living children, one 14, one 12 and one 10. The children, bereaved by death of their little brothers, sit silent and frightened in a dark corner of the room. The parents, two short, emaciated worn people, look terribly pale, their eyes are tired and red-rimmed with sleeplessness. The man – a clerk at the local people's committee – speaks in a dull voice, the woman stands silent, gazing into the void or keeping her eyes on the ground, raising her voice only when the questions are directed to her.

'On Wednesday, March 5th, I left the house very early, before six in the morning,' the man says, 'because we were having a conference at the office at six. It was still dark, I noticed nothing. My father came out of the house after six, he found the flies.'

'What flies?'

'The ones dropped by the Americans during the night. All night their planes had circled low over our heads.'

'Where were the flies?'

'In the yard, then on that stone in front of the door and at a few feet from the house. There were others in front of the neighbouring houses. My father found three piles of them.'

'Was your wife at home?'

'I was here,' the woman says, 'preparing breakfast. I looked out from the kitchen but by then grandfather had begun cleaning away the flies.'

'About what size were those piles?'

'The size of my palm. There must have been 50–60 flies in one.'

'Were they alive?'

'Very much alive. Some of them could even fly. The envelope was lying beside them, torn.'

'The envelope?'

'The Americans dropped them in white envelopes,' the man replies, 'in square envelopes. People brought in a number of them to the people's committee. It was only at the people's committee that I learned that the Americans had dropped insects upon our district. And only in the afternoon, when I got home did I learn from my father that they had been dropped on our house also.'

The man showed his hand up to the knuckle.

'The envelopes were about this size.'

'Was there some mark or writing on them?'

'No. There was nothing on the envelopes. But leaflets were found near them which had been dropped simultaneously with the flies.'

'What kind of leaflets?'

'American leaflets, printed in Korean.'

'What did they say?'

'Something in connexion with March 1st.' (March 1st is a traditional holiday of the Koreans, anniversary of the national anti-Japanese uprising of March 1st, 1919.)

'What was done with the flies?'

'My father swept them into a pile on the side of the bomb crater in front of the house, threw bits of wood on them and burned them.'

'Were the children already up?'

'Yes, of course. They always rise at dawn. The three older ones had gone to school, but the two small ones were there with my father while he swept together and burned the flies. He told me in the afternoon that he had constantly had to shoo them away because they considered the whole thing an amusing game.'

'Did your father know about the bacteriological warfare?'

'He did. We read about it in the papers. We knew that we were not to drink unboiled water. We also knew that they had begun vaccinating the population of the town.'

'Has your family been vaccinated at the time?'

'Not yet. The turn of our borough hadn't come yet.'

'What did the old man do after he had finished burning the flies?' I ask the woman.

'He washed his hands and came into the room with the children to have breakfast.'

'When were they taken ill?'

'The following afternoon,' the man replies. 'My father came down with it first, then the 6-year-old and then the little one.'

'What were the first symptoms of the disease?'

'It began with sickness. They vomited everything they had eaten. They had an attack of ague. The lips of the little one were parched. The skin of my father's hands was completely dry. Their stools were like dirty water. The same evening I went for the doctor. He gave them injections and isolated them from the rest of the family. In the morning he returned but their condition had worsened. The doctor took them to the epidemic hospital. My father died at ten in the morning, my 6-year-old son at eight in the evening, and the little one at ten.'

'Did your father suspect what was wrong with him?'

'He fell ill very suddenly and got steadily worse and worse. He hardly spoke at all. He only complained. Once he asked me: "Don't you think, son, that it was the flies that made me sick?" That was all he said.'

'What was your father's occupation?'

'He was a mason. He built houses. This house was also built by him. But now he was very old. He lived at home, swept the yard, kept the house clean. Months passed without his ever leaving the house.'

'Have you sometimes made plans for the future of your children?'

'In the case of the older ones, yes. But the youngest were still very little. We only hoped that we would all live to see the end of this war. It happened differently. They murdered the most helpless.'

The voice of this simple man is now deeper, more bitter, more determined.

'Why did they murder them? Why are they using bacteria against us? I want to know the reason! Let the Americans tell me!'

The mother, who had lost her youngest, her dearest child looks at the ground, the ground that would bear new life in the approaching spring, then lifts her head. Her poor, tortured face is calm but tears stream out of her eyes.

'Punish the criminals!' is all she says.

This is what Kim Djun, physician at the Pyongyang municipal hospital, who had treated Han San Kuk and his grandchildren, has to say:

'On March 6th, at 8 o'clock in the evening, the father of the two sick children came to the hospital and told us that his father was constantly vomiting. I immediately went with him. The old man was in a very bad condition, the children were somewhat better.'

'Did you know right off that it was cholera?'

'The vomiting, diarrhoea and watery stools looked very suspicious but I was not yet sure of its being cholera. I gave them Ringer injections, camphor and dextrose. Next morning I visited them again. By then I had no doubts left. I had them taken to the epidemic hospital. We could do nothing to save them. After death we performed an autopsy on them and established cholera.'

'Who established it?'

'Han Ton Sun, bacteriologist, chairman of the committee for the prevention of epidemics in Pyongyang.'

I spoke also to Han Ton Sun.

'On the morning of the 5th I received a few specimens from the flies dropped in the neighbourhood of Han San Kuk's house. In part of these flies, submitted to bacteriological tests, we found cholera germs. The tests were performed by me and the well-known bacteriologist Kim Nak Ce. We then put the whole area under quarantine, surrounded it with armed guards and began disinfecting and vaccinating. By then Han San Kuk and his two grandchildren had already contracted the disease.'

'How long does it usually take for this disease to kill?'

'That depends on the age and physical condition of the patient. Usually about thirty-six hours.'

'Did you make the bacteriological examination establishing the cause of death?'

'Yes, together with Kim Nak Ce. We received the autopsy material on the night of 8th March and on the 10th we found the cholera germs.'

'How does cholera infection usually spread?'

'Mostly by hand.'[1] The germs pass at meals, from the hand to the mouth and from there into the organism. There is no doubt that the old man and the children contracted cholera when sweeping together and burning the flies.'

'To what do you ascribe the circumstance that the cholera did not spread?'

'As I said before, we took preventive measures as soon as we established the presence of cholera germs in the flies. Thus we kept the disease from spreading. We have already lifted the quarantine from the district and are keeping isolated only the block where we had the three cases of cholera. For the last two weeks we have been regularly disinfecting here. In a few days we shall probably lift the quarantine also here.

'Without these measures, however, the germ infected flies of the Americans could have spread a cholera epidemic all over Pyongyang.'

'How long have you been a physician?'

'Ten years. The last eight years I have been engaged exclusively in bacteriological research and the prevention of epidemics.'

In Pyongyang bacteriological warfare has three victims, a 68-year-old man and two children. It is against these that the germ war is being carried on. These are the targets of the American military forces. The helpless, the old, the children. It is upon these that they rain down hundreds of thousands of cholera-infected flies and other epidemics. Can there be crime more monstrous than this? Can humanity tolerate it?

The old mason who had been building houses all his life and the two children who thought the death-bearing flies to be toys are buried beyond the limits of the town. Their grave is unmarked and contains only the ashes of their burned bodies. Even these ashes are buried seven metres deep and there is a two metre high mound over them. An unmarked grave among the mountains. Not even the parents know its location. No one will ever take flowers to that grave. No mother, no son, no brother will ever stand beside it. A silent grave among silent mountains.

But humanity will never forget that grave. Hundreds of millions are standing around it with tears in their eyes saying 'farewell and a peaceful rest' to the old Korean mason and the two little Korean boys. And hundreds of millions raise their fists roaring the words of the Korean mother:

'Punish the criminals!'

[1] In fact, almost always cholera epidemics are water-borne.

A considerable part of the Scientific Report – both the summary and conclusions which were most widely circulated and the appendices which made up the bulk of the full volume – was devoted to the testimonies of the captured American Air Force Officers. There is no tally between the B.W. incidents reported from the North Korean sources and those mentioned in the various confessions. They form two quite separate groups, coinciding neither in time nor in place. One group of testimonies considered by the Scientific Commission consisted of depositions concerning materials stated by the Chinese or North Koreans to have been dropped by American aircraft; the other group consisted of testimony by American airmen about occasions when they considered they had used bacterial weapons.

Consideration was also given in detail to the types of containers supposed to have been used by American aircraft. But again it should be noted that the evidence was of two kinds. On the one hand the Chinese or Koreans stated what they had seen being dropped or which they considered had been dropped, on the other were statements by the captured Americans linked with this evidence about what they reckoned they had used.

Under the chapter heading 'Testimonies of Captured Intelligence Agents' the Commission dealt in fact with the testimony of only one such agent, a Korean, who together with a Chinese made up the sum total of such intelligence agents to be produced as evidence for the statement: '. . . that since the beginning of the war agents had been sent into North Korea with the precise object of obtaining and sending back epidemiological information related to bacterial warfare . . . '

The Korean agent in question told the Commission very little and, as the report puts it: '. . . in replying to questions, he was rather reticent, perhaps to shield collaborators . . .'. However, '. . . the witness made it clear that before his illicit entry into North Korea he had been given no indication that bacterial warfare was being carried on. He had only heard that there were numerous epidemics in the North and that the armies of the South . . . were employing the most modern scientific weapons with good results.' He learned of bacterial warfare only from reading public notices, that is notices put up by the communist authorities. The Commission concluded – somewhat reluctantly it would seem – that his evidence 'bore the stamp of truth', but dismissed him as seeming to be 'a rather mercenary personality'.

An early section of the report discussed briefly allegations of the use of infected plant material at Chong-Ju in Korea and in more than ten other localities in North-east China and North Korea. 'In one case,' it was noted, 'the descent of the material was seen personally by a British war correspondent.' This case was not detailed in the appendices.

The cases dealt with in the appendices were six in number. Two were concerned to show that on two occasions leaves were dropped over districts of Manchuria and North Korea respectively of plants only distributed south of the 38th Parallel and never seen to the north. In neither case was it alleged that they were infected with bacterial growth. The other four cases made up a mixed bag.

The first case told how on March 20th, 1952, the Deputy Political Instructor of Chinese volunteer detachment in North Korea '. . . saw four American Sabre jet planes and a dark mass dropping. The mass broke up at the height of about 300 metres. Then soya-bean stalks and pods and some sort of tree leaves began to fall down. These scattered over an area about 200 metres in width and 500 metres in length, there being on the average 2–3 soya-bean stalks and pods and 15–16 leaves per square metre. . . .' The samples put to laboratory test were infected with purple spot fungus *Cercospora sojina* Hara.

The second incident was earlier still, on the morning of February 28th. Here again, the witness was a Chinese soldier, who saw two American planes drop 'five big roundish objects' at a spot east of Kaesong from which large numbers of tree leaves were dispersed over about a square kilometre. Laboratory tests showed them to be infected with a strain of *Glomerella* fungus capable of attacking pear, apple and cotton plants. The third case was on July 10th when a Manchurian farmer saw an American plane fly over, after which he found a large number of leaves 'dispersed from the air' into a field of about 10,000 square metres. Tests of samples showed them to be peach leaves infected with pear and apple ring fungus, highly parasitic in orchards.

The last case told of how on March 19th another Manchurian

farmer '. . . discovered a certain quantity of corn (i.e. maize) kernels scattered beside a river . . .'. Without mentioning the presence of any plane the laboratory report went on: '. . . since the major part of the dropped corn kernels had been burned by the peasants immediately after their discovery, only a small sample was sent to this laboratory for examination . . .'. The tested kernels were found to be infected with a smut, *Thecaphora sp.* 'hitherto unknown in China'.

Passing reference, again, is made in the report to the use of bacterial infections directed against animals. 'When the discovery of *Pasteurella multocida* (*septica*) on certain disseminated vectors was confirmed, it seemed at first to have little importance since it is so common an infection of laboratory animals. There are reasons, however, for supposing that it might be used as a weapon against domestic stock.'

These reasons are based on evidence of airplanes being seen over various districts of Manchuria adjoining the Korean frontier, followed by the finding of insects and spiders subsequently found to be infected with *P. multocida*. In one case a farmer's ducks died after foraging for food near some of these spiders. The ducks were autopsied and found to be infected with *P. multocida*, though no mention was made of the disease diagnosed which would normally be fowl cholerax, pasteurellosis. A similar case concerned the ducks of a local poultry breeding station, of which sixty died over a period of nine days in April, 1952, after being seen eating flies and spiders supposedly dropped on a local river by American aircraft. Here again *P. multocida* was isolated but the actual cause of death was not stated.

However, so little attention was paid in the report to either of these two sets of evidence – infected plants and the infection of domestic stock – that the Scientific Commission evidently did not consider them worth more than a formal mention. As far as the Commission's main work is concerned, they can be ignored.

This then is the substance of the scientific evidence presented to support the communist case that the Americans had carried out bacterial warfare against the forces and people in North Korea.

A large part of the full report and appendices was devoted to the evidence of various captured American officers as to how they personally carried out B.W. raids and how they considered the American authorities were organizing their campaigns. At the time these confessions were published in Peking the men concerned were still prisoners and considerable doubt was expressed from the very beginning in non-communist circles as to the veracity of the statements. Following their release as a result of the cease-fire agreement of August 1952 the men gave detailed depositions as to the pressures put upon them to fabricate the confessions. But these were unnecessary, since the Scientific Report itself had quite clearly demonstrated the unsubstantiated nature of their confessions. At the time the Commission was in North Korea, confessions made some months later stated quite specifically that the officers concerned were carrying out B.W. raids in the area. Yet the six scientists who made up the investigating commission were told nothing. The various confessions considered by the Commission list definite places in communist territory where the American flyers stated they had dropped B.W. containers. These cases would be the ones which would have given the Commission the full evidence it needed, for if the Americans could be so specific as to the time and place of their individual B.W. attacks, then it would be expected that the communist authorities for their part would be able to produce the evidence of the effect of these specific raids. But nowhere was this ever done, either in the pages of the Scientific Report or elsewhere.

The 'perfect proof' envisaged by the Commission was for a plane to be forced down with its biological cargo intact and the crew ready to confess all. This was considered unlikely so the Commission right at the beginning contented itself with seeking a direct connexion between materials thrown out of a plane and pathogenic infections of objects beneath. Even this the Commission concluded to be 'rarely or never encountered', but added that it was satisfied that cases had occurred 'which come near enough to it to be decisive'. Yet in its interrogations of the American airmen, at no time did the Commission make any attempt to corroborate their long and circumstantial stories with direct evidence of the effects of their supposed raids.

The basic feature of all the evidence is its circumstantial nature. Quite simply American planes were seen – or stated to have been seen – over various spots at certain times. Later objects or creatures were found which on laboratory test were demonstrated as carrying pathogenic bacteria. In some cases deaths resulted, in the majority nothing further happened. In some cases stated as conclusive evidence neither planes nor bacteria were cited, merely insects capable of becoming vectors of disease. In any normal court of law the evidence presented in the Scientific Report would have been dismissed as totally inconclusive.

But this does not mean that it was false. Quite the contrary. The scientific evidence given in the appendices shows that a large number of Chinese and Korean scientists carried out the work demanded of them by the communists without having to fake anything. The charges show themselves to be false in the light of their own evidence. At the same time this very evidence helps us to decide for ourselves how the communists were able to put up such a sham campaign on such an elaborate scale involving so many people whose personal integrity was beyond doubt.

CHAPTER ELEVEN

# The Hidden Hands

At the very least the bacterial warfare evidence produced by the communists against the American forces would bring in a verdict of not proven in a properly constituted court of law. Indeed, the essence of the charges are legal rather than scientific. If the Democratic Lawyers' Commission had carried out its investigation juridically, it would have to have acquitted the 'defendants' for sheer lack of proof, even of the most circumstantial kind. To this extent the Scientific Commission was of no more value. Its vast accumulation of documents and statements filled in the details of a number of significant events, but did nothing more towards proving the communist charges.

What the Scientific Report shows is the wholly unscientific nature of the Commission's work. Statements and propositions were accepted without question if they fitted in with the communist charges, the most glaring occasions being the acceptance of the American confessions without any attempt to check them from the North Korean or the United Nations authorities. In Dr Zhukov-Verezhnikov and Dr Pessoa the Commission had a bacteriologist and a parasitologist. Yet serious errors were made in the report on matters directly within their specialist spheres. Indeed, all the six scientists – with the possible exception of the bio-chemist, Dr Needham – were reasonably competent to assess directly most of the detailed evidence presented by the Chinese and North Koreans for its scientific validity and relevance: Dr Andreen headed a clinical laboratory in a large hospital, Mr Malterre was an animal physiologist and Dr Olivo a professor of anatomy, while the seventh member joining right at the end of the investigation was a micro-biologist, Dr Grazioso. Certainly all six of them should have been able to approach the subject with scientific detachment.

That they were obviously aware of this is shown by the complex arrangements described in the report for the hearings of evidence from Chinese and Korean witnesses so that the Commission should be '. . . protected against any criticisms that it did not succeed in apprehending (*sic*) the full mind of Chinese and Korean witnesses and specialists . . .'. We are left in no doubt by the voluminous appendices that 'the full mind' was duly recorded. Equally clear is the complete misinterpretation by the Scientific Commission of what the witnesses and specialists told its six members.

In assessing the various incidents highlighted in the Scientific Report we have to remember one very important factor common to them all. The whole period in question was one of war. Fighting and bombing had devastated the areas of North Korea, while in the whole of China – and most particularly in Manchuria – the population was being subjected to a concentrated hate campaign against the West in general and the United States in particular. The main organization conducting the campaign in China was the Chinese Committee for World Peace and against American Aggression, set up shortly after the Korean war began in the summer of 1950 and headed by the writer Kuo Mo-jo, who was also the chief Chinese representative on the World Peace Council in Prague. A reference was made earlier to the many mass meetings organized as part of this campaign in all the main cities and towns of the Chinese mainland. This technique was first tried during the Korean war and as time went on it was refined and considerably enlarged in its scope until by the 1960's the mass demonstrations were being measured in hundreds of thousands of people rather than in tens of thousands.[1]

At the same time the Communist Chinese health authorities were conducting the first of their periodic campaigns to clean up – in the literal sense – the more noisome parts of the towns. Everywhere people were being exhorted to destroy rats, mice, flies, mosquitoes, house and garbage flies, everything that could carry bacteria and spread disease. It was in this context that the bacterial warfare scare played such an important role: it acted as a spur to

[1] Appendix VI gives a detailed account of how an organized series of such mass meetings were conducted throughout mainland China during one week in June 1960.

people to redouble their efforts against the enemies of good health and it also stirred their hatred of the communist political enemy, personified in the West as represented by the American forces in Korea.

In North Korea itself the pattern was much the same, except that there was the obviously greater anti-American accent. Not that the health aspect was neglected, for Korea faced far greater risk of epidemics breaking out, with the wide-spread destruction of shelter and sanitary facilities in the fighting areas and those parts in the path of the advancing and retreating forces of both sides.

It is against this background of mass political agitation and turmoil that we must judge the value of the many eye-witness accounts of strange sights in the sky produced as scientific evidence throughout the report. The K'uan-Tien incident followed a flight of American fighters overhead (in itself a common occurrence) when a 'bright cylindrical object' was seen to drop from one of them. Several days later the evidence of a heap of feathers and spiders was found by a schoolboy on the search. On another occasion four hundred people at a village meeting saw a 'greyish object' fall from a plane. They were immediately put to work on a mass search and eventually came across a large amount of feathers. On another occasion – not mentioned in the Scientific Report – a Press correspondent told in a dispatch how he saw a mass fall from a plane.

The Scientific Report stresses the importance of these eye-witness accounts because they were made by ordinary people, too unsophisticated to make up elaborate stories. For this reason, the Commission declared, their evidence was completely dependable.

But this is an old fallacy. Hallucinations in time of stress can be traced back to the oldest civilizations recorded. Best described, perhaps, are the delusions at the various periods of the Black Death in Europe during the Middle Ages. In Britain during the Second World War there were many scare stories arising from things seen in the skies. A new 'secret weapon' of the Germans in the summer of 1940 turned out to be gossamer webs floating in the breeze. Many an eye-witness of an air-raid from afar swore to have seen a particular target blown up, when nothing had dropped near it.

It also has to be remembered that if you are looking for something, you are the more likely to spot it in your imagination. This is especially so if you are looking into a low lying sun, as was the case with a number of the eye-witness accounts cited in the Scientific Report. The human eye can be the most unreliable testimony. The more unreliable it is, the more emphatic you are as to its reality!

Over and over again the Scientific Report – like the other reports made before it – details of the types of bomb casings found in the region of B.W. incidents. Some of the casings from the earlier incidents were quite obviously propaganda leaflet bombs of a type used extensively by the U.N. forces in Korea. The Scientific Commission devoted a chapter to this subject in the report, based on communist exhibition material and on the American Air Force Officers' confessions.

The Commission was obviously not happy about the bomb question, for what at first thought would have been a simple matter was complicated by containers which destroyed themselves! These containers, in the words of the Commission: '. . . either break into pieces so small that their discovery is unlikely, or containers which set fire to themselves and disappear after delivering their cargo. . . .' In fact, the report revealed in an almost ingenuous manner: '. . . there runs a streak of unavoidable confusion due to the fact that even when eye-witnesses were on the spot when a container was delivered, they did not always succeed in finding it, partly because quite naturally they did not quite know what to look for, and when they did find it their descriptions were sometimes not as detailed as they might have been. This confusion was unfortunately not cleared up by the testimonies of the captured Air Force Officers, whose status as pilots and navigators did not seem to have entitled them to very precise and detailed information on bombs and containers. . . .' So rather reluctantly the report concluded that the findings 'must therefore be accepted with all due reservations'.

Immediately afterwards the report dealt with the spraying of infected insects by American planes as claimed to have been seen by a Chinese soldier, commenting with a degree of candour lacking elsewhere: '. . . it seems unlikely that this could have been anything else than a deduction from the fact that large numbers of insects were found anomalously on the snow over an oblong area of 6 by 3 miles after its passage. Nevertheless all four American pilots are quite specific and concordant that in five separate lectures they were told that spraying could and would be done. . . .' On this basis, therefore; 'the Chinese volunteer may have been right in his deduction', and the technique of spraying was covered fully.

Paper packets are referred to among the other types of containers as well as self-destroying paper containers, of which latter the Commission rather obviously saw nothing! The first group was undoubtedly brought in by the communists to distract people from picking up and reading propaganda leaflets after raids. The presumed use of the latter was based on an article on the subject which had appeared in the Japanese weekly *Mainichi* in January 1952, an article cited over and over again as part of the argument that the claimed American use of B.W. in Korea was a continuation of the work done during the Second World War by the Japanese in Manchuria.

This work had been highlighted a couple of years previously at a Soviet show trial of twelve Japanese officers and N.C.O.s held in the Far Eastern administrative centre of Khabarovsk at the end of December 1949. It was put on without any preliminary notice and took place without any Western correspondents being present. For one thing they would have found it difficult to get to Khabarovsk from Moscow at that time, and in any case Western observers were specifically excluded by the Soviet authorities. The defendants were found guilty of 'manufacturing and employing bacteriological weapons' at various centres in Manchuria before 1945. The chief expert witness at the trial was Dr Zhukov-Verezhnikov.

Selections from the hearings at the Khabarovsk trial were published later in 1960 as a book of over 500 pages. This made constant references to Japanese preparations for a B.W. attack on the Soviet Union and gave details of the production potentials of cholera, plagues and other germs from the Japanese production units in Manchuria, as well as of the mass breeding of fleas to act as vectors of plague bacilli.[1] Alleged experiments with prisoners were given, including a Russian and Americans. These last were being used, the testimony said, to study the effects of B.W. agents on Anglo-Saxons, for it was the Japanese intention to launch bacterial warfare directly on the United States and on England, as well as on Russia.

Epidemic diseases of man and beast were all listed at the trial – typhus, cholera, glanders, anthrax and above all, plague. The part of the indictment dealing with the use of B.W., as distinct from its preparation, only gave two plague incidents. One, at Nimpo, near Hankow, in September 1940, was described circumstantially without any proof from Chinese sources, other than an unspecified newspaper report. The second was the Changteh incident in November 1941, to which more detailed reference will be made later.

The report gave much evidence on the Japanese production facilities in Manchuria for the mass output of bacteria of various kinds. Monthly figures quoted by one defendant for the two production units were at the theoretical level of 300 kg. of plague germs, 800–900 kg. of typhoid 300 kg. of paratyphoid, 600 kg. of anthrax and a ton of cholera germs. Evidence was also given of experiments on animals and humans. Significantly no indictments on these counts were brought against the Japanese war criminals in the War Crimes Trials at Tokyo, either by the Russians or by the Western Allies.

It is somewhat surprising that the Russians did not bring the matter up, for the summing up of the Military Tribunal which presided over the Khabarovsk trial was quite strong in its accusation that the accused '. . . performed experiments in infecting people with the germs of plague, cholera, anthrax and gas gangrene which were cultivated in the laboratories. The majority of the people infected died in horrible agony. Those who recovered were again subjected to experiments, and finally they were killed. . . .' These accusations were featured prominently in the Soviet Press in the

[1] Published in English as *Materials on the Trial of Former Servicemen of the Japanese Army charged with Manufacturing and Employing Bacteriological Weapons*, Moscow, 1950.

early weeks of 1950 but nothing further was done about them. Nothing, that is, until two years later when the Korean B.W. campaign was started on the theme that the Americans were cynically making use of the experience gained by the Japanese war criminals. In this way the Korean events were presented as the political continuation by the Americans of Japanese imperialism.

In October 1950 the Institute of Law of the Soviet Academy of Sciences published a book on the international significance of the Khabarovsk trial and its findings under the title *Bacteriological War – the Criminal Tool of Imperialist Aggression.*[1] While recapitulating the material presented at the trial, the book underlined the fact that the Americans were currently experimenting with bacterial warfare methods, linking this with Nazi work done during the Second World War.

This recapitulation led on to a description of American atrocities in Korea in the autumn of 1950 (the period when these atrocity stories started in the communist Press). This was linked by implication with charges that the Americans were preparing to use biological weapons in their 'aggressive plans', helped by fascist and Japanese experts.

Published as it was by the Academy of Sciences in Moscow, this book had more than a nominal official standing. A Czech translation of it was published in Prague some months later and a second edition was published in the spring of 1952. A note was added to this second edition pointing out on the basis of the material just published at that time in Pyongyang how the warnings in the book had proved true and how the Korean people were now suffering bacterial warfare. This Czech book was published by the official Army publishing house in the relatively large edition of 12,400 copies for the second edition alone. The original Soviet book had a print of 20,000 copies.

These books were intended for specialist readers, not for the general public. Their function was to provide agitators and Party lecturers with background material for meetings and lectures.

[1] M. Yu. Raginskiy, S. Ya. Rozenblit, L. P. Smirnov, *Bakteriologicheskaya prestupnoye orudiye imperialisticheskoy agressii*, Akademiya Nauk Soyuza S.S.R., Moscow, 1950. Published in Czech as *Bakteriologická válka zločinny nastroj imperialistické agrese*, Naše Vojsko, Prague, 1952.

Their main interest lies in two ways. The original Moscow edition 'predicted' the bacterial warfare issue in Korea within a little over three months of the war starting. The second edition of the Czech translation was set up ready for printing early in December 1951: the note on the significance of the new series of B.W. allegations in Korea must have been added while the book was printing.

As a scientific indictment the Khabarovsk trial report carries little weight. It showed intention and research on the part of the Japanese, but then the same could be said about every major protagonist in the last war – Soviet, German, British and American research centres were in operation testing the ways of bringing out effective bacterial weapons. Some of the work dated to pre-war years, for Marshal Voroshilov in 1938 was publicly boasting of the Soviet work being done in the B.W. field. The main purpose of the Khabarovsk trial was to underline the theme of Japanese aggression during the war and to postulate the new power in Asia, the U.S.A., as an ever greater threat to peace. As the prosecution put it when summing up at Khabarovsk: '. . . let all those who are contemplating new crimes against mankind and preparing new means for the wholesale extermination of human beings remember that the world has not forgotten the lessons of the Second World War. Peace and security is being guarded by millions of common people, by the mighty force of democratic forces headed by the great Soviet Union. It is a mighty and all-conquering force which will be able to check and sternly punish all instigators of a new war. Let your verdict sound as a stern reminder of this, Comrade Judges.'

If one single aspect stands out from the welter of information in the trial report, it is the significance given to the production of plague bacillae, *Pasteurella pestis*, and their vectors, fleas.

Plague is as old as the history of man and beast. It is a disease of the rodent, showing itself with fever and swelling of the lymphatic glands. It develops very quickly and its mortality is high. The main rodent it is associated with is the black rat, which spread the disease to Europe in the thirteenth century when it was brought back in the entourage of the returning Crusaders. In its turn each rat supports its own colony of parasitic fleas, of a species equally ready to feed on rat or man.

Normally fleas using a rat as host will feed on it as long as it remains alive. But as soon as it dies – as it will if plague-infected – they desert the cooling body for another. If no more rodents are to be found then the infected fleas will seek the next best thing, man, transmitting *P. pestis* to him by biting. This was the case with such classic plague epidemics as the Black Death of the Middle Ages and with outbreaks in India and other Asian countries of the nineteenth and early twentieth century. The rat took the plague with it to every part of the world and it was by programmes of rodent control that we were able to reduce plague to the exceptional occurrence it is today.

It is only by maintaining such strict controls that we are able to confine it to occasional small outbreaks, so small that they never make news. But Asian memories are long and the possibility of a plague epidemic among humans is a constant fear in the Far East. This was most certainly so in Manchuria and North Korea at the time of the Korean fighting, even though normally Korea was not considered a plague area. The devastation of war and the breakdown this meant for the public health services together with the influx of large numbers of Chinese soldiers from the endemic areas of North China increased the plague potential.

In fact, the Scientific Report only mentioned one epidemic of plague in North Korea and that superficially. Instead they dealt in detail with a single case, that of the man in Kang-Sou who found some fleas floating in a water-jar after a plane had been heard overhead the previous night. He died of bubonic plague a few days later 'probably bitten by other fleas of the same sending'. The uncertainty of the Scientific Commission on this point was shared by one of the senior Chinese experts testifying before them, Dr Choi Hyun-Soo, Chief of the Mobile Epidemic Prevention Corps, who told them cautiously: '. . . as to whether the patient was bitten by the fleas, he supposed, with the members of the Commission, that this must have occurred but wondered also whether a sufficient inoculum of the bacilli might not have been obtained by the patient having simply washed in the water in which the fleas had floated. . . .' The fleas collected were examined over a period of three weeks and indicated only light infection with *P. pestis*.

But more important than this flimsy testimony was that of Dr

Chen Wen-kuei, President of the South-west Branch of the Chinese Medical Association and seconded at that time to the North Korean epidemic prevention service. Dr Chen, himself a bacteriologist, emphasized on this occasion – and the point was stressed throughout the report – that the fleas identified were human fleas *Pulex irritans* and not the rat flea or any other species of flea.

The Soviet member of the Commission, Dr Zhukov, also stated at this time that two of the Japanese tried at Khabarovsk had made it clear that they had been working with the human flea. The identifications throughout the Scientific Report are of *P. irritans* not the *X. cheopis* Oriental rat fleas normal to this part of Asia as the plague vector.

Whatever the Japanese defendants may have said at Khabarovsk, the record published by the Russians in 1950 made no reference whatever to *P. irritans*. Instead the vague term 'flea' was used throughout. But the mass breeding systems described were those used normally in plague research centres for breeding large numbers of *X. cheopis*. There is no indication that the Japanese breeding stations in Manchuria ever worked on the mass production of human fleas.

Indeed, there is every reason why they should not have done so. In the first place the human flea is difficult to breed artificially under laboratory conditions, unlike its rodent-haunting cousin. It is just not worth while trying to do so for the rat flea does a better job as a vector of plague bacilli, which again is not the job for *P. irritans*, which is selective in its choice of Man as a host and so is unlikely to transmit *P. pestis* from a rat. So it is noteworthy that both the parasitologist Dr Chen and the bacteriologist Dr Zhukov should place such a deliberate stress on *P. irritans*. Dr Chen went out of his way to stress how '. . . he had himself established at the time of the Changteh attacks that the Japanese were disseminating plague-infected fleas mixed with rice husks and cotton wool . . .'. In fact there was only one Changteh attack, that of November 1941, when rice grains – but no fleas – were found on the ground after a Japanese plane had flown over this Chinese town early one morning. Some days later a number of people in the town went down with bubonic and suspected bubonic plague and died.

On this flimsy circumstantial material Dr Chen wanted the then government in Chungking to accuse the Japanese of using bacterial warfare. His report was rejected by the Chinese Nationalists and by most of the Allied Government missions in Chungking. A copy went to the Soviet mission and presumably found its way to Moscow, where it was evidently kept on file for later use. How big a role it played in the background of the Khabarovsk trial is for conjecture and it was never produced in evidence there. But it certainly played its part in 1952 as a convenient flashback link of the present with the past.

Of all the people on the Commission Dr Needham the British biochemist would have been expected to remember it well, since he was in China towards the latter part of the war. Yet none of his writings in the later 40's made any reference to the deliberate spreading of plague by the Japanese, though he wrote in general terms about the problems of epidemics in China. It was only when he became a member of the Scientific Commission in 1952 that such matters came into his head.

At a Press conference in London on his return from China in September 1952, Dr Needham declared that in 1944 it had been part of his duty as a British official in China to report to the British Government that the Japanese were and had been disseminating plague-infected fleas in China. Dr Needham at that time was an officer of the British Council in Chungking and had the honorary rank of Scientific Counsellor at the Embassy. In July 1945, he wrote an account of a journey he had made in the second quarter of 1944 in South-east China. In this somewhat belated report he noted briefly that he had met Dr Chen Wen-kuei, who had told him about the Ningpo episode of 1940 and the Changteh incident of 1941. When he recalled that same journey in his book *Science in China* published in 1948 he omitted the Chen interview completely. The meeting of Dr Needham with Dr Chen four years later in North Korea apparently helped to refresh his memory to the extent of alleging events that even Dr Chen had not specified.

Undoubtedly the unfortunate man who went to the water jars at Kang-Sou died of plague. The 'fleas' he saw floating – as we are told at second hand – might well have been midges or any other small insects. Equally, small numbers of fleas might have been deliberately planted there. There had been no time for the bacilli to multiply in the fleas' guts and on balance everything pointed to the occurrence as a natural one exploited for political ends.

Even more so was the Hoi-yang incident, when two young Chinese officers saw a dense mass of human fleas advancing on them, of which phenomenon the Commission declared: '. . . such a witches' Sabbath was certainly not called together by any natural means . . .', but rather dropped by American aircraft. On the contrary, such large massings of fleas are possible and have been recorded many times, particularly from battle areas. Typical testimony of this comes from the U.S. Department of Agriculture's Yearbook for 1952, which dealt with insects. Discussing fleas and disease one of the authors noted how in the Second World War he watched '. . . the pests jump in all directions from the wrinkles in the pantaloons of Arabs while he was studying the effects of D.D.T. in Egypt; boil up into his clothes from the straw in abandoned pillboxes and from cave floors occupied by refugees in Sicily, where he was investigating mosquitoes and sand-flies; and emerge by thousands from the ground litter of a small, abandoned native village along a mountain stream in the Philippines. Regardless of locality, race and colour, they were after human blood. . . .'

So there was every likelihood that the Hoi-yang fleas were a natural event. All but a few were destroyed immediately. These few were sent for laboratory test and although the direct smear examination showed no *P. pestis* present a guinea-pig injected with an emulsion of the fleas died after nine days. This bacteriological examination was carried out a month after the event by Dr Chen Wen-kwei, who concluded that *P. pestis* was present in the specimen fleas tested. An unconvincing examination.

Similarly with the Kan-Nan voles, those 700 which suddenly turned up in the village on the borderlands of Inner Mongolia. Their appearance was unusual, but not impossible in nature. Those making the zoological examination of the single vole saved could not identify it from comparative materials readily available. From this the Commission came to the conclusion that the Kan-Nan voles had been bred artificially at a breeding centre in Japan, working on parental strains originating in North-east China!

Natural occurrences were considered briefly but dismissed on the grounds that rivers to the east and west of Kan-Nan would have to be crossed. Possible migrations from other points of the compass were ignored.

But another China traveller, working quite independently, provided a more feasible answer to the Kan-Nan puzzle. He was Ivor Montagu, the old-time British Communist who has played such a big role in the work of the World Peace Council. At the time the Scientific Commission was making its inquiries in Shenyang and Kan-Nan itself, Mr Montagu was attending a World Peace Council meeting in Prague. At that meeting he acquired a skin and skull of a Kan-Nan vole: on the evidence of the Scientific Report it would appear that these were the remains of the one and only Kan-Nan vole to be preserved, so the Commission itself never actually saw a specimen of the 700 they discussed in such detail. On his return from Prague, Mr Montagu took this skin and skull to Dr T. C. S. Morrison-Scott of the Natural History Department of the British Museum in London. He asked Dr Morrison-Scott to identify the vole, because he wanted to be quite sure that it was not normally found in the Kan-Nan area.

The Chinese zoologists who examined the vole from Kan-Nan made their comparisons on the basis of Japanese work in 1941, from which they could give no definite identification. For his part Dr Morrison-Scott was quite emphatic in identifying the vole as a sub-genus, the existence of which was first established in 1901 by a Russian, Kastchenko. The species, he said, is widely distributed in Eastern Siberia, Manchuria and other parts of China and he considered that Mr Montagu could get more detailed information about the vole from the Russians, who were so much better informed about it.

The Commission went to great lengths to establish the validity of the thesis that the voles had been dropped by plane. It will be remembered that the animals had supposedly been dropped in paper containers. This impression is largely given by implication. A reference to the possible use of paper containers in the Japanese *Mainichi* article made it tempting for the Commission '. . . to suppose that a battery of them had been used in the Kan-Nan incident, but for this there is no specific evidence . . .'. The obvious thought having also occurred to the Commission members they qualified even this guarded statement: '. . . one corollary of paper containers for rodents would be that the animals might have to be kept in at least a semi-anaesthetized condition during the flight, to prevent them from gnawing their way out . . .'. So, they concluded with a rider which completely destroyed their half-case: '. . . the Commission places these points on record only for the purpose of drawing attention to possibilities . . .'. This confession neatly summed up the recurring major theme of the whole 600 pages of the report.

The second of the three epidemic diseases covered was anthrax. This killer disease is widespread all over the world and may attack all domestic animals and man, as well as many wild animals. Only birds possess any real immunity. It is caused by the *Bacillus anthracis*, the spores of which are the hardest to destroy. They resist drying for at least a couple of years and can remain latent in the soil for up to eighteen years and still be capable of infecting animals. Even the strongest disinfectants only kill them with difficulty and they can resist boiling for up to half an hour. Infection in animals is usually by the mouth and the alimentary tract. The actual bacilli are delicate and probably destroyed by the gastric juices, but the spores are unaffected and begin to vegetate. They invade the walls of the intestine and reach the bloodstream, where they find ideal conditions for rapid growth. Anthrax in man usually occurs by infection through abraded skin, though spores can be inhaled through dust in the air when handling infected pelts. In most cases the attacks are sudden and death comes quickly.

So it is hardly surprising that anthrax bacilli were found on flies, spiders and feathers picked up off the ground outside the Chinese town of K'uan-tien following their discovery nine days after American planes had been seen overhead. The possibility of natural ground contamination was not considered by the Commission, which was more concerned at the possibilities of the feathers being used as packing to protect the flies and spiders when they were dropped from the aircraft. The listed fatal cases of respiratory anthrax cited from Liaotung and Liaohsi in Manchuria fell into the pattern of inhalation of infected dust from an infected area during an anti-vermin campaign. Here the beetle *Ptinus fur* joined with flies and feathers as a carrier.

Last of the three epidemic diseases discussed by the Scientific Report is cholera. This is again a widespread disease, particularly in Asia. It is faecal-borne and the main vehicle is drinking water, with food, flies and direct contact also being important. It is a rapid and painful disease, between thirty and eighty per cent fatal. But, like other water-borne diseases, it is not automatically infectious: it all depends on the physical condition of the individual at the time he takes in the cholera vibrio, which under normal circumstances might well be destroyed by his gastric juices.

The specific cholera case considered by the Scientific Commission was that of the unfortunate young Korean couple who ate some clams they had picked up on a hillside. These clams, it was argued circumstantially, must have been dropped by American aircraft in an attempt to pollute a nearby reservoir. Great stress was laid on the claim that cholera had been unknown in Korea for many years.

It was certainly true that while faecal-borne diseases were as rife in Korea as in China the controls imposed by the Japanese when they ruled Korea had kept cholera in check. But the wartime devastation following 1950 had changed that situation completely and by 1952 there was every probability of cholera outbreaks in the past or present fighting areas. Clams are popular delicacies among the Korean peasants and, as the Commission itself noted, the two who died had not eaten any since the war broke out. There was every temptation for them to eat the clams and every likelihood that in their raw state they would be infected with some kind of bacteria. As to how the clams got on to the mountainside, they could have easily been dropped there by someone walking along as dropped by Americans flying overhead.

Of far more point in this connexion is the case from Pyongyang, described by Tibor Meray and others in great detail, but given only briefly in an appendix by the Scientific Commission, which did not mention any of the deaths. This Pyongyang incident throws particularly strong light on the way the communists ran the B.W. campaign. It will be remembered how very strongly it affected

Meray at the time. He described how he and his party drove to the house of the cholera victims, but was stopped by an armed guard at a barricade. He had already been vaccinated against cholera, but he had had to don a complete set of rubber clothing, including boots and gloves. Over it all he had put a white coat and an air-filtering mask. As they went over the barricade, they were all sprayed from head to toes with a disinfecting solution. When they left the dead man's house they were once again sprayed, even more thoroughly.

Following the Hungarian Revolution of 1956, Tibor Meray was one of the group of Hungarian journalists to leave the country. He settled in Paris and in May 1957 published a number of articles in the newspaper *Franc-Tireur* under the general heading 'The Truth about Bacterial Warfare'. In these articles he looked back on the stories he had written in 1952 and on everything he had been told by the communists in Korea. He checked on their stories with scientists at the Pasteur Institute in Paris and these articles were the outcome of his 'self post-mortem'.

Most revealing is what he tells us of the Pyongyang incident. His vaccination, given half an hour before going to the site, was useless. He needed two, at a week's interval, and even then immunity would not have been certain for some days. This vaccination, the protective clothing, the sprayings with disinfectant, were all part of what he called a dreadful comedy, a comedy which he related in all its terrifying detail. Such was the cynicism of those behind it all, he noted in *Franc-Tireur*, that they did not even bother to get their numbers right: he was told that three were dead, while the visiting International Lawyers' delegation was at the same time told that the figure was two dead.

The incidents involving plant fungi, like those of fowl septicaemia, are mentioned in detail in the appendices, but with relatively little comment made on them in the actual report. In all the cases, the evidence was highly circumstantial and could equally as easily be explained – in a more convincing manner or in terms of natural phenomena. All the diseases listed were contagious and serious, but not directly to human beings.

A wide variety of insects and spiders was detailed throughout the Report. A number of them were notorious carriers of disease organisms: the stable fly and house fly, bluebottle, mosquitoes and fleas. Others, such as the beetle *Ptinus fur*, are store pests. Some of the insects and spiders mentioned were quite harmless. But in general those cited as vectors (the human flea *Pulex irritans* being the exception) were the objects of the widespread health drives taking place in China and North Korea at the time the Scientific Commission was doing its work. There was every reason to wipe out these pests, whether they were actual bacterial carriers or not. For an anti-pest drive, it was better to be all-embracing rather than selective.

Though imagination played a great part in witnesses' accounts, there is no doubt that in the majority of the cases, infected insects or materials were found. No combatant wishing to wage bacterial warfare effectively would have resorted to the methods described. They were just too crude to succeed. Even at the time of Korea the state of B.W. research in the West and in the communist world had got well beyond the stage represented by the communist propagadists, which were those supposedly developed by the Japanese in the early 40's.

The evidence produced in the Scientific Report did nothing to substantiate the charges against the Americans. Some of it, indeed, was an effective repudiation. The small quantity of *P. pestis* in the Hoi-Yang fleas, for instance showed that they had been infected for too short a time for them to have been loaded at an American base, flown over, dropped, been picked up and then taken to a laboratory for bacteriological examination. Which raises the question of how many of the incidents were natural occurrences and how many were deliberately planted? Which in its turn raises the further question of whether any natural occurrences were later exploited with deliberate plants.

In its work the Scientific Commission was presented with a series of incidents. An American plane was seen overhead. Objects were found on the ground afterwards. Later still bacteria of various kinds which were stated to have been found in or on these objects, were isolated in laboratories. Guinea-pigs which died under test in these series were autopsied and pronounced as dead as a result of the bacteria found on the objects picked up after the plane had passed over. The whole sequence was analysed in each case as a progressive factor, each stage directly resulting from the one before and leading on to the one after.

But all the evidence for this was indirect, with separate people or groups of people giving testimony at each stage. The evidence relating to the planes was valueless as in a number of cases there is little doubt that the objects found on the ground were there naturally, notwithstanding the Scientific Commission's opinion to the contrary. This would be the case with the anthrax spores, the 'witches brew' of fleas at Hoi-Yang and the Kan-Nan voles.

The actual cholera incident in Pyongyang described by Tibor Meray had a genuine basis, as far as the actual occurrence was concerned (though there seemed to be discrepencies over the number of fatalities). But elsewhere in his *Franc Tireur* articles Meray recalled an incident at the Hungarian field hospital in Korea named after the then Hungarian communist leader Matyas Rakosi. This hospital served several villages. Early one morning someone in one of these villages found some flies in bags on the ground. They were concluded to be the results of a B.W. attack. Later in the day, Meray said, one of the Hungarian doctors (who believed the B.W. propaganda) told him indignantly that some of the peasants were claiming that these flies had not been dropped by American planes, but had been put there by Chinese soldiers.

In this same connexion Meray also told another story which happened after he had filed some of his early B.W. dispatches in Pyongyang for his Budapest paper. In these dispatches he had mentioned the evidence as being found by Chinese soldiers. Shortly afterwards he was instructed officially to delete the references to Chinese soldiers and just refer to the evidence as having been found.

If the actual evidence were planted, as seems very probable with the clams at Dai-Dong, then we can be sure that the necessary infectivity was there ready to be revealed during actual laboratory tests, carried out in the normal way by scientists on the job.

But where natural events were used, the laboratory tests would not necessarily prove anything. This was so where the human flea played such a vital part. In North Korea at this time in 1952 the Chinese plague expert, Dr Chen Wen-kuei, was playing an active role, as the Scientific Report told us, with the reminder that

Dr Chen wrote the report of the Changteh incident in 1940 of an alleged Japanese B.W. attack which was rejected by the authorities at the time. In that 1940 incident no fleas were found, but Dr Chen concluded that plague-infected fleas had been used by the Japanese.

In his evidence before the Scientific Commission Dr Chen was quite specific that the human flea *P. irritans* had been used as a vector for plague attacks by the Americans in Korea. He went on to a rhetorical question: had the Japanese twelve years earlier used human fleas? The answer he quoted without contradiction from Dr Zhukov-Verezhnikov the Soviet bacteriologist, who, '. . . after hearing my report, confirmed the fact that the bacteriological weapons used by the Japanese war criminals were indeed infected human fleas, entirely the same as those now used by the American aggressors . . .'. Curiously enough, in the report of the Khabarovsk trial at which Dr Zhukov was the principal expert witness, nothing is said about the species of flea used by the Japanese at their experimental stations in Manchuria. But the production techniques are described as those for the rat flea. This, it will be remembered, is a far more efficient vector of plague than *P. irritans*, which is difficult (though not impossible) to breed under laboratory conditions and which is at best an inefficient carrier of plague.

Dr Chen and Dr Zhukov adopted a united front on the flea question, a connivance that apparently escaped the other members of the Commission, even the parasitologist, Dr Pessoa from Brazil. Scientifically they would have been on firm ground if they had stuck by the rat flea *Xenopsylla cheopis*. But if they had done that they would not have been able to exploit the Hoi-Yang 'witches' brew'.

A strong point made in the Scientific Commission report was the academic probity of the scientific witnesses interrogated, many of them Western trained. Most of the evidence recorded in the report's appendices is straightforward, of a nature that would not call for any falsifications or fabrications. Even the contradictory evidence of Dr Chen could have been given with a genuine belief in its truth. The real fault lay with the individual members of the Scientific Commission, who were ready – and seemingly eager – to accept everything presented to them on its face value as evidence of

American guilt, without any attempt at applying their normal scientific detachment and inquiring assessment. Between them – and even excluding the Soviet Dr Zhukov as likely to be politically biased – they commanded sufficient background knowledge of the issues involved for them to accept and reject the scientific testimony for what it was worth. In the event, the six scientists showed themselves so eager to make the political points that they drew conclusions for themselves which bore no resemblance to the evidence they were supposedly sifting.

It will be recalled that the B.W. propaganda campaign was preceded by one devoted to accusations of the most depraved forms of bestiality by American forces against the Korean population. It is significant that these early horror stories made very little impression on the world outside communist propaganda circles. After the first few months little attempt was made to follow up the reports, for instance, of the Women's International Democratic Federation delegation of 1951.

But the germ warfare accusations received world-wide publicity. The campaign rode on the crest of a wave of anti-American fervour that had hitherto been unknown. It created controversy among scientists in all countries, with well-known figures taking one side or the other.

Looking back on this campaign, it may be wondered why it should have raised such feelings, when accusations of more tangible atrocities excited no response. In the first place, of course, the atrocity accusations just did not ring true. They were just too far-fetched.

With bacterial warfare there was – and still is – a strong sense of the unknown. Unknown because it is a weapon unseen, bringing with it all the primitive fears aroused in Man by an invisible evil. These fears can provide his imagination with all the details that would otherwise be lacking, as was shown time and time again in the testimonies of the peasants given before the Scientific Commission and duly recorded in their report as being 'too simple, too concordant and too independent to be subject to doubt'.

The exploitation of such fears is nothing new in psychological warfare. In 1918, the British propaganda organization – then newly set up – circulated rumours of a Spanish influenza epidemic inside

Germany. Later on, in the Second World War, another British propaganda unit had the job of spreading plague rumours behind the German lines on a sector of the Eastern front, to help demoralize the local population in the face of advancing Red Army forces. The Soviet Union itself also suffered a B.W. propaganda attack from Stalin during the purges of the 1930's. In 1933 he accused one group of setting out to destroy the collective farm cattle by injecting them with anthrax and plague, and helping to spread meningitis among horses.

Stalin also charged the kulaks with introducing potato beetles into the potato crops, spreading rust in the wheat, boll weevils in the cotton, mixing dust with the grain compulsorily purchased by the State and with allowing crops to rot in the field and the barn. Of course, there was an element of truth behind these charges at the time for the collectivization drive was being carried out at an intense pitch and peasant resistance was strong. At the same time Stalin undoubtedly exaggerated the state of affairs as a deliberate propaganda policy of alienating the sympathy of the workers for the peasants. His strictures on this occasion were duly preserved in his collected works and in the volume *Problems of Leninism*, which was a Party handbook right into the middle of the 1950's.

So it was hardly surprising when one part of these charges came up again. This time the place shifted to Eastern Europe in the summer of 1950. On June 30th that year the Soviet Government presented a Note to the United States Government transmitting a protest from the East German régime against the alleged dropping by American planes of Colorado or potato beetles over many districts of Eastern Germany.

On the previous day the Czechoslovak Government had issued a proclamation over Prague radio stating that 'the American imperialists and their agents were spreading the beetle all over the western areas of Czechoslovakia with the aim of 'destroying the prosperity of the people's democracies'. An official Note to the American Government on July 10th developed this theme, contending that the beetle had appeared simultaneously in all areas bordering Western Germany (then the American Zone), that it had often been found on roof-tops and in other places where it would not normally exist, and that many little boxes, some still full of beetles, had been found as well as broken bottles in which beetles had been carried. All the allegations were denied by the Americans.

On July 12th an agreement for mutual assistance against the potato beetle was signed in Prague between the Czechoslovak and East German Governments. During July and into August the communist Press and radio of the two countries carried heavy propaganda on the theme of imperialist potato beetles and measures taken to combat them. By the middle of August the subject had been dropped and its place in anti-American propaganda taken up by events in Korea, where the United Nations forces were in retreat.

Those, such as myself, who were in Czechoslovakia at this time will remember the patent absurdity of the charges as carried by the communist Press. The colorado potato beetle *Leptimotarsa decimlineata* is the most dangerous pest of the potato crop. Its larvae feed on the plant leaves at the critical developing period for the tubers. If infestations are allowed to build up, whole crops can be destroyed. The complete life cycle of the beetle lasts about forty days, so that it can breed and infest twice in a growing season. Being a winged beetle, it can spread rapidly across land areas, though sea channels such as the English Channel are usually a reasonably good barrier to migration. For this reason – and with strict control over potato imports – countries such as Britain are normally free of the beetle. But this is not so in continental Europe, where inter-governmental measures to control the pest are constantly in force.

When the beetle epidemic broke out in neighbouring areas of Eastern Germany and Czechoslovakia in the early summer of 1950, the East German régime had only just been recognized by the Prague government. So the outbreak found both governments unprepared for joint action. There is no doubt that the epidemic could have had a serious effect on the major food crop of both countries – at a time when they were still continuing with food rationing, so the official anxieties were well-founded.

As a short-term measure, the charges against the Americans were intended to divert public attention from laxities on the part of the communist régimes. At the same time they were intended to help build up the image of rapacious American imperialism.

Looking back on that short campaign, we can now see its link with the Korean B.W. campaign, which was to start in earnest nearly two years later on the signal from Moscow Radio's Korean Service. It seems certain that the beetle campaign itself was of Czechoslovak origin, and it seems equally certain that it owed much to the ideas contained in Stalin's accusations of 1933.[1]

After 1954 the specifically Korean B.W. charges were dropped by the communists. But more general accusations against the West have been preferred as the opportunities have arisen. In 1956 for instance, the Moscow satirical magazine *Krokodil* linked American A-bomb generals, B.W. agents and the Radio Free Europe transmitters together as three forms of Western aggression against the People's Democracies. This was at the time of the Hungarian uprising. Three years later, in June 1959, *Izvestia* and the English-language *Moscow News* dwelt on the American B.W. theme, at a time when evidence on the effectiveness of B.W. and other weapons was being presented in Washington as part of the normal routine. A Soviet textbook on bacteriology published in 1958 had a special section in the B.W. campaign. This section was omitted from the English translation.

In July 1960, the B.W. bogey was raised once again, this time in Slovakia with a report on the activities of the frontier guards in the Bratislava Party daily *Pravda* which claimed: '. . . hundreds of foreign agents who came to our country with ampules containing pest germs, with weapons, leaflets and with bloodthirsty ideas, have had to raise their hands at gunpoint . . .'. These specific accusations were part of a general uproar being raised all over Eastern Europe in the Party Press at the time as part of the anti-American drive following the U2 affair and the cancellation of the Paris Summit Conference.

Six months later, a home service broadcast by Moscow Radio on January 2nd, 1961, made the innuendo that the cholera research centre of the South-east Asia Treaty Organization in Dacca,

[1] In the 1939 trials of Radek and other alleged Trotskyites in Moscow one of the accused, Knyazev, confessed to having received instructions from the Japanese Intelligence Service to use bacterial means in time of war to contaminate Soviet troop trains, canteens and army sanitary centres. This incident – small at the time – may well have motivated the Khabarovsk stage trial ten years later.

Pakistan, was being used as a research laboratory for B.W. and that 'U.S. military specialists in bacterial warfare are showing particular interest in the establishment of this centre'. Quoting 'usually well-informed circles' at the Dacca station, the broadcast reported that 'experiments on the various methods for the artificial spreading of cholera would be carried out under the direction of the American experts'. Dacca was allegedly chosen as the site of the experiments since cholera epidemics appear frequently in the region. In January 1963, Moscow Radio raised the B.W. question again briefly.

In Communist China and North Korea, travellers' accounts tell us that bacterial warfare exhibitions are still standard equipment on the anti-Western propaganda shows. In June 1960, when the Chinese and North Koreans celebrated the tenth anniversary of the outbreak of the Korean war, the long list of American crimes denounced at the mass meetings, detailed in plays and films and mimed in opera and dance included bacterial warfare.[1]

In Czechoslovakia in 1960 civil defence lecturers were still using the Korean B.W. material as background for talks on the use of bacterial weapons and methods of combating them.

The bacterial warfare charges were directly associated with a war in which both communist and non-communist forces were engaged fighting each other. When that fighting finished, so did its propaganda. Outside China and Korea, little or no reference to that period is made in the communist world. It is no longer a source of inspiration for novelists or playwrights in the U.S.S.R. or Eastern Europe, no films are made there which recall the fighting deeds of the Chinese or North Koreans, or which dwell on the effects of the United Nations action.

China and Korea are different, in that they were directly involved. In these cases, the propaganda stories are highlighted on propaganda occasions, such as the tenth anniversary of the outbreak of the war in June 1960 already mentioned.

This period of the early 1950's marked the end of the Stalinist era, in the sense that Stalin himself was still in control. The B.W. campaign was a Stalinist concept, like that of 1933, but set in the

[1] This is shown by the official account of these manifestations given as Appendix VI.

context of the whole world. The campaign ran at full spate right into the beginning of 1953. Stalin died in March of that year and the Korean truce was signed in the summer. By the early autumn, moreover, the then premier Malenkov was claiming that Russia had the H-bomb, a more powerful propaganda weapon in the modern world than any handful of bacteria.

The repatriation of American forces from North Korea following the truce agreement closed an interesting and puzzling chapter of the B.W. history, which has only been mentioned in passing here. Among the Americans repatriated were all those who had made long and widely publicized confessions to carrying out bacterial warfare missions against North Korea. At the time these were made, there was every doubt as to their veracity, for none of the confessions tied in with the evidence produced by the communists. It has already been noted that the material given in the Scientific Report does not connect one single incident described by the American prisoners with any incident given by the North Korean or Chinese authorities. The very language used in the confessions was just not true to character. Following their release and return home, all the men concerned told in detail how their confessions had been forced from them over long periods of interrogation and privation.

As Dr Needham, one of the Scientific Commission members, himself has said, we do not need the airmen's testimonies to assess the charges made. For Dr Needham the confessions merely added extra weight to the charges, for us they are irrelevant since they were false at the time and later repudiated in full by those making them.

But they are significant in this case history of a communist propaganda campaign in depth for three reasons. They show how even senior officers – as some of those were who confessed – can be broken down under skilful and systematic pressures and made to serve propaganda purposes against all their natural instincts. In these cases – as in various others – it has also to be remembered that a leading role in the interrogations was played by two Western communist-sympathizing journalists, the London *Daily Worker* correspondent Alan Winnington and the Australian correspondent in Korea of the French communist paper *Ce Soir* Wilfred Burchett.

They brought into the processes an understanding of Western behaviour not possessed by the Chinese or North Korean interrogators.

The early 60's saw Winnington in East Berlin as *Daily Worker* correspondent, with Burchett working from Moscow stringing for various Western papers, his Korean work well behind him.

Secondly, the airmen's confessions are interesting for the way in which they were accepted completely at their face value by the Scientific Commission, which itself interviewed two of the officers, declaring itself to be quite satisfied that it had heard willing and voluntary statements from them.

Lastly, the very repatriation of these men – in the full knowledge that they would immediately recant once past the American check-point – suggested that the whole B.W. structure was being allowed to drop to pieces.

The campaign was built up on lies, and very few of them, at that. At the time, when B.W. lectures were being given in British P.O.W. camps in North Korea, many prisoners believed that the Americans were carrying out bacterial warfare. How long such beliefs persisted cannot be said. It is likely that in some people the belief still persists that the West used bacterial warfare, without them specifically connecting the belief with Korea. If so, then the Korean B.W. propaganda campaign can be said to be still with us.

# *Appendices*

APPENDIX ONE

# *Communist Bloc Prestige Periodicals*

A wide range of prestige and propaganda periodicals primarily intended for non-communist readers abroad are published by the State and other official organizations in the communist countries. A list of the major publications available on subscription is given here, based with one or two exceptions on data given in the official 1963 catalogues. In some cases (marked n.a.) price details were not available. In the case of Czechoslovak publications no complete list was available for 1963 and the data in part refer to earlier years. The North Korean list was for 1962 and no official data was available for Albania, North Vietnam or Mongolia, though they are all known to publish at least one foreign language prestige magazine.

The main criteria for the publications listed is that they are specially edited for foreign readership, that they are lavishly produced and that in most cases their subscription rates are less than their costs of production, usually being nominal when postage is taken into account: *Peking Review* for instance is dispatched from Peking to Europe air mail for 24s. a year.

This list is by no means exhaustive, as it is confined to publications obtainable by subscription. In addition many similar magazines are sent out on specially selected mailing lists by Communist Bloc trade union, youth, student, peace and other mass organizations to potential sympathizers outside the communist world.

It should also be remembered that magazines and papers in Bloc country languages are offered at low subscription rates, particularly those from the U.S.S.R. and China, and to a lesser extent from Poland and Hungary. In many cases these are intended for possible sympathizers among Bloc ethnic minority groups in Western Europe, South-east Asia and Latin America.

U.S.S.R.

| *Publication* | *Frequency p.a.* | *Postal Subscription* | *Languages* |
|---|---|---|---|
| *Culture and Life* | 12 | 10/- | Russian, English, French, German, Spanish |

| *Publication* | *Frequency p.a.* | *Postal Subscription* | *Languages* |
|---|---|---|---|
| *International Affairs* | 12 | 14/– | Russian, English, French |
| *Moscow News* | 52 | 12/– | English, French, Spanish (three distinct editions) |
| *New Times* | 52 | 14/– | Russian, English, Spanish, German, French. (Some East European countries publish their own language editions) |
| *Oeuvres et opinions* | 12 | 12/– | French |
| *Soviet Film* | 12 | 15/– | Russian, English, French, Spanish, German, Arabic |
| *Soviet Literature* | 12 | 12/6 | English, Spanish, German, Polish |
| *Soviet Union* | 12 | 10/– | Russian, English, Arabic, Spanish, German, Urdu, Finnish, French, Hindi, Japanese, Hungarian, Chinese, Korean, Serbo-Croat, Vietnamese, Mongolian, Rumanian |
| *Soviet Woman* | 12 | 10/– | Russian, English, Spanish, German, Hindi, Japanese, Chinese, Korean |
| *Femmes de nos jours* | 12 | 10/– | French (this concentrates more on fashion, etc. with *Soviet Woman* as the political journal) |

All the above are listed for postal subscription from Moscow. In addition there are other publications published abroad on subscription: e.g. the *Soviet Weekly* published by the Soviet Embassy in London is sent in quantity to British colonial and ex-colonial territories under plain postal wrappers; similarly the fortnightly *Soviet Land* is circulated widely in India, Burma and Cambodia in fourteen languages, including Burmese, Nepali, Hindi, Bengali, Urdu, Telugu, Tamil, Malayalam, Kannada, Punjabi, Gujarati, Marathi and Oriya.

### COMMUNIST CHINA

| *Publication* | *Frequency p.a.* | *Postal Subscription* | *Languages* |
|---|---|---|---|
| *Chinese Literature* | 12 | 15/- | English |
| *China Pictorial* | 12 | 15/- | Chinese, Mongolian, Tibetan, Chuang, Uighur, Korean, English, Russian, French, Japanese, Spanish, Indonesian, German, Hindi, Vietnamese, Arabic, Swedish. |
| *China Reconstructs* | 12 | 10/- | English, Spanish, French |
| *Evergreen* (youth magazine) | 6 | 5/- | English |
| *Peking Review* | 52 | 20/- | English (in Spanish and French fortnightly) |
| *People's China* | 12 | n.a. | Japanese, French, Indonesian, also Esperanto version. |
| *China's Sports* | 6 | 5/- | English |
| *Women of China* | 4 | 4/- | English |

As at the beginning of 1963, Peking had allowed some relaxation on the ban imposed some years earlier on the export of Chinese language periodicals other than the leading communist papers. Chinese-reading subscribers in 1963 had the choice of 51 nationally published papers and magazines, all at cheap subscription rates. Regional and local papers were not included on the permitted list.

### POLAND

| *Publication* | *Frequency p.a.* | *Postal Subscription* | *Languages* |
|---|---|---|---|
| *Daily News* | 365 | 228/8 | English, French, Russian |
| *Demokratis* | 52 | 33/6 | Greek |
| *Economic Survey* | 24 | 55/- | English, Russian |
| *Mosaic* | 12 | 16/- | English, French, German, Russian |

| Publication | Frequency p.a. | Postal Subscription | Languages |
|---|---|---|---|
| *Little Mosaic* | 12 | 11/6 | English, French, German, Russian |
| *Materials and Documents* | 24 | 128/– | English, French, German, Russian |
| *Polish Perspectives* | 12 | 23/– | English and French |
| *Pola Esperantista* | 6 | 6/– | Esperanto |
| *Polish Review* | 12 | 11/6 | English |
| *Polish Maritime News* | 12 | 28/– | English |
| *Poland* | 12 | 18/– | Polish, English, French, German, Russian, Spanish, Swedish, Czech |
| *Polish Foreign Trade* | 4 | 39/– | English, French, Russian, German, Spanish |
| *Radar* | 12 | 8/– | Polish, English, German |
| *Weekly Review* | 50 | 86/– | English, French, Spanish, German, Russian |

## CZECHOSLOVAKIA

| Publication | Frequency p.a. | Postal Subscription | Languages |
|---|---|---|---|
| *Czechoslovak Co-operator* | 4 | 6/– | English, French, Spanish |
| *Czechoslovak Youth* | 10 | 6/– | English, French, Spanish, German |
| *Czechoslovak Trade Unions* | 12 | 9/– | English, Russian, French, German, Italian, Swedish, Spanish |
| *Czechoslovak Life* | 12 | 6/– | English, French, Swedish, German |
| *Czechoslovak Film* | 12 | *n.a.* | English, French, German, Spanish |
| *Czechoslovak Sport* | 6 | 3/– | English, Russian, French, Spanish |
| *Czechoslovak Woman* | 12 | *n.a.* | English, Spanish, German, Russian, French |
| *Prague Newsletter* | 24 | *n.a.* | English |
| *In the Heart of Europe* | 12 | 6/– | German |

| Publication | Frequency p.a. | Postal Subscription | Languages |
|---|---|---|---|
| *Solidarity* | 12 | 12/6 | English, French |
| *New Orient* | 6 | 5/– | English |

No full 1963 subscription list was available at the time of compilation and in some cases the prices are those for earlier years, though they are not likely to have changed much. One or two publications may have been discontinued either in their entirety or in specific language editions.

HUNGARY

| Publication | Frequency p.a. | Postal Subscription | Languages |
|---|---|---|---|
| *Weekly Bulletin* | 52 | 145/– | French, English, German |
| *Hungara Vivo* | 4 | 11/– | Esperanto |
| *Hungarian Review* | 12 | 13/– | English, French, German, Russian |
| *Hungarian Travel Magazine* | 4 | 14/6 | English, French, German |
| *Hungarian Law Review* | 3–4 | 29/– | English, French |
| *Hungarian Exporter* | 12 | 21/6 | English |
| *Hungarian Foreign Trade* | 4 | 26/– | English, French, German |
| *New Hungarian Quarterly* | 4 | 17/6 | English |
| *Hungarian Church Press* | 24 | 86/– | English, German |

RUMANIA

| Publication | Frequency p.a. | Postal Subscription | Languages |
|---|---|---|---|
| *Arts in the Rumanian People's Republic* | 2 | 47/7 | English, French, German, Russian |
| *Co-operation in Rumania* | 2 | 16/1 | English, French |
| *Information Bulletin of the Chamber of Commerce of the People's Republic of Rumania* | 12 | 28/7 | English, Russian, French, Spanish, German |

| Publication | Frequency p.a. | Postal Subscription | Languages |
|---|---|---|---|
| *People's Rumania* | 12 | 28/7 | Russian |
| *Rumania* | 12 | 28/7 | Chinese |
| *Rumania for Tourists* | 4 | 28/7 | English, Russian, French, German, Spanish |
| *Rumanian Foreign Trade* | 4 | 28/7 | English, Russian, French, Spanish, German |
| *Rumanian Review* | 4 | 14/3 | English, French, German, Russian |
| *Rumania Today* | 12 | 28/7 | English, French, German, Spanish |

## BULGARIA

| Publication | Frequency p.a. | Postal Subscription | Languages |
|---|---|---|---|
| *Bulgaria* | 12 | \$4.50 | Russian, Polish, Czech, German |
| *Bulgarian Foreign Trade* | 6 | \$1.50 | German, English, Russian, Spanish, French |
| *Bulgaria Today* | 12 | \$2.00 | French, German, English, Spanish, Esperanto |
| *Bulgarian Resorts* | 6 | \$1.50 | Russian, German, English, French |
| *Bulgarian Trade Unions* | 6 | \$2.50 | Spanish, Russian, French, English |
| *New Bulgaria* | 12 | \$3.00 | English, French, Arabic |

## EASTERN GERMANY

(G.D.R. – German Democratic Republic)

| Publication | Frequency p.a. | Postal Subscription | Languages |
|---|---|---|---|
| *Al Majallah* | 12 | 5/– | Arabic (only for circulation in Arabic-speaking countries) |
| *G.D.R. in Word and Picture* | 12 | n.a. | German, Polish, Russian, Czech (only for circulation in communist countries), also Chinese |

| Publication | Frequency p.a. | Postal Subscription | Languages |
|---|---|---|---|
| *G.D.R. Review* | 12 | 11/– | German, Danish, English, Spanish, Finnish, French, Swedish (only for circulation in capitalist countries) |
| *G.D.R. Sport* | 4 | DM. 5.00 | German, English, French, Swedish, Spanish, Russian |
| *Democratic German Report* | 26 | DM. 4.00 | English |
| *F.D.G.B. Review* (trade union review) | 6 | n.a. | German, English, Swedish, Spanish, French |
| *German Foreign Policy* | 6 | DM. 20.40 | English |
| *Foreign Affairs Bulletin* | every 10 days | 21/– | English, French, Spanish |
| (weekly in German) | | 58/– | |
| *Jena Review* | 6 | DM. 13.50 | German, English, Russian (not for circulation in West Germany, West Berlin or Austria) |
| *News* | 12 | n.a. | English, French (only for circulation in Africa) |
| *Review* | 12 | n.a. | Spanish (only for circulation in Latin America) |
| *Speak German* | 12 | n.a. | German/English (only for circulation in capitalist countries, except Spain, Portugal) |
| *Saut as-Sadaka* | 12 | n.a. | Arabic |
| *Voix de l'Amitie* | 12 | n.a. | French (for Africa) |
| *Picture News* | 12 | n.a. | English (for Asia) |
| *Echo d'Allemagne* | 12 | n.a. | French |

It will be noted that according to the official catalogue, certain publications and groups of G.D.R. publications are for circulation only in specific areas, with bans imposed on their being sent elsewhere.

### ALBANIA

| *Publication* | *Frequency p.a.* | *Postal Subscription* | *Languages* |
|---|---|---|---|
| *L'Albanie Nouvelle* | 6 | n.a. | French, possibly also English |

### NORTH KOREA

| *Publication* | *Frequency p.a.* | *Postal Subscription* | *Languages* |
|---|---|---|---|
| *New Korea* | 12 | n.a. | Russian, Chinese, English Japanese |
| *Korea* (pictorial) | 12 | n.a. | Russian, Chinese, English, Japanese, French |
| *Korea News* | 36 | n.a. | Russian, English |

APPENDIX TWO

# Communist Publications in the United Kingdom 1963

1. The principal publications for which the Communist Party of Great Britain (C.P.G.B.) is ultimately responsible are:

*Daily Worker*. Published by the Daily Worker Co-operative Society Ltd. and owned by the People's Press Printing Society Ltd., edited by George Matthews, member of the C.P. Political Committee; average daily circulation in 1962, approximately 60,000.

*Comment*. A 'Communist weekly review' first published from the headquarters of the C.P.G.B., January 1963, and edited initially by Dennis Ogden and later by Arthur Jordan. The successor to *World News* (1954–1962) *World News and Views* and *Inprecorr*.

*Marxism Today*. Monthly theoretical journal of the Communist Party; edited by James Klugmann.

*Bulletin*. Published fortnightly by the London District Committee of the C.P.

*Labour Monthly*. A 'Marxist commentary on political events' published by the Trinity Trust; founded and edited by R. Palme Dutt, Vice-Chairman of the C.P.

*Challenge*. Published monthly by Challenge Publications Ltd. for the Young Communist League and edited by Anne Devine; circulation approximately 10,800.

*Country Standard*. Published quarterly by Jack Dunman, C.P. National Agricultural Organizer.

*Education Today and Tomorrow*. Published bi-monthly by the C.P. Education Advisory Committee; edited by Ian Gunn.

*Music and Life*. Published quarterly by the Music Group of the C.P.; edited by Alfred Corum.

*Our History*. Published quarterly by the Historians' Group of the C.P.

*Party Life*. A bi-monthly discussion journal on problems of C.P. organization and leadership, First published October 1962, it was discontinued in October 1963.

2. The following periodicals are published by communist-controlled organizations in the United Kingdom:

*Anglo-Soviet Journal.* Published quarterly by the Society for Cultural Relations with the U.S.S.R. and edited by H. C. Creighton.

*British-Soviet Friendship.* Published monthly by the British-Soviet Friendship Society,* and edited by Pat Sloan.

*British-Soviet Newsletter.* Published monthly by the British-Soviet Friendship Society.*

*Peace Campaign.* Published bi-monthly by the British Peace Committee.*

*Irish Democrat.* Published monthly by the Connolly Association and edited by Desmond Greaves.

*Labour Research.* Incorporating 'Social Service News', published monthly by the Labour Research Department.*

*L.R.D. Fact Service.* Published weekly by the Labour Research Department.*

*Tenants' Leader.* Published bi-monthly by the National Association of Tenants and Residents.

3. Other periodicals published in the United Kingdom which reflect communist sympathies in varying degrees include:

*The African Communist.* Published quarterly for the South African Communist Party and printed by the Farleigh Press, Herts.

*Anglo-Russian News Bulletin.* Published monthly by the Anglo-Russian Parliamentary Committee and edited by W. P. Coates.

*China Trade and Economic Newsletter.* Published monthly by the British Council for the Promotion of International Trade.

*From the Current Press.* A selection of Press comment on foreign trade published fortnightly by the British Council for the Promotion of International Trade.

*Greek News Agency Bulletin.* Weekly survey of Greek news published from 376 Gray's Inn Road, W.C.1.

*Malayan Monitor.* Published monthly by the editor, H. B. Lim from 57 Charlwood Street, S.W.1.

*West Indian Gazette and Afro-Asian Caribbean News.* Published monthly from 250 Brixton Road, S.W.9 and edited by Claudia Jones.

4. Pro-communist publications circulating among trade unionists include:

*Platform.* Published monthly for bus workers and edited by George Moore from 21 New Wanstead, E.11.

*Metal Worker.* Published monthly for workers in the engineering, shipbuilding and allied trades by the Engineering and Allied Trades Shop Stewards National Council.

5. The following organs of international communists organizations, are available in the United Kingdom in an English edition:

*World Marxist Review.* Published monthly by S. C. Easton from the

headquarters of the C.P.G.B. English edition of *Problems of Peace and Socialism* a journal of international communism with editorial offices in Prague.
*World Trade Union Movement*. Published monthly in London by the World Federation of Trade Unions;* English editor, T. F. McWhinnie.
*Women of the Whole World*. Published monthly by the Women's International Democratic Federation,* in Berlin.
*World Student News*. Published monthly by the International Union of Students* in Prague.
*World Youth*. Published bi-monthly by the World Federation of Democratic Youth,* in Budapest.
*Democratic Journalist*. Published monthly by the International Organization of Journalists* in Prague.
*Scientific World*. Published quarterly by the World Federation of Scientific Workers* in London.

* Proscribed by the Labour Party.

APPENDIX THREE

# *Organizations Proscribed by the Labour Party, 1963*

Membership of a proscribed organization is incompatible with membership of the Labour Party

| *Date of Proscription* | *Organization* |
|---|---|
| 1947 | British Soviet Society |
| 1947 | British Soviet Friendship Houses Ltd. |
| 1943 | Common Wealth |
| 1924 | Communist Party of Great Britain |
| 1942 | Labour Research Department |
| 1941 | Marx House |
| 1940 | Militant Labour League |
| 1947 | Scottish-U.S.S.R. Society |
| 1940 | Student Labour Federation |
| 1948 | International Youth Council in Britain |
| 1948 | The World Federation of Democratic Youth |
| 1949 | Women's International Democratic Federation |
| 1950 | League for Democracy in Greece |
| 1950 | British Peace Committee |
| 1951 | Welsh Peace Council |
| 1951 | Socialist Fellowship |
| 1951 | Union Movement (Fascist) |
| 1952 | British Youth Festival |
| 1952 | International Women's Day Committee |
| 1952 | People's Congress for Peace |
| 1952 | West Yorkshire Federation of Peace Organizations |
| 1953 | World Federation of Trade Unions |
| 1953 | The International Union of Students |
| 1953 | The International Association of Democratic Lawyers |
| 1953 | The International Organization of Journalists |
| 1953 | The World Federation of Scientific Workers |

| *Date of Proscription* | *Organization* |
|---|---|
| 1953 | World Peace Council |
| 1953 | British-Soviet Friendship Society |
| 1953 | British-Polish Friendship Society |
| 1953 | British-China Friendship Association |
| 1953 | British-Czechoslovak Friendship League |
| 1953 | British-Rumanian Friendship Association |
| 1953 | The Committee for Friendship with Bulgaria |
| 1953 | British Hungarian Friendship Society |
| 1953 | Medical Association for the Prevention of War |
| 1953 | Artists for Peace |
| 1953 | Musician's Organization for Peace |
| 1953 | Authors' World Peace Appeal |
| 1953 | Teachers for Peace |
| 1953 | Scientists for Peace |
| 1953 | National Assembly of Women |
| 1959 | The Newsletter |
| 1959 | Socialist Labour League |

The following organizations have been proscribed by the Labour Party, but are now believed to exist no longer:

Independent Socialist Party
National A.R.P. Co-ordinating Committee
National Council of Anglo-Soviet Committees (and Subsidiaries)
National Council for British Soviet Unity.
Russia Today Society
British Union of Fascists
Independent Labour Association of Wolverhampton
Scottish Peace Council
Anti-Fascist Relief Committee
British Anti-War Council
British Anti-War Movement
European Workers' Anti-Fascist Congress
Friends of Soviet Russia
Friends of Soviet Union
International Class War Prisoners' Aid
League Against Imperialism
Left Wing Movement
Minority Movement
National Anti-War Council
National Charter Campaign Committee
People's Convention

Railwaymen's Vigilance Committee
Relief Committee for the Victims of German and Austrian Fascism
Relief Committee for the Victims of German Fascism
Workers' International Relief
The Link
New Party (Oswald Mosley Organization)
Popular Front Campaign
Socialist League
United Peace Alliance

APPENDIX FOUR

# *International Communist Fronts 1945-62*

## *A Chronology of Major Events*

This chronology of major international communist front events from 1945 to mid-1962 is not exhaustive. It is confined to those of propaganda significance, which were used at the time to publicize current front policies and activities. Lesser meetings have been omitted, in particular those of the various front councils and executive committees meeting more than once a year. The exception to this is the World Peace Council, which by its loose structure involves every meeting of its council and executive bureau as a platform for its current propaganda line. The International Broadcasting and Television Organization (O.I.R.T.) has not been listed below nor have its meetings been included in the chronology. It is largely a technical organization concerned with the co-ordinating of radio and television services between the Communist Bloc countries and its influence has so far not spread very far outside – Cuba excepted – though it is in contact with the European Broadcasting Union on intra-European radio and T.V. exchanges, as well as with some African bodies (but not China).

The International Fronts are listed below, together with the initials by which they are usually known. Where the initials do not reflect the English names, they are based on the original French titles. The numbers listed under each front refer to the reference numbers of the events listed in the chronology.

| | |
|---|---|
| W.P.C. WORLD PEACE COUNCIL (1949) Nowadays more commonly called World Council of Peace. | Headquarters originally Paris, whence expelled 1951. Moved first to Prague, then to Vienna 1954. Banned by Austrian Government 1957. Invited to Prague but never moved there. No official H.Q. currently but operates under cover of International Institute for Peace (see below) |

Ref. Nos.: 19, 31, 32, 39, 40, 42, 43, 44, 45, 47, 53, 61, 64, 70, 74, 77, 86, 95, 104, 115, 121, 123, 132, 143, 146, 158, 163.

I.I.P.: INTERNATIONAL INSTITUTE FOR PEACE (1957)
Ref. Nos.: 96, 107, 112.

Set up in Vienna in 1917 to provide a legal cover for the W.P.C. (above) and thus avoid its expulsion.

A.A.P.S.O.: AFRO-ASIAN PEOPLE'S SOLIDARITY ORGANIZATION (1957)

Started by a W.P.C.-backed Conference of Asian nations for the Relaxation of International Tension in Delhi, 1955, which set up an Asian Solidarity Committee there. Movement extended by Cairo conference, December 1957 to include Africa. Present name adopted and a permanent secretariat established in Cairo.

Ref. Nos.: 104, 134, 142.

I.M.A.: INTERNATIONAL MEDICAL ASSOCIATION (1954)

The Association originated at the W.P.C.'s Warsaw Peace Congress in 1950 and was originally known by the name of its first event, the World Congress of Doctors held in Vienna 1953. It was formally registered there as such in December 1955, but in October 1957 it was reconstituted and its title changed to that currently used.

Ref. Nos.: 50, 76, 102, 153.

I.C.P.T.: INTERNATIONAL COMMITTEE FOR THE PROMOTION OF TRADE (1951)

This organization was a direct offshoot of the World Peace Council, which in 1951 set up an International Initiating Committee to organize the Moscow Economic Conference of April 1952. At this conference the initiating committee was perpetuated with the title Committee for the Promotion of International Trade with headquarters in Vienna. Later the present title was adopted. A second conference was proposed for 1953 and again for 1955, but they came to nothing. The Committee was disbanded in 1956 but a number of national affiliates still exist, such as the one in the United Kingdom.

Ref. No.: 40.

W.F.T.U.: WORLD FEDERATION OF TRADE UNIONS (1945) — Original headquarters in Paris, whence expelled 1951. Moved to Vienna, where banned 1956 as endangering Austrian neutrality. Then moved to present headquarters in Prague.

Ref. Nos.: 1, 9, 20, 26, 27, 33, 38, 48, 49, 59, 65, 75, 84, 101, 103, 113, 116, 117, 124, 141, 148, 152, 156.

F.I.S.E.: WORLD FEDERATION OF TEACHERS' UNIONS (1946) — Originally founded in 1946, it became a Trade Department of the W.F.T.U. (above) 1949. Unlike other W.F.T.U. trade departments it leads a largely independent existence. Until 1952 the F.I.S.E. headquarters were in Paris, from which they were expelled, moving to Vienna from whence they were again expelled in 1956. For a while they operated from a private office in Paris before moving to Prague in 1959.

Ref. Nos.: 21, 29, 57, 99, 136.

W.F.D.Y.: WORLD FEDERATION OF DEMOCRATIC YOUTH (1945) — The headquarters were in Paris until expulsion 1951. They then moved to Budapest, where they have since been except for the period of the 1956 Hungarian uprising, when they were evacuated to Prague.

Ref. Nos.: 2, 8, 11, 13, 14, 15, 21, 24, 37, 49, 54, 55, 63, 71, 73, 79, 97, 98, 105, 114, 115, 119, 126, 127, 131, 135, 137, 150, 164, 165.

I.U.S.: INTERNATIONAL UNION OF STUDENTS (1946) — The headquarters have always been in Prague.

Ref. Nos.: 6, 11, 14, 28, 37, 55, 56, 73, 79, 82, 85, 90, 97, 118, 126, 138, 144, 150, 151, 155, 164, 166.

W.I.D.F.: WOMEN'S INTERNATIONAL DEMOCRATIC FEDERATION (1945) — The headquarters were in Paris until expulsion 1951, since when they have been in East Berlin. They share their offices with the P.I.C.M. (below).

Ref. Nos.: 3, 18, 41, 52, 78, 88, 111, 130, 133, 160, 162.

P.I.C.M.: PERMANENT INTERNATIONAL COMMITTEE OF MOTHERS (1955) — The headquarters have been shared in East Berlin with the W.I.D.F., of which the Committee is an offshoot, since the P.I.C.M. was formed.

| | |
|---|---|
| I.A.D.L.: INTERNATIONAL ASSOCIATION OF DEMOCRATIC LAWYERS (1946) | Originally in Paris, after expulsion in 1950 the headquarters were set up in Brussels, where they have been ever since. |

Ref. Nos.: 7, 12, 17, 25, 34, 46, 60, 62, 72, 87, 139, 154.

| | |
|---|---|
| W.F.S.W.: WORLD FEDERATION OF SCIENTIFIC WORKERS (1946) | The headquarters have always been in London, with regional centres in Calcutta Prague and Paris. |

Ref. Nos.: 5, 16, 35, 58, 80, 91, 92, 100, 128, 129, 149, 168.

| | |
|---|---|
| I.O.J.: INTERNATIONAL ORGANIZATION OF JOURNALISTS (1946) | Originally in London, the headquarters were moved to Prague in 1947, where they have remained. |

Ref. Nos.: 4, 10, 23, 30, 89, 108, 109, 110, 125, 140, 147, 159, 167.

| | |
|---|---|
| F.I.R.: INTERNATIONAL FEDERATION OF RESISTANCE FIGHTERS (1951) | The Federation was formed at a congress in Vienna, 1951, organized by its predecessor the International Federation of Former Political Prisoners of Fascism, which had been founded in 1947 in Paris, but which did not include Resistance fighters. The F.I.R. headquarters were in Warsaw until 1952, when it moved to Vienna with a small secretariat in Paris. |

Ref. Nos.: 36, 51, 66, 68, 69, 81, 94, 120, 122, 145, 157, 161.

| *Ref. No.* | | *Date* | *Place* | *Organization* | *Event* |
|---|---|---|---|---|---|
| 1. | 1945 | October | Paris | W.F.T.U. | 1st World Trade Union Congress |
| 2. | | November | London | W.F.D.Y. | World Youth Conference |
| 3. | | December | Paris | W.I.D.F. | 1st Congress W.I.D.F. |
| 4. | 1946 | June | Copenhagen | I.O.J. | Foundation I.O.J. |
| 5. | | July | London | W.F.S.W. | Foundation Meeting W.F.S.W. |
| 6. | | August | Prague | I.U.S. | 1st World Student Congress |
| 7. | | October | Paris | I.A.D.L. | Founding Congress I.A.D.L. |
| 8. | 1947 | March | Cuba | W.F.D.Y. | Latin American Youth Conference |
| 9. | | April | Dakar | W.F.T.U. | Pan-African Trade Union Conference |
| 10. | | June | Prague | I.O.J. | 1st Congress I.O.J. |
| 11. | | July–August | Prague | W.F.D.Y./I.U.S. | 1st World Youth Festival |
| 12. | | July | Brussels | I.A.D.L. | 2nd Congress I.A.D.L. |
| 13. | 1948 | February | Calcutta | W.F.D.Y. | S.E. Asian Youth Conference |
| 14. | | February | Mexico City | W.F.D.Y./I.U.S. | Latin American Youth Conference |
| 15. | | August | Warsaw | W.F.D.Y. | Conference of Working Youth |
| 16. | | September | Dobris (C.S.R.) | W.F.S.W. | 1st Assembly W.F.S.W. |
| 17. | | September | Prague | I.A.D.L. | 3rd Congress I.A.D.L. |
| 18. | | December | Budapest | W.I.D.F. | 2nd Congress W.I.D.F. |
| 19. | 1949 | April | Paris–Prague | W.P.C. | 1st World Peace Congress |
| 20. | | June–July | Milan | W.F.T.U. | 2nd World Trade Union Congress |
| 21. | | August | Warsaw | F.I.S.E. | 1st Congress F.I.S.E. |
| 22. | | August | Budapest | W.F.D.Y./I.U.S. | 2nd World Youth Festival |
| 23. | | September | Brussels | I.O.J. | 2nd Congress I.O.J. |
| 24. | | September | Budapest | W.F.D.Y. | 2nd World Youth Congress |
| 25. | | October | Rome | I.A.D.L. | 4th Congress I.A.D.L. |

| Ref. No. | | Date | Place | Organization | Event |
|---|---|---|---|---|---|
| 26. | | November–December | Peking | W.F.T.U. | Trade Union Conf. of Asian and Australasian Countries |
| 27. | 1950 | March–April | Montevideo | W.F.T.U. | South American Trade Union Conference |
| 28. | | August | Prague | I.U.S. | 2nd World Student Congress |
| 29. | | August | Vienna | F.I.S.E. | 2nd Congress F.I.S.E. |
| 30. | | September | Helsinki | I.O.J. | 3rd Congress I.O.J. |
| 31. | | November | Warsaw | W.P.C. | 2nd World Peace Congress |
| 32. | 1951 | February | East Berlin | W.P.C. | Council Meeting |
| 33. | | March | East Berlin | W.F.T.U. | European Workers' Conference Against German Rearmament |
| 34. | | April | East Berlin | I.A.D.L. | 5th Congress I.A.D.L. |
| 35. | | April | Paris/Prague | W.F.S.W. | 2nd Assembly W.F.S.W. |
| 36. | | June | Vienna | F.I.R. | Foundation Congress F.I.R. |
| 37. | | August | East Berlin | W.F.D.Y./I.U.S. | 3rd World Youth Festival |
| 38. | | October | Bamako | W.F.T.U. | African Workers' Conference |
| 39. | | November | Vienna | W.P.C. | Council Meeting |
| 40. | 1952 | April | Moscow | W.P.C. | World Economic Conference (C.P.I.T. founded) |
| 41. | | April | Vienna | W.I.D.F./I.M.A. | International Conference in Defence of Children |
| 42. | | July | East Berlin | W.P.C. | Council Meeting W.P.C. |
| 43. | | October | Peking | W.P.C. | Asian and Pacific Peace Conference |
| 44. | | November | Helsinki | W.P.C. | Nordic Peace Conference |
| 45. | | November | East Berlin | W.P.C. | 2nd Conference for the Peaceful Solution of the German Problem |
| 46. | | November | Rio de Janeiro | I.A.D.L. | 1st (Latin-American) Continental Conference of Jurists |

| Ref. No. | | Date | Place | Organization | Event |
|---|---|---|---|---|---|
| 47. | | December | Vienna | W.P.C. | People's Congress for Peace |
| 48. | 1953 | March | Vienna | W.F.T.U. | International Social Security Conference |
| 49. | | March | Vienna | W.F.T.U./W.F.D.Y. | International Conference in Defence of the Rights of Youth |
| 50. | | May | Vienna | I.M.A. | 1st World Congress of Doctors |
| 51. | | May | Stuttgart | F.I.R. | 1st International Conference of Former Resistance Fighters |
| 52. | | June | Copenhagen | W.I.D.F. | 3rd Congress W.I.D.F. |
| 53. | | June | Budapest | W.P.C. | Council Meeting W.P.C. |
| 54. | | July | Bucharest | W.F.D.Y. | 3rd World Youth Congress |
| 55. | | August | Bucharest | W.F.D.Y./I.U.S. | 4th World Youth Festival |
| 56. | | August | Warsaw | I.U.S. | 3rd World Student Congress |
| 57. | | August | Vienna | F.I.S.E. | World Congress F.I.S.E. |
| 58. | | September | Budapest | W.F.S.W. | 3rd Assembly W.F.S.W. |
| 59. | | October | Vienna | W.F.T.U. | 3rd World Trade Union Congress |
| 60. | | October | Guatemala | I.A.D.L. | 2nd (Latin American) Continental Conference of Jurists |
| 61. | | November | Vienna | W.P.C. | Council Meeting W.P.C. |
| 62. | 1954 | January | Vienna | I.A.D.L. | International Conference of Lawyers for the Defence of Democratic Liberties |
| 63. | | May | East Berlin | W.F.D.Y. | Conference of European Youth Against the European Defence Community (E.D.C.) |
| 64. | | May | East Berlin | W.P.C. | Council Meeting W.P.C. |
| 65. | | June | East Berlin | W.F.T.U. | European Trade Union Conference Against the E.D.C. |

| *Ref. No.* | | *Date* | *Place* | *Organization* | *Event* |
|---|---|---|---|---|---|
| 66. | | June | Copenhagen | F.I.R. | International Medico-Social Conference |
| 67. | | August | Rio de Janeiro | W.I.D.F. | Latin American Women's Conference |
| 68. | | November | Vienna | F.I.R. | 2nd Congress F.I.R. |
| 69. | | November | Vienna | F.I.R. | International Resistance Rally |
| 70. | | November | Stockholm | W.P.C. | Council Meeting |
| 71. | | December | Vienna | W.F.D.Y. | International Gathering of Rural Youth |
| 72. | 1955 | January | Calcutta | I.A.D.L. | Congress of Asian Democratic Lawyers |
| 73. | | February | São Paulo | W.F.D.Y./I.U.S. | South American Youth Festival |
| 74. | | April | Delhi | W.P.C. | Conference of Asian Nations for the Relaxation of International Tension |
| 75. | | April | Leipzig | W.F.T.U. | Conference of European Workers Against German Rearmament |
| 76. | | June | Japan | I.M.A. | International Medical Conference on Radioactivity |
| 77. | | June | Helsinki | W.P.C. | World Peace Assembly |
| 78. | | July | Lausanne | W.I.D.F. | World Congress of Mothers (P.I.C.M. founded) |
| 79. | | August | Warsaw | W.F.D.Y./I.U.S. | 5th World Youth Festival |
| 80. | | September | East Berlin | W.F.S.W. | 4th Assembly W.F.S.W. |
| 81. | | October | Brussels | F.I.R. | International Conference on Legislation and the Rights of Resistance Fighters |
| 82. | | December | Vienna | I.U.S. | International Conference of Editors of Student Periodicals |
| 83. | 1956 | February | Geneva | P.I.C.M. | 1st Permanent International Committee of Mothers' Meeting |
| 84. | | April | Turin | W.F.T.U. | International Conference on the Forty Hour Week |

| Ref. No. | | Date | Place | Organization | Event |
|---|---|---|---|---|---|
| 85. | | April | Prague | I.U.S. | Seminar on the Problems of Students in Colonial Countries |
| 86. | | April | Stockholm | W.P.C. | Council Meeting W.P.C. |
| 87. | | May | Brussels | I.A.D.L. | 6th Congress I.A.D.L. |
| 88. | | June | Budapest | W.F.T.U./W.I.D.F. | World Conference of Women Workers |
| 89. | | June | Helsinki | I.O.J. | International Meeting of Journalists |
| 90. | | August | Prague | I.U.S. | 4th World Student Congress |
| 91. | | October | Prague | W.F.S.W. | East European Regional Conference |
| 92. | 1957 | February | Paris | W.F.S.W. | West European Regional Conference |
| 93. | | April | Lausanne | P.I.C.M. | 2nd Meeting of P.I.C.M. |
| 94. | | June | Moscow | F.I.R. | International Physicians' Conference |
| 95. | | June | Colombo | W.P.C. | Council Meeting |
| 96. | | July | Vienna | I.I.P. | Constituent General Meeting |
| 97. | | August | Moscow | W.F.D.Y./I.U.S. | 6th World Youth Festival |
| 98. | | August | Kiev | W.F.D.Y. | 4th Assembly (replaced former W.F.D.Y. Congress) |
| 99. | | August | Warsaw | F.I.S.E. | World Conference of Teachers |
| 100. | | August | Warsaw | W.F.S.W. | 5th Assembly W.F.S.W. |
| 101. | | September | Prague | W.F.T.U. | International Seminar for Women Trade Unionists |
| 102. | | September | Cannes | I.M.A. | 2nd World Medical Congress |
| 103. | | October | Leipzig | W.F.T.U. | Fourth World Trade Union Congress |
| 104. | | December | Cairo | W.P.C. | Afro-Asian People's Solidarity Conference |
| 105. | 1958 | January | Budapest | W.F.D.Y. | Conference of Leaders of European Children's Organization's |
| 106. | | February | Sofia | P.I.C.M. | 3rd Meeting of P.I.C.M. |

| Ref. No. | | Date | Place | Organization | Event |
|---|---|---|---|---|---|
| 107. | | April | Vienna | I.I.P. | Constituent Meeting of Economic Commission |
| 108. | | April | Warsaw | I.O.J. | Conference of Editors of Journalist Union Journals |
| 109. | | May | Bucharest | I.O.J. | 4th Congress I.O.J. |
| 110. | | May | Bucharest | I.O.J. | International Conference of Reporters |
| 111. | | June | Vienna | W.I.D.F. | 4th Congress W.I.D.F. |
| 112. | | June | Vienna | I.I.P. | Meeting – Cultural Commission set up |
| 113. | | June | East Berlin | W.F.T.U. | European Trade Union Conference Against Atomic War |
| 114. | | June | Brussels | W.F.D.Y. | Seminar for Leaders of Children's Organizations |
| 115. | | July | Stockholm | W.P.C. | Congress for Disarmament and International Co-operation |
| 116. | | July | Prague | W.F.T.U./W.F.D.Y. | 1st World Conference of Young Workers |
| 117. | | September | Cairo | W.F.T.U. | Trade Union Conference in Support of Algeria |
| 118. | | September | Peking | I.U.S. | 5th World Student Congress |
| 119. | | October | Budapest | W.F.D.Y. | International Conference on Youth Tourism |
| 120. | | November | Vienna | F.I.R. | 3rd Congress F.I.R. (1st Session) |
| 121. | 1959 | February | Cairo | W.P.C. | Afro-Asian Youth Conference |
| 122. | | March | Vienna | F.I.R. | 3rd Congress F.I.R. (2nd Session) |
| 123. | | May | Stockholm | W.P.C. | Council Meeting – 10th Anniversary Meeting |
| 124. | | May | Goerlitz | W.F.T.U. | Conference of European Trade Unions for a German Peace Treaty |
| 125. | | June | Prague | I.O.J. | International Conference of Foreign Affairs Editors |
| 126. | | July | Vienna | W.F.D.Y./I.U.S. | 7th World Youth Festival |
| 127. | | August | Prague | W.F.D.Y. | 5th Assembly W.F.D.Y. |
| 128. | | September | Warsaw | W.F.S.W. | 6th Assembly W.F.S.W. |

| Ref. No. | | Date | Place | Organization | Event |
|---|---|---|---|---|---|
| 129. | | September | Warsaw | W.F.S.W. | International Symposium on Science and Under-developed Countries |
| 130. | | December | Kungalv | W.I.D.F. | International Women's Conference on Disarmament |
| 131. | 1960 | February | Bucharest | W.F.D.Y. | Balkan and Adriatic Youth Rally |
| 132. | | March | Havana | W.P.C. | Latin American Peace Meeting |
| 133. | | April | Copenhagen | W.I.D.F. | International Assembly of Women |
| 134. | | April | Conakry | A.A.P.S.O. | 2nd International Conference, Afro-Asian People's Solidarity Council |
| 135. | | April | Baghdad | W.F.D.Y. | Afro-Asian Youth Festival |
| 136. | | July | Conakry | F.I.S.E. | World Teachers' Conference |
| 137. | | July | Havana | W.F.D.Y. | Latin American Youth Congress |
| 138. | | October | Baghdad | I.U.S. | 6th World Student Congress |
| 139. | | October | Sofia | I.A.D.L. | 7th Congress I.A.D.L. |
| 140. | | October | Baden | I.O.J. | 2nd International Meeting of Journalists |
| 141. | | November | Warsaw | W.F.T.U./I.L.O. | International Trade Union Seminar |
| 142. | 1961 | January | Cairo | A.A.P.S.O. | Afro-Asian Women's Conference |
| 143. | | March | Mexico | W.P.C. | Latin American Peace Conference |
| 144. | | March | Casablanca | I.U.S. | Seminar on economic Problems |
| 145. | | March | Liége | F.I.R. | 3rd Medical Conference |
| 146. | | March | New Delhi | W.P.C. | Council Meeting W.P.C. |
| 147. | | May | Bamako | I.O.J. | 1st All-African Journalists' Conference |
| 148. | | May | Vienna | W.F.T.U. | European Conference on the Forty Hour Week |
| 149. | | July | Cambridge | W.F.S.W. | West European Regional Conference |
| 150. | | July | Moscow | W.F.D.Y./I.U.S. | World Youth Forum |

| Ref. No. | | Date | Place | Organization | Event |
|---|---|---|---|---|---|
| 151. | | August | Hanoi | I.U.S. | International Students' Seminar |
| 152. | | September | East Berlin | W.F.T.U. | International Conference on the German Question |
| 153. | | September | St Vincent d'Aoste | I.M.A. | 3rd World Medical Congress |
| 154. | | November | East Berlin | I.A.D.L. | International Lawyers' Conference on the German Problem |
| 155. | | November | Prague | I.U.S. | 15th Anniversary Ceremonial Meeting and Symposium |
| 156. | | December | Moscow | W.F.T.U. | Fifth World Trade Union Congress |
| 157. | | December | Vienna | F.I.R. | 10th Anniversary Ceremony. |
| 158. | | December | Stockholm | W.P.C. | Council Meeting |
| 159. | 1962 | February | Warsaw | I.O.J. | Conference on the History and Theory of the Press |
| 160. | | March | Vienna | W.I.D.F. | Conference on Disarmament |
| 161. | | April | Warsaw | F.I.R. | International Conference on History of the Resistance |
| 162. | | July | Havana | W.I.D.F. | Congress of Women of the Americas |
| 163. | | July | Moscow | W.P.C. | Congress for Disarmament and Peace |
| 164. | | July | Helsinki | W.F.D.Y./I.U.S. | 8th World Youth Festival |
| 165. | | August | Warsaw | W.F.D.Y. | 6th Assembly W.F.D.Y. |
| 166. | | August | Leningrad | I.U.S. | 7th World Student Congress |
| 167. | | August | Budapest | I.O.J. | 5th Congress I.O.J. |
| 168. | | September | Moscow | W.F.S.W. | 6th Assembly W.F.S.W. (also Symposium) |

APPENDIX FIVE (A)

# *Hate Propaganda, 1952*

A colour film entitled *The Silvery Dust* – a version of A. Yakobson's satire *The Jackals* which was included in the repertoire of the Maly Theatre, Moscow – was first shown in the U.S.S.R. at the end of 1953. Some idea of the virulence of this propaganda piece can be gained from the reviews published in the Moscow *Literary Gazette* of November 14th, 1952 and in *Pravda* on December 10th, 1952, when the text of the play first appeared in a Russian translation from the Estonian.

(1) The *Literary Gazette* review.

In American parlance there is saying: 'self-made man' a man who, so they say, has won a place in society by his own efforts. Samuel Steel is such a 'self-made man'. He became a well-known figure among American chemists soon after his patron and teacher, Professor O'Connell, suddenly died on the eve of completing experimental work in the sphere of chemical warfare against crop pests.

Devoted to the family of his teacher, Samuel Steel immediately married his widow. Devoted to the work of his teacher, Samuel Steel just as rapidly took over his laboratory as a legacy and began to publish his scientific studies under his own name.

He is quite a respectable American gentleman – Samuel Steel. It is true, there is one strange trait in his character: even today, twenty years later, he becomes irritable when he is reminded of the sudden death of Professor O'Connell. But this is not surprising. He does not like to remember the death of his patron and teacher in the first place because, as a true 'self-made man', he dispatched O'Connell to the other world with his own hand, not relying on fate, and in the second place he has no time to remember it since he is occupied with experiments in 'silvery-grey dust' – a new means of the mass slaughter of people. In the course of completion of his 'work', in which the War Department of the U.S.A. is interested as customer, and the Southern Trust of the dye industry is interested as future supplier of 'silvery-grey dust', Professor Steel encounters difficulties. He wishes to conduct his final experiments upon people.

'Just one transport plane, filled with Koreans or Chinese, and I myself will contrive for you an excellent method of killing people,' he assures representatives of the War Department and the Southern Trust of the dye industry. But the War Department, although in principle of course it does not object to helping Steel, nevertheless owing to the necessary formalities cannot promise the prisoners earlier than in three weeks' time. But Steel has weighty grounds for being in a hurry.

Kurt Schneider, in the recent past a Nazi officer who made experiments on people in one of the Nazi death camps and who has now found in the U.S.A. not only a safe refuge but also the best sphere for application of his inclinations and capabilities, comes to the help of the professor. Making use of the acquaintances which he has acquired – Schneider is connected either with the secretary of the governor of the state through gangsters, or with gangsters through the secretary of the governor of the state (it is not so simple to understand this dependence in American conditions!), he receives permission to try out his 'silvery-grey dust' on Negro youths – participants in a demonstration of peace partisans, who have been condemned through provocational accusation to death by the electric chair.

Kurt Schneider – the executive assistant of Samuel Steel – has another job, too. He has been attached to the professor by the Southern Trust of the dye industry, and in this capacity he informs the bosses of the Trust that Steel, who is threatened by the disclosure of the circumstances of O'Connell's death, is ready to communicate this discovery, and accordingly the profits, to the Dye Cartel which is blackmailing him through gangsters, thus fooling the Southern Trust of the dye industry.

The friends of Steel's youth, a general from the War Department and a member of the board of the Southern Trust of the dye industry, MacKennedy, and one of the directors of the Trust, Upton Bruce, decide to save their future profits. Only a few days ago they were anxiously inquiring about Steel's health, giving him gifts, kissing the hand of his wife, drinking wine at his table, recalling the shared amusements of their youth, and now they decide to get him out of the way, for it is not profitable for them that he should live. MacKennedy 'in a friendly way' explains to him the reason for this decision: 'It is clear that you would not voluntarily concede the share which is due to you as inventor for the same price as Dr Schneider –' And Kurt Schneider prepared to poison his patron Steel, as Steel once poisoned O'Connell. However, he prepares to do this by an improved method: science in America is making advances.

Such are some of the characters in the new play by August Yakobson *Jackals*; such is the outline of the plot.

The author has called his new work a dramatic satire, and the play fully justifies such a definition. . . .

The play not without reason has the title *Jackals*. 'A jackal is a beast of prey belonging to the dog family,' states the dictionary. Not a single trait of the evil predatory nature of the characters in the play has been invented; they have been borrowed from the inhabitants of the American political jungle. But there is still another trait which is characteristic of jackals: 'It is distinguished by its cowardly nature,' adds the dictionary. And the characters of A. Yakobson's play, who belong to the camp of aggression, are all the time in a state of fear. First of all they fear each other . . .

They fear each other. But they fear the people still more. 'I am not a pessimist nor a coward,' suddenly exclaims Bruce, the most cold-blooded of the jackals, when he hears of the growth of protests against the condemnation of the Negro youths: 'but sometimes I feel alarmed.' And he has something to be afraid of! Scene by scene in the play, in full accordance with historical truth, there is shown the growth of the forces of the camp of peace partisans, preparing the rightful and prophetic finale of the play: the destruction by the people of the devilish invention of Professor Steel.

The dramatic character of the development of the action of the play grows by reason of the fact that the dramatist has concentrated all the events which take place within the walls of one house, has linked together the majority of the characters with a pre-history of complex personal relationships, love and hatred. But this is far from being an artificial method in the interests of increasing the tension. No! In it there is demonstrated again the central theme of A. Yakobson's work, expressed in the title of his play *Two Camps*, one of the leading themes of contemporary art, the theme of mankind divided into two camps, the theme of the invisible frontier which cuts across towns, homes and the souls of people.

The journalistic generalization of events and speeches in the play is obvious. But this does not lend to the schematic impoverishment of the characters. All the negative characters, and they are at the centre of attention of the dramatist, are endowed with sharply accentuated individual traits, which are emphasized as far as the grotesque . . .

The world of bourgeois relations destroys everything human in the people who defend it. The wife of Professor Steel, a mother with a blind love for her son, kicks a negro woman who has served in her household for fifteen years, when she implores her mistress to come to the defence of her boy. Steel's son Harry, who is young but a very promising member of the Ku Klux Klan, wants to repeat his father's crime – to poison his rival in a sports competition. He steals from his father's laboratory a phial containing the deadly dust and himself falls victim to his criminal design. Thus in the retribution of father and son there is revealed the inescapable law: criminal designs recoil on their originators. It is with justification that the play about the invention of a deadly dust by Professor Steel logically ends with the death both of Steel himself and of his son, who wished to make use of his father's discovery.

The play of A. Yakobson is written with the red-hot pen of a dramatist-journalist. In it light and shade, love and hatred are powerfully defined. Everything in it breathes loathing and contempt for Steel, MacKennedy, Bruce and their Ridgway-like prototypes, respect and love for the common people of America, black and white – the champions of peace. The words of A. M. Gorky are fully applicable to A. Yakobson's play: 'To be impartial is to be without feeling. We are people of feeling. We hate passionately and shall be partial – understand us like that!'

(2) The *Pravda* review.

The Estonian playwright August Yakobson, author of the widely known plays *Life in the Citadel*, *The Flight Without a Front* and *Two Camps*, has published a play entitled *The Jackals*. The author calls it a dramatic satire. One reads A. Yakobson's new work with absorbing interest. The playwright has created a vivid, sharply satirical picture of present-day imperialist America, depicting its way of life and its political morality with typical portraits and situations. . . .

A. Yakobson shows in his play the everyday affairs of the warmongers, their misanthropic 'philosophy' – which fully corresponds to their actual behaviour – their cruelty, their jackal-like cowardice, their hatred of the forces of peace and progress and their craven panic in the face of these forces, the brutish struggle among them for the dollar, their claims to world domination. Indeed, before us unfolds a monstrous, bloody tragi-comedy in which the leading role is played by profit – 'business' – that business which dominates everything, in which murder has become an essential component, in which hypocrisy appears in especially revolting form, in which everything is corrupt and contaminated by crime – in short, before us is the so-called 'American way of life'.

A. Yakobson's play is distinguished by the tense drama of the action, by the discerning development of the subject matter.

We are present at a meeting of three old friends, school companions who have done well in life. Before us are the main characters of the play, the prominent scientist and chemist, Professor Steel, who is working on an 'important invention'; his colleague MacKennedy, a professor and general employed by a research division of the War Department and, moreover, a board member of the dye industry's Southern Trust; and

Upton Bruce, one of the directors of this trust, one of the monopoly bosses. . . The War Department and the trust are interested in Steel's invention, but MacKennedy dwells on tender recollections of friendship, reminiscences of his childhood and youth and sentimental reflections. He also has friendly, familiar words for Steel, 'old times, my friend', expressions of concern for his health, and raptures and compliments over his scientific talent. 'You're like all true cultural figures – people who enrich our great age by their discoveries!' MacKennedy exclaims in his raptures over Steel.

But just what are Professor Steel's services to his age? It develops that the important scientific discovery on which the 'cultural figure' is working is a 'silver-grey powder' for the mass destruction of human beings. In response to a demand by Bruce and MacKennedy that he speed the work to its conclusion Steel delivers an ultimatum: he needs 'real material' in order to test his 'formula'.

At this stage his 'scientific research' on the monkeys he has experimented with no longer satisfies him. He needs human beings. 'Don't give me monkeys for the experiments, but a shipment of Koreans or Chinese; load just one transport plane with them and I'll perfect an excellent way for you to become masters of the world!' says Professor Steel.

A. Yakobson authentically re-creates the true nature of present-day American reality . . . The playwright gives an equally true picture of the 'American way of life' throughout the remainder of the play. Six young Negroes have been sentenced to death in the electric chair on the brazen accusation so common in American life of 'raping a white woman', an accusation which could only be conceived in the distorted, misanthropic minds of foul racists. Actually, it was decided to punish these young people for their active participation in the fight for peace. Is this not typical of the 'American way of life?'

Professor Steel decides to use his own money to buy these young Negroes for his experiments with the aid of gangsters who have connexions with the governor's secretary. This plan is based on the belief that no one would find out about this 'business', that everyone would think the six Negroes died in the electric chair when actually they would die as 'experimental material' in Professor Steel's laboratory. . . .

A struggle ensues for Professor Steel's invention, for the 'silver-grey powder'. A second trust – the Dye Cartel – is competing with the Southern Trust of the dye industry, the interests of which are represented by Bruce and to some extent by MacKennedy (whom Bruce incidentally suspects of 'treachery'). The Dye Cartel's representatives blackmail Steel, demanding that he sell the 'powder' to their organization; unless he does so, they threaten to expose a secret they have dug up from Steel's past, a secret which, if made public, could bring the professor up for trial as a common criminal.

Steel wavers but finally is frightened into meeting the blackmailer's demands, thus deciding to 'betray' the Southern Trust. Bruce and MacKennedy hear about this from Kurt Schneider, Steel's colleague, who has been assigned by the Southern Trust to spy on him. Schneider is a very expressive figure in present-day fascistized U.S.A.: a chemist and doctor, a 'scientist' in Hitler's army, who went through the school of professional murderers in the Gestapo. It may be assumed that the doctor burned no inconsiderable number of human beings in the fiendish ovens of the Hitler death camps.

The sincerity of MacKennedy's comradely outbursts and especially his concern for Steel's health may be fully judged if one considers that MacKennedy manifests this concern at a time when he and Bruce have already decided to kill Steel. Steel's 'liquidation' is in their view a very profitable business because the secret of his 'powder' can be obtained with the help of Schneider, and this 'cultural figure' asks far fewer dollars for his services than does Professor Steel.

Present at Steel's 'liquidation', MacKennedy runs true to form. He asks Steel to sit in the chair which is to serve as the place for the professor's torture: 'Keep calm, my friend! And sit down, please sit down!' Steel cries, 'Scum' and MacKennedy upbraids him: 'School chum, old friend – why use such course expressions?' Steel is wrathful: 'Crook!' 'You keep interrupting me, Sam, old pal,' MacKennedy politely reprimands him.

This entire scene is a model of mordant satire . . . Without going outside the walls of the home of one of the warmongers, the action of *The Jackals* reveals the characteristics of the whole warmonger camp . . .

The 'law of the jungle', extolled by MacKennedy and all these Bruces and Steels, turns against them: such is the logic of this 'law'. Professor Steel's 17-year-old son Harry, Ku Klux Klan member and ardent young advocate of Negro lynchings, is by an irony of fate, or, rather, by the 'law of the jungle', the first victim of the 'silver-grey powder', the first 'experimental human' on whom his father's formula is tested. Harry has eavesdropped on the conversation about the 'formula' and has stolen a container of 'powder' in order to poison his rival in sports. But the lead container opens in Harry's pocket, and he writhes in the throes of death.

In his dramatic satire A. Yakobson exposes the criminal nature, the cunning, the unprecedented vileness yet unprecedented folly, stupidity and inhumanity of all the desires, designs and pretensions of the 'commanders' of present-day America. These are the dreams of the present-day American Khlestakovs,[1] expressed by MacKennedy: 'The Roman patricians used to say, "*Ubi bene, ibi patria*". Where one prospers is one's homeland. But our children and grandchildren perhaps will say: "*Ubi terra, ibi* America". Where land is, there is America'.

Thus cosmopolitanism is shown as the reverse of the rapacious imperialism which dreams of turning the whole world into a colony of the American monopolists. The words of the American Khlestakov are repeated by the American Korobochka,[2] depicted in the person of Professor Steel's wife, the trivial, foolish Doris. She translates, so to speak, the 'learned' words of MacKennedy into ordinary, everyday language: 'There is only the United States of America in the whole world – what is wrong with that? Go to Europe, and it is America there, just as it is here. Go to Asia – it is America there too, just as it is here. Go to Africa, or Australia, it does not matter where, everywhere it is America, just as here. But today the Chinese or the Russians – God knows who – do whatever they like. What is the good of that?'

The old woman has said it! But the point is that her words are essentially very little different from those screamed every day by the American Press, proclaimed by American politicians and by all kinds of 'geopoliticians' and other fascists in American dress. . . .

The artistic merits, the talent shown in A. Yakobson's satire, are above all due to the fact that the author has produced typical characters, views and situations. . . .

A. Yakobson portrays the fascist transformation going on in the U.S.A. He gives some devastating passages which characterize the true essence of contemporary American 'democracy'. Here for example is a report written up by some gutter journalist: 'Six Negroes, sentenced to death last week, were sent to the electric chair last night. The Press protests in the name of democratic principles that its representatives were not allowed to witness the execution.' It would be difficult to characterize the essence of the contemporary American democracy of hangmen more precisely and accurately!

Stark fear seizes the two-legged beasts portrayed in the play the instant mention is made of the people of progressive forces, of fighters for peace. When a group of active fighters for peace who have freed the young Negroes from the laboratory and have revealed the secret of the 'silver-grey powder' appear in Steel's home after his death, what dues, what real powder is left of the 'supermen', the pretenders to

[1] Khlestakov – main character in Gogol's play *The Inspector General* – is the archetype of an idle boaster and schemer.

[2] Korobochka – a peasant woman in Gogol's novel *Dead Souls* – is depicted as ignorant, superstitious and grasping.

domination over all peoples, who break down so completely in their panic of fear!

It is a very good thing that the heroes in A. Yakobson's play, the fighters for peace, first among them Alan O'Connell, do not merely deliver good speeches but act a real struggle. . . .

A. Yakobson has written an inspired and genuine play. The next word lies with the theatres, which are given the opportunity of creating a pungent, satirical production.

APPENDIX FIVE (B)

# *Hate Propaganda, 1962*

*The 'Animal Morals and Manners' of U.S. Troops: broadcast for Soviet Servicemen over Radio Volga for Soviet Armed Forces Abroad, 24th June, 1962.*

Excerpts from a talk on international themes entitled 'The Animal Morals and Manners of the U.S. Military':

In the rotten capitalist world, the spirit of individualism, of personal benefit, enrichment, lust, hostility, and competition prevail. The richest capitalist country, the U.S.A. the backbone of the capitalism, incorporates the most abnormal characteristic features of the entire system of imperialism in its detestable animal morals. Nowhere else in the world has the cult of business, enrichment, and usury been developed to such an extent than in the U.S.A. today. 'Make money', this expression has become daily usage for the Americans.

From childhood, the whole American way of life deforms the soul of man; it educates him in the spirit of servility towards the dollar. To obtain riches, all means are justified. For gaining and profit you may slander, defraud, rob, and kill. This is the monstrous philosophy determining the conduct of the monopolists, industrial bosses, and bankers. For example, the U.S. Press reports that in the U.S.A. blood and blood plasma that had been stored too long and was useless has been sold by commercial firms to hospitals. The directors of such firms doing business in human blood simply changed the dates on the labels. This knavish practice cost many people their lives. However, the businessmen are not embarrassed by this. To them, human life can be sold for a cent, for them, what is most important is profit. Business has no compassion, not for the sick, the aged, or for children.

It is not incidental that only in the U.S.A. have violence and cruelty assumed such vast dimensions. According to a U.S. magazine, more than 3,000,000 crimes were recorded in the U.S.A. in 1961. In the past ten years, incidents of crime doubled. In Washington crime reached such dimensions as to make the city known in Congress as the 'capital of horrors'. Congress was called for an increase in the capital's police force, because even an evening walk near the brightly-illuminated White House is dangerous.

The American way of life with its mental devastation of the people, the constant existence of a huge army of unemployed, and the feverish war hysteria, cause a multitude of mental diseases among the population. Every tenth American, according to the Press, suffers from one form of mental disorder or another. There are 5,500,000 chronic dipsomaniacs and about 150,000 addicts in the U.S.A. Young Americans who enlisted are subject to a mental stupification. Many become professional murderers. The population of those countries where U.S. military bases are located virtually groans as a result of the excesses of the U.S. soldiers. Murder and robbery, scuffles and violence, speculation and contraband – such are the heroic deeds of thousands of U.S. military personnel overseas.

Recently, the West German paper *Rheinische Post* carried three items with startling headings: 'U.S. soldier Kills Farm Worker', 'Life Imprisonment for U.S. Soldier', 'Soldier Robs 30 Cars'. . . . Recently in West Berlin, two Americans attacked a 40-year-old German taxi driver and cruelly maltreated him . . . The U.S. military ruthlessly violates the national sovereignty of those countries where the feet of its soldiers march, where Yankee imperialism stretches out its paws. In Western Germany alone, the U.S. occupants commit about 500 excesses each month, including a tenth of all murders, robberies, and other forms of violence.

In the past seven years in Japan, U.S. soldiers and sailors committed 66,000 crimes, in other words one crime per hour. According to the South Korean Press, a few days ago a U.S. soldier . . . had his service dog attack a 14-year-old boy . . . The criminal soldier was allowed to go to his barracks undisturbed.

The U.S. military authorities in the Pentagon shamelessly and openly plant the most evil traits in U.S. soldiers. A directive 'The Conduct of Military Personnel and its Rule', issued by the U.S. Defence Department, teaches: a word such as honesty is a particularly artificial and an abstract concept. The word morals is to be treated only humorously. A directive of this kind is not characterized by a special burden. Even the insane Hitler, in his works calculated to train the fascist murderers, called consciousness a useless chimera. The entire system of the ideological training of U.S. troops is designed to turn them into professional murderers. The U.S.A. does not conceal this. . . .

In countries where power is concentrated in the hands of a small group of monopolists, cruelly exploiting millions of people and making big profits, the imperialist law of the jungle and abominable capitalist morals prevail. As the rottenness of imperialism advances, the more clearly do the detestable characteristics of the morals of bourgeois society appear. Only after the collapse of the imperialist order will its detestable morals belong to the past for ever, the main principle of which is '*Homo Homini Lupus Est*'.

APPENDIX SIX

# *Art for Propaganda's Sake*

The tenth anniversary of the outbreak of the war in Korea coincided with the Far Eastern tour of the then President Eisenhower in June 1960. The occasion was used by the communist authorities in mainland China for a mass anti-American propaganda drive on a highly organized basis, using the full resources of the stage, the cinema and the graphic arts. In its September 1960 number the English-language Peking monthly *Chinese Literature* devoted a special section to these under the general title 'Art Activities in the Anti-U.S. Imperialism Propaganda Week'. The three articles in the section are reproduced in this appendix because they describe clearly and in communist terms the use to which the arts are put in communist propaganda. Each of them is written by a political activist in his respective field: Chou Wei-chih, composer of the Korean campaign tune 'March of the Chinese People's Volunteers' and a member of the secretariat of the Chinese Musicians' Union; Yuan Wen-shu, film critic and director of the official China Institute of Film Art, and Hau Chun-wu, a political cartoonist and secretary-general of the Chinese Artists' Union. The editorial preamble to the section gives us the essential background significance of the Week:

During the angry tide of the Chinese people's unanimous and resolute opposition to U.S. imperialist aggression and the wrathful condemnation of the tour of the Far East and Taiwan made by warmonger No. 1, the 'god of plague' Eisenhower, our capital Peking and other big cities including Shanghai, Tientsin, Shenyang, Wuhan, Canton, Chungking and Sian, observed June 21 to June 27 as a 'Propaganda Week to Oppose U.S. Imperialist Aggression, for Resolute Liberation of Taiwan and Safeguarding of World Peace'.

The U.S. imperialists, who have committed countless crimes against the peoples of the world, are now meeting with severe condemnation and resolute resistance from all the peoples of the world; and in Asia, Africa and Latin America there have arisen tremendous struggles involving millions of people. We in China have always considered it our sacred duty to support the struggles of the peoples of different lands in the world against U.S. imperialism. In order to lay bare the aggressive nature of U.S. imperialism, to oppose gangster Eisenhower's tour in the West Pacific, to reaffirm our people's resolution to liberate Taiwan, to carry forward the struggle against the aggressive war plots of U.S. imperialism and to defend world peace together with all the peoples of the world, we have launched a nation-wide, large-scale propaganda campaign to oppose U.S. imperialist aggression, resolutely liberate Taiwan and defend world peace.

China's revolutionary art has always been a powerful weapon against imperialism. During the last ten years, in such past struggles as the movement to resist U.S. aggression and aid Korea and the campaign to oppose the occupation of Taiwan by U.S. imperialism, Chinese writers and artists have written and produced innumerable works in various art forms to oppose U.S. imperialism. They have effectively aroused and educated the masses and dealt powerful blows against the enemy.

In this large-scale propaganda week we showed films, gave stage performances, held art exhibitions and used other mediums to show the struggle against U.S. imperialism. The Hall of the War to Resist U.S. Aggression and Aid Korea in the Military Museum of the Chinese People's Revolution was formally opened in Peking during this period. In this propaganda week, Chinese cultural workers, actors and artists fully demonstrated the strength of art as a weapon and made a forceful attack on the enemy. The following three articles report some of the activities of the theatre, the film world and Chinese art circles during this campaign.

At the end of June, Peking actors and artistes, together with all the citizens of the capital, all the people of China, and the peoples of the whole world, carried out a campaign to deal heavy blows at U.S. imperialism and to submit the 'god of plague' to heavy fire from all sides. The weapon used in this case was theatrical art. During the 'Propaganda Week to Oppose U.S. Imperialist Aggression, for Resolute Liberation of Taiwan and Safeguarding of World Peace', held throughout China theatre workers were very active, putting on many performances at different places and doing a splendid job of agitation and propaganda.

Nearly fifty groups with several thousand members in Peking took part in the performances against U.S. imperialism. From June 21st to June 27th all Peking theatres put on shows opposing U.S. imperialism, while performances were also given in the streets, squares and parks of Peking. Government offices, schools, factories and communes also organized propaganda teams to give performances in the streets.

Of the several hundred items shown, a few plays, songs, variety shows and dances were old favourites; but the great majority were specially written and staged for the occasion within two–five days. These items opposing U.S. imperialism made use of a great variety of themes. From different angles, the artistes forcefully exposed the crimes committed by the U.S. imperialists at different times against the peoples of the world. The forms used embraced a great variety too: modern plays and operas, topical dramatic sketches, traditional operas, variety shows, chorus singing, dancing and acrobatics.

One of the past favourites re-edited and staged again was *Long Live Our Heroes!* This play, put on by the Peking People's Art Theatre, shows how the Chinese People's Volunteers in Korea defended their tunnels against the U.S. imperialist aggressors and finally won a great victory. *The Iron and Steel Transport Troops*, staged by the China Youth Art Theatre, reflected the stirring deeds in the autumn of 1951 when the Korean and Chinese peoples' forces smashed Van Fleet's 'autumn offensive'. *Friendship*, produced by the Comrades-in-Arms Theatre Group, is the story of the Korean heroine Kim Sun Ok who went behind the enemy lines to save platoon leader Ho Ming of the Chinese People's Volunteers. This play pays tribute to the noble friendship, sealed in blood, of the Korean and Chinese peoples who fought in a common cause. Both in their ideological content and stage technique these plays reached a fairly high level. They had run continuously for months in the past, always to full houses.

One of the most noteworthy of the new productions was *On The 38th Parallel*, Presented by the Theatre Group of the Political Department of the People's Liberation Army. This is in some way a sequel to *Long Live Our Heroes*! which showed how courageously the Korean and Chinese people smashed the enemy's so-called 'biggest offensive' and forced the aggressors to sign an armistice agreement. *On The 38th Parallel* further exposes U.S. imperialism as the most vicious of aggressors, unwilling to accept defeat. This play reveals how, just after signing the armistice agreement, while negotiations were still going on to fix the military demarcation line, the U.S. imperialists were already plotting a 'new offensive'. It discloses vividly how, to attain their criminal objective, the U.S. imperialists again and again sent agents across the line to carry out espionage and various acts of military provocation. But the high degree of vigilance of the Korean and Chinese peoples' forces and the Korean people brought about the thorough exposure of the enemy's plots, so that the representatives of U.S. imperialism were strongly condemned by the people and finally had to stand trial before the Military Armistice Commission as defendants. These penetrating sketches make very evident the gangster nature of U.S. imperialism which makes aggression its 'state policy' and will resort to all means to attain its ends. Faking peace while actually preparing for war, talk of easing tensions while actually intensifying aggression, have been the trickery used by the U.S. imperialists all along.

Similar in theme is the new play of the China Youth Art Theatre, *Fresh In Our Memory*. It portrays how between 1945 and 1949 the U.S. imperialists instigated the Kuomintang reactionaries to launch a civil war and carry out frenzied attacks on the liberated areas, and how they were thoroughly defeated in the end. Here the U.S. imperialists are clearly exposed as the most vicious, most cunning enemy of the Chinese people. Their so-called 'Executive Headquarters' for military mediation was a shameful tool intended to deceive the people by negotiations while pinning down the People's Liberation Army and enabling the Kuomintang troops with American assistance to acquire sufficient strength to attack the liberated areas. This play also shows the use made of U.N.R.R.A. for spying. The reactionaries tried to take advantage of the distribution of relief materials to collect information in the liberated areas. In short, they attempted to use both the 'Executive Headquarters' for military mediation and U.N.R.R.A. to attack the Chinese Communist Party from two sides, hoping the Chinese people would be fooled and fall into their trap. Their trick was seen through, however, by Chairman Mao Tse-tung and the Chinese Communist Party. The people showed a high sense of vigilance and a strong fighting spirit. While still negotiating for peace in the country, we strengthened our military defences, ready to deal mortal blows to the reactionaries if they dared to attack. Finally Chiang Kai-shek's régime was thoroughly overthrown and the aggressive forces of U.S. imperialism were driven out of the mainland of China. The strong contempt and hatred for U.S. imperialism in these two plays are like two powerful missiles which accurately hit their mark. These plays have completely exposed to their audiences the gangster fact of U.S. imperialism, its blatant lies and shameless behaviour.

Another new play was the political satire *The 'God of Plague'*, written and staged by the Experimental Drama Theatre of the Central Drama College. The staging was rather unusual. The play opened with weird music, to the accompaniment of which a group of revolting and ludicrous warmongers crossed the stage making disgusting gestures. These were the U.S. gangster chief Eisenhower, his colleagues Herter, Allen Dulles and the chairman of the U.S. joint chief-of-staff Twining, as well as the lackeys of U.S. vassal states supported by U.S. imperialism. A description of the deliberate sabotage of the Four-power Conference of Government Heads by U.S. imperialism and of Eisenhower's tour of the Far East pulls the mask off U.S. imperialism and directs biting satire at the comical figure cut by the enemy. The whole play breathes contempt for the enemy, and the negative characters are successfully drawn: arrogant, cold-blooded Herter; wily, venomous Allen Dulles; and, most outstanding of all, Eisenhower, who appears like a chameleon, now pretending to be 'kind' and 'gentle', now revealing his true ferocity; sometimes making gestures of 'peace', sometimes clamouring for war. The portrayal of such a figure clearly reveals the true nature of the U.S. imperialists.

An outstanding feature of these performances to oppose U.S. imperialism was the use of full-length plays to extol the courageous struggle of the Japanese and South Korean peoples against U.S. imperialism and its lackeys. For instance *Angry Waves*, staged by the Peking People's Art Theatre, describes the mass struggle of workers, peasants, fishermen, students and other circles in South Korea, who united to oppose the establishment of U.S. military bases, to oppose the war plots of the U.S. imperialists in collusion with Syngman Rhee; it depicts the heinous rule of the reactionaries and their oppression and persecution of the South Korean people, who finally succeeded in overthrowing Syngman Rhee. Again *Advance, Brave People of Japan!* produced by the Children's Theatre, deals with the determined mass struggle of the Japanese people led by the Japanese Communist Party and other anti-imperialist, patriotic, democratic forces to oppose the signing of the aggressive new Japan–U.S. 'Security Treaty' and to overthrow the traitorous Kishi government.

Both these plays depict the leading role of the working class in this struggle, and the strong resolution with which the working people and youth are opposing U.S. imperialism and its lackeys. Even when the latter have been overthrown or announced their resignation, the people will not slacken their vigilance or give up the struggle. They resolutely oppose the formation of another government like that of Kishi; they refuse to be deceived by another traitor like Huh Chung. The people of Japan and South Korea announce to the whole world: the struggle will not stop till U.S. imperialism is driven out of Japan, driven out of South Korea, till the traitorous governments are overthrown, till the people have gained a complete victory.

In addition to these plays, there were modern operas like *Smash the Invaders!* song and dance shows like *Song of the Volunteers* and *The Chinese and Korean Peoples Fight Shoulder to Shoulder*, traditional operas like *Eisenhower's Sorrow* and *Storm Over the Pacific*, as well as topical dramatic sketches, choruses, solo-singing, dances, ballads, acrobatics and puppet-plays. From different angles all these lively performances paid tribute to the anti-U.S. struggle of the peoples of the world, the friendship of the Korean and Chinese peoples and that among peoples of different lands in a common fight; they dealt blows to the aggressive war policy of U.S. imperialism, exposing its plots, its faking peace while actually preparing for war, talk of easing tension while actually intensifying aggression; they once more laid bare the true nature of the paper tiger and the despicable character of its lackeys Kishi and Syngman Rhee and others; they also proved that U.S. imperialism has been, still is and will continue to be the deadly enemy of the people of China, the peoples of Asia, Africa and Latin America, and all the people of the world, thus forcefully refuting the fallacies of the modern revisionists in Yugoslavia who argue that the aggressive nature of imperialism has changed.

Chinese actors and artistes are playing their part in the struggle against U.S. imperialism. Let us, together with all the peoples of the world, carry to a new, victorious stage the struggle to oppose the aggressive U.S. war policy and to defend world peace. May the storm of revolution rise in every corner of the globe and go from strength to strength, until the aggressive war policy of U.S. imperialism is completely smashed, until the heinous colonialist rule of the U.S. imperialists is completely overthrown, until the people's world-wide struggle against U.S. imperialism has gained a total victory and true, lasting peace in the world has been realized!

'A hurricane is lashing the shores of the West Pacific. But fiercer than the raging forces of nature is the rising storm of the Asian people's struggle against U.S. imperialism.' These were the opening words of the documentary film *Storm in Asia* shown in June during the large-scale film exhibition of the 'Propaganda Week to Oppose U.S. Imperialist Aggression, for Resolute Liberation of Taiwan and Safeguarding of World Peace,' held in various cities in China. The screen showed angry waves pounding the coast with such violence that the hardest rocks must be ground into sand in the end. And this has a profound symbolic significance. For in the mounting tide of opposition to U.S. imperialist aggression and for the defence of world peace by the peoples of the world, U.S. imperialism and its lackeys in various lands face certain destruction at the hands of the people.

More than twenty documentary and feature films were shown, all truthfully and forcefully exposing the vicious nature of the U.S. aggressors. *Storm in Asia* is a fine documentary which gives a general view of the indomitable struggle of the Asian peoples against U.S. imperialism and its lackeys. Using actual shots of the most recent events it re-enacts the mounting wrath of the Asian peoples against the American imperialists, exposing their talk of peace while preparing for war, their claim to be easing tension when in fact they are intensifying their aggression. The documentary evidence in this film is used concisely and forcefully to present scene after scene of the patriotic and just struggles of the people against U.S. imperialism in Japan, South Korea and Turkey, bringing home the anger of the peoples of Asia and their determination to resist U.S. imperialism and its lackeys. This film shows the U.S. imperialist army trampling over Japanese land while its owners, homeless, are forced to wander from place to place; it shows American guided missiles fired over Japan, the aggressors' flag flying arrogantly over Japanese soil, the aggressors' troops molesting women, looting and killing . . . It shows the lackeys of U.S. imperialism, Kishi and Syngman Rhee, using tanks, armoured cars, bayonets, clubs and water hoses to attack unarmed patriots. Through Eisenhower, the 'god of plague', is working hand in glove with his henchmen, the foundations of U.S. imperialism are crumbling. Before the gate of the Diet building in Tokyo, outside the president's residence in Seoul, on the streets of Istanbul, the wrathful crowds surge like angry billows, like a hurricane or an erupting volcano rushing at and destroying U.S. imperialism and its agents. The film also presents unforgettable, historic shots of the defeat of U.S. imperialism by the Chinese and Korean peoples on the battlefields of Korea, disclosing the real face of the American paper tiger and strengthening the people's confidence in the victory of their struggle.

Another documentary, *Exposure of the 'God of Plague'*, marshals many convincing facts to lay bare the aggressive designs of U.S. imperialism under its peaceful guise. The chief representative of U.S. imperialism, the 'god of plague' Eisenhower, with sinister intent assumes a smiling face, disguising himself as a 'peace envoy', and tries to deceive the world. But fire cannot be contained in a paper wrapper. This film goes on to show how the world's people recognize the true nature of the 'god of plague' through their own historical experience and through actual struggles. When this 'god of plague' goes on his wretched gangster tour to the Western Pacific, the people 'welcome' him not with cheers or flowers but with angry fists opposing U.S. imperialist aggression. Wherever the 'god of plague' goes, he is like 'a rat running across the street with everyone saying: "Hit him".' In Japan, in South Korea, in the Philippines, throughout the whole of Asia, the seeds of hatred sown by U.S. imperialists have grown and ripened, and the 'god of plague' deserves to enjoy his own fruit. In a brief space of time, the reactionary lackeys fostered by U.S. imperialism are overthrown one by one – Syngman Rhee, Menderes, Kishi. This further proves that the people's strength is invincible. As Chairman Mao has said: The days of imperialism are numbered. The imperialists have done every kind of evil and all the oppressed peoples of the world will never forgive them. There are also shots in this film of the tremendous barrage of shells fired from the Fukien front to 'greet' and 'farewell' the 'god of plague' when he came to China's territory Taiwan, now occupied by U.S. imperialism, telling him of the inevitable failure of his plot to carry out aggression against China.

The U.S. imperialists constantly boast about their science and their 'civilization'. All seeing the documentaries *News from the Korean Front* and *Oppose U.S. Germ Warfare* must realize what fearful crimes are perpetrated when modern science is controlled by the imperialists. The 'science' of U.S. imperialism has produced weapons of mass destruction; it has razed innumerable cities and villages in Korea to the ground, and murdered hundreds of thousands of innocent people. U.S. 'science' equipped rats and insects with germs to spread fatal diseases to men and even to the cattle and crops in the fields. It is obvious that to achieve their aim of aggression and plunder, the U.S. imperialists will resort to any crime. These two documentaries make it clear that U.S. imperialism is the most vicious force for evil in the world, and that all the peoples of the world are wrathfully condemning the U.S. imperialist aggressors.

The crime of the U.S. imperialists who sent U-2 planes to invade the Soviet Union thus sabotaging the Four-power Conference of Government Heads has appeared on the screen. Of course, the gangsterism of U.S. imperialism in carrying out espionage is nothing new. The documentaries *The Criminal U.S. Military Reconnaissance Balloons* and *Exhibition of the Criminal Evidence of U.S. Air-dropped Agents* testify to a long record of such criminal acts. Eisenhower himself sometimes discloses the 'truth'. Just as a thief caught red-handed claims that he was earning an 'honest living'. Eisenhower has openly admitted: 'Since the beginning of my administration I have issued directives to gather, in every feasible way,' what the U.S. deemed to be 'information required . . .' These two documentaries, the criminal act of the U-2 plane and Eisenhower's shameless confession point to one conclusion: the aggressive nature of imperialism has not changed. In China we have a proverb: 'It is easier to change rivers and mountains than it is to change a man's nature.' This applies perfectly to U.S. imperialism to-day.

*The Battle of Sangkumryung* and the new productions *Heroic Island* and *Eagles of the Sea* were among the good feature films shown during this film exhibition. *The Battle of Sangkumryung* deals with the fiercest, and most difficult battle of the Korean war, the world-famed battle which struck terror into the U.S. aggressors. *Eagles of the Sea* and *Heroic Island* present the Chinese People's Liberation Army's fight against U.S.

imperialism among the south-east coast of China. These films introducing fights at different times and in different localities have one feature in common – they thoroughly expose the aggressive nature of U.S. imperialism and glorify the heroes, fighting it, affirming our people's confidence in the ultimate victory against the enemy and recording the great successes already won.

U.S. imperialism is utterly vicious. Sangkumryung is a hill less than four square kilometres in area, yet the U.S. aggressors pounded it with a daily average of more than 300,000 shells. The film shows not only the braggadocio of the enemy, but the true nature of this seemingly powerful paper tiger. Strategically, we should despise this enemy but tactically take him seriously. It reveals vividly that weapons are not the decisive factor in determining victory or defeat in war; the decisive factor is the man holding the gun and the nature of the war he is engaged in. Although the aggressors were equipped with modern weapons, could wipe out whole sectors of the hillside and sometimes cut our tunnel fighters off from supplies and all other contact, our heroic troops held out for twenty-four days with scarcely any food or water till they won the final victory Their tremendous strength stemmed from the consciousness that they were fighting for a just cause. The bombardment of the U.S. imperialists could not shake the resolve of these men armed with patriotism and internationalism. This is why, after the aggressors suffered one heavy blow after another at Sangkumryung, they were forced to sit down to negotiate and sign a cease-fire. And this points out another important lesson: the best way to treat an aggressor is to strike back fiercely. Our films graphically illustrate this truth pointed out by Chairman Mao: 'Imperialism and all reactionaries are paper tigers.'

The heroic feats done in this just war were too many to count, and countless heroes appeared. In *The Battle of Sangkumryung*, Company Commander Chung-fa, Political Instructor Meng Teh-kuei and the scout Yang Teh-tsai display boundless loyalty to their country, the people and the peace cause, and the indomitable heroism of proletarian, internationalist fighters. Meng Teh-kuei is blinded in the battle, yet he leads the few men left to defend the position, repelling many frenzied enemy attacks. The last thing he considers is his own safety or comfort; his one thought is how best to defend the position. Similarly, at the crucial moment when we are launching a big counter-attack, the young scout Yang Teh-tsai sees that enemy fire is holding up his comrades' advance. Without hesitation he rushes up and with his own body blocks the enemy machine-gun to silence its fire, giving his young life for victory in the battle. The noble qualities of men like these illustrate the just nature of the war fought by the Chinese People's Volunteers to resist U.S. aggression and aid Korea. Only proletarian fighters guided by Marxism-Leninism and Mao Tse-tung's thought, inspired by the great spirit of patriotism and internationalism, and dedicated heart and soul to the cause of justice, can develop such heroism and fine moral qualities.

In accordance with a good tradition in Chinese literature and art, our films do not portray the cruelty of war in naturalistic manner, neither do they show the sufferings of individuals in a sentimental way, nor use tear-provoking, pessimistic, gloomy scenes. Of course, the basic question is the nature of the war. A just war against aggression helps to safeguard world peace. If some men die or are wounded in the war it is for the happiness of millions. *The Battle of Sangkumryung* makes use of the heroism of the Volunteers to inspire others and strengthen their will to fight. In the cruel battle of Sangkumryung, though there was no food or water in the tunnels, the men sang of their homeland, of peace and the justice of their cause. Surrounded by the enemy, they could still cheerfully catch squirrels and crack jokes. In the same way in *Heroic Island*, however fierce the enemy bombardment, the men and women in the underground city on Lotus Island lived and worked as usual, discussing the people's commune and young people's marriage. In *Eagles of the Sea*, though the gunboat sank and the men were floating beyond sight of land, they were not easily dismayed by difficulties and felt no despair. In fact they spoke confidently of finding a new ship and going out to fresh battles. This revlutionary optimism is common in China today; and to express this noble spirit through the medium of films is the great and glorious task of those of us in the film industry.

On 17th and 19th June, while the Chinese People's Liberation Army at the Fukien front was using thousands of guns to bombard Quemoy, still occupied by Chiang Kai-shek and the U.S. imperialists, to 'greet' and 'farewell' the 'god of plague' Eisenhower who came to our territory Taiwan to spread disaster and trouble, Chinese artists were busy using thousands of brushes to support the struggle of the peoples of the world against U.S. imperialism. Many cities in China held exhibitions, and the Chinese Artists' Union in Peking also held an art exhibition of the 'Propaganda Week to Oppose U.S. Imperialist Aggression, for Resolute Liberation of Taiwan and Safeguarding of World Peace'. This exhibition displayed political cartoons, posters, oil paintings and traditional paintings, done recently.

The exhibition received keen support from Chinese cartoonists, poster artists, painters in ink and water-colours and in oils, woodcut artists and the staff and students of art schools in the capital. Noted cartoonists like Mi Ku and Fang Cheng, the popular woodcut artists Ku Yuan, Li Hua and Wu Pi-tuan, and Wang Shu-hui a painter in the traditional style, were among those who contributed exhibits. Many of them worked day and night to produce good works extolling the people's victories and dealing blows at the warmongers' plots.

The gouache 'Chairman Mao Tse-tung with the Peoples of Asia, Africa and Latin America' by the woodcut artists Wu Pi-tuan and Chin Shang-yi has marked clarity and strength, and conveys comprehensively and profoundly the Chinese people's sympathy and support for all oppressed peoples. The same theme was the subject of the large traditional-style painting 'The Just Voice of the Chinese People', a collective work by the second-year students of the Department of Traditional Painting of the Central Institute of Fine Arts. This presents a great ocean of men at a big demonstration held in Tien An Men Square in support of the Japanese people's struggle. Though the artists have made use of the symmetry and balance of traditional Chinese art this painting suggests great forces mobilized and unleashed. The use of red as the main colour further strengthens the militant atmosphere. Several artists chose as their theme our bombardment of Quemoy to 'greet' the 'god of plague' Eisenhower. Some used oils to depict the heroic People's Liberation Army, some used cartoons and posters to portray the panicky plight of Eisenhower. All expressed the Chinese people's determination to liberate Taiwan.

The ludicrous and pitiful position of the U.S. imperialists in this anti-imperialist storm of the Asian peoples was another theme chosen by many artists. Many cartoons evoked laughter by stripping the masks from the ugly faces of Eisenhower, his Press secretary Hagerty and Kishi confronted with the aroused Japanese people. Tsao Chen-feng's 'A Much Profitable Trip', which shows Eisenhower with both cheeks slapped by the Asian people, is a fine cartoon, sharply sarcastic and humorous. Chiang Fan's cartoon 'Chain Reaction' portrays the broken bits from the statue of Syngman Rhee, pulled down by the people of South Korea, flying out and hitting the U.S. imperialists.

The Chinese artists did not confine themselves only to the struggles of the peoples in Asia; many paid equal attention to the struggles of the African and Latin American peoples. The third-year students of the Department of Graphic Art of the Central Institute of Fine Arts produced a woodcut series entitled: 'Peoples of the World Unite! Down with U.S. Imperialism! This forcefully presents the awakened people of Africa, the armed struggle of the Algerians, the wrath with which the people of Latin America drove out the U.S. invaders, and China's six hundred and fifty million resolutely supporting the just struggle of the people of other lands.

Considerable interest was aroused by posters in this exhibition showing how heroically Chinese and Koreans fought side by side against U.S. imperialism and expressing support for the Vietnamese people's struggle. A number of these posters, produced during the War to Resist U.S. Aggression and Aid Korea, recalled those days and strengthened our people's determination in the struggle against U.S. imperialism.

The cartoonists, with pens trenchant as scalpels, did not spare the modern revisionists who try to whitewash U.S. imperialism. Mi Ku's cartoon 'Gilding the Exterior' and Fang Cheng's 'Good Service' are scathing exposures of modern revisionism and won high praise. The fawning, sycophantic subservience of modern revisionism to its imperialist masters was clearly depicted here by these cartoonists.

Once again the fighting tradition of Chinese artists and their determination to safeguard world peace have been strongly demonstrated by this exhibition. Chinese artists made their contribution in the long period of anti-imperialist struggles in the past, and now that a broad united front on a world scale has been formed against imperialism, Chinese artists are throwing themselves with even greater enthusiasm into this struggle. As Chairman Mao has said, the days of imperialism are numbered. Before the coffin of U.S. imperialists is finally nailed down, when the noose is tightening around their necks we shall continue ceaselessly to deal blows at them, and this exhibition is one of these powerful blows.

# *Index*